D1520707

THE

PUBLICATIONS

OF THE

SURTEES SOCIETY

VOL. 213

AND

CUMBERLAND & WESTMORLAND
ANTIQUARIAN
&
ARCHAEOLOGICAL
SOCIETY

Record Series Vol. XX

Hon. General Editors

R. H. BRITNELL and M. M. HARVEY

THE

PUBLICATIONS

OF THE

SURTEES SOCIETY

ESTABLISHED IN THE YEAR
M.DCCC.XXXIV

VOL. CCXIII

JOHN DENTON'S
HISTORY
OF
CUMBERLAND

EDITED
BY
ANGUS J. L. WINCHESTER

THE SURTEES SOCIETY
AND
CUMBERLAND & WESTMORLAND ANTIQUARIAN
& ARCHAEOLOGICAL SOCIETY

THE BOYDELL PRESS

© The Surtees Society 2010

All Rights Reserved. Except as permitted under current legislation
no part of this work may be photocopied, stored in a retrieval system,
published, performed in public, adapted, broadcast,
transmitted, recorded or reproduced in any form or by any means,
without the prior permission of the copyright owner

First published 2010

A joint publication of
The Surtees Society and of
Cumberland & Westmorland Antiquarian &
Archaeological Society
published by The Boydell Press
an imprint of Boydell & Brewer Ltd
PO Box 9, Woodbridge, Suffolk IP12 3DF, UK
and of Boydell & Brewer Inc.
Mt Hope Avenue, Rochester, NY 14620, USA
website: www.boydellandbrewer.com

ISBN 978–0–85444–068–9

ISSN 0307–5362

DA
670
.C9
D46
2010

A catalogue record for this book is available
from the British Library

The Surtees Society acknowledges the generous financial
support of the Aurelius Charitable Trust
in the production of this volume

Details of other Surtees Society volumes are available
from Boydell & Brewer Ltd

This publication is printed on acid-free paper

Printed in Great Britain by
CPI Antony Rowe, Chippenham and Eastbourne

CONTENTS

JOHN DENTON'S HISTORY OF CUMBERLAND

In Memoriam

David John Williams Mawson (1930 – 2006)

ACKNOWLEDGEMENTS

The editor and publishers would like to record their thanks to the Dean and Chapter of Carlisle Cathedral for permission to publish the text of the Machell MS of John Denton's history, and to Viscount Coke and the Trustees of the Holkham Estate for permission to publish extracts from Holkham Hall MS 760.

This volume has been several years in the making, during which time I have accumulated a large debt of gratitude to a large number of people. I should like to record particular thanks as follows. The late David Mawson, to whose memory this volume is dedicated, pioneered the serious study of the surviving manuscripts of John Denton's history and was unstinting in his help and encouragement, even as illness curtailed his energies. This edition owes much to his careful groundwork and extensive knowledge. The British Academy provided a small research grant to enable a detailed textual comparison of the different manuscripts to be undertaken, and this work was ably carried out at Lancaster University by Eleanor Straughton and John Marsh. Cumbria Archive Service contributed towards the cost of preparing the Map, reproduced on p. xiv. Individual archivists and librarians have been unfailingly generous in answering queries and providing access to material in their keeping: special thanks are due to Stephen White, Carlisle Library, who supplied copies of manuscripts in the Jackson Collection; David Bowcock, Susan Dench and Tom Robson of Cumbria Record Office, Carlisle; Steven Tomlinson, Department of Special Collections and Western Manuscripts, Bodleian Library; Amanda Saville, librarian at Queen's College, Oxford; Suzanne Reynolds, curator of manuscripts at Holkham Hall, Norfolk; Roger Simms, Manx National Heritage Library, Douglas; and Annette Lawrence, Lancaster University Library. Numerous scholars, both colleagues at Lancaster and in the wider historical world, have willingly shared their specialist knowledge in the pursuit of footnote references; it is a pleasure to record thanks to: John Broad, Jan Broadway, Hugh Doherty, Alexander Grant, Andrew Jotischky, Oliver Padel, Tim Padley, Richard Sharpe, David Shotter, Keith Stringer, John Thorley, Mary Wane and Susan

Whyman. Finally, I am indebted to Margaret Harvey, joint general editor of Surtees Society, for her guidance and her sharp eye for detail. I take full responsibility for the edition and for any errors or omissions it may contain.

Angus J. L. Winchester
Lancaster University
July 2009

ABBREVIATIONS

Accompt	*An Accompt of the most considerable estates and families in the county of Cumberland … by John Denton of Cardew*, ed. R. S. Ferguson, CWAAS Tract Series No. 2 (Kendal, 1887).
Book of Fees	*Liber Feodorum. The Book of Fees commonly called Testa de Nevill, reformed from the earliest MSS by the Deputy Keeper of the Records. Part I (AD 1198–1242)* (London, 1920).
Britannia	W. Camden, *Britain, or a Chorographicall Description of … England, Scotland and Ireland*, trans. P. Holland (London, 1610).
Cal. Charter R	*Calendar of Charter Rolls*, 6 vols [Hen. III to Hen. VIII] (London, 1903–27).
Cal. Close	*Calendar of Close Rolls*, 47 vols [Ed. I to Hen. VII] (London, 1892–1963).
Cal. Docs Scotland	*Calendar of Documents relating to Scotland preserved in Her Majesty's Public Record Office, London*, ed. J. Bain, 4 vols [1108–1509] (London, 1881–88).
Cal. IPM	*Calendar of Inquisitions Post Mortem and other analogous documents*, 20 vols [Hen. III to Hen. V] (London, 1904–95).
Cal. Pat.	*Calendar of Patent Rolls*, 72 vols [Hen. III to Eliz. I] (London, 1891–1982).
Cal. SP Dom.	*Calendar of State Papers, Domestic*, 12 vols [Edw. VI to Jas. I] (London, 1856–72).
CFH	C. Roy Hudleston and R. S. Boumphrey, *Cumberland Families and Heraldry*, CWAAS Extra Series XXIII (Kendal, 1978).
Complete Peerage	G. E. C[okayne], *The Complete Peerage of England, Scotland, Ireland, Great Britain and the United Kingdom: extant, extinct and dormant*, revised edition, 14 vols (Vols 1–13: London, 1910–1959; Vol. 14: Stroud, 1998).
CRO	Cumbria Record Office.
Curwen, *Castles*	J. F. Curwen, *The Castles and Fortified Towers of Cumberland, Westmorland and Lancashire North-of-the-Sands*, CWAAS Extra Series XIII (Kendal, 1913).

CW1	*Transactions of Cumberland & Westmorland Antiquarian & Archaeological Society*, old series (1866–1900).
CW2	*Transactions of Cumberland & Westmorland Antiquarian & Archaeological Society*, new series (1901–2000).
CW3	*Transactions of Cumberland & Westmorland Antiquarian & Archaeological Society*, third series (2001–).
CWAAS	Cumberland & Westmorland Antiquarian & Archaeological Society.
Denton, *Perambulation*	*Thomas Denton: a Perambulation of Cumberland 1687–1688, including descriptions of Westmorland, The Isle of Man and Ireland*, ed. A. J. L. Winchester with M. Wane, Surtees Society Vol. 207 and CWAAS Record Series Vol. XVI (Woodbridge, 2003).
Dict. LDPN	D. Whaley, *Dictionary of Lake District Place-Names*, English Place-Name Society Regional Series 1 (Nottingham, 2006).
DUL	Durham University Library, Archives and Special Collections.
EEA 30: Carlisle	*English Episcopal Acta 30: Carlisle 1133–1292*, ed. D. M. Smith (Oxford, 2005).
FF Cumb.	F. H. M. Parker, 'A calendar of the Feet of Fines for Cumberland, from their commencement to the accession of Henry VII', *CW2*, 7 (1907), pp. 215–61.
Gilpin	Annotations in Gilpin MS (see Appendix I, no. [11]).
H	Holkham MS (see Appendix I, no. [7]).
Holm Cultram	*The Register and Records of Holm Cultram*, ed. F. Grainger and W. G. Collingwood, CWAAS Record Series Vol. VII (Kendal, 1929).
J	Jackson MS (see Appendix I, no. [3]).
L & P Hen. VIII	*Letters and Papers, Foreign and Domestic, of the Reign of Henry VIII, preserved in the Public Record Office, the British Museum and elsewhere in England*, 23 vols in 38 (London, 1862–1932).
Lanercost	*The Lanercost Cartulary*, ed. J. M. Todd, Surtees Society Vol. 203 and CWAAS Record Series Vol. XI (Gateshead, 1997).
M	Machell MS (see Appendix I, no. [1]).
Monasticon	W. Dugdale, *Monasticon Anglicanum: a history of the abbies and other monasteries … in England and Wales*, ed. J. Caley *et al.*, 6 vols (London, 1846).
ODNB	*Oxford Dictionary of National Biography.*
OE	Old English
OED	*Oxford English Dictionary.*
ON	Old Norse

Plac. Abbrev.	*Placitorum Abbreviatio, Richard I – Edward II*, ed. G. Rose and W. Illingworth (London, 1811).
PNC	A. M. Armstrong, A. Mawer, F. M. Stenton and Bruce Dickens, *The Place-Names of Cumberland*, English Place-Name Society Vols XX–XXII (Cambridge, 1950–52).
PRO	The National Archives, Kew: Public Record Office.
Rot. Chart.	*Calendarium rotulorum chartarum et inquisitionum ad quod damnum*, ed. J. Caley (London, 1803).
Rot. Litt. Claus.	*Rotuli litterarum clausurum in Turri Londinensi asservati*, ed. T. D. Hardy, 2 vols (London, 1833–44).
Sharpe, *Norman Rule*	R. Sharpe, *Norman Rule in Cumbria 1092–1136*, CWAAS Tract Series XXI (Kendal, 2006).
St Bees	*The Register of the Priory of St Bees*, ed. James Wilson, Surtees Society Vol. 126 (Durham, 1915).
Summerson, *Aglionbys*	H. Summerson, *'An Ancient Squires Family': a history of the Aglionbys, c. 1130–2002* (Carlisle, 2007).
VCH Cumb.	*The Victoria History of the County of Cumberland*, ed. James Wilson (London, 1901–5; reprinted 1968).
Wetheral	*The Register of the Priory of Wetherhal*, ed. J. E. Prescott (London and Kendal, 1897).

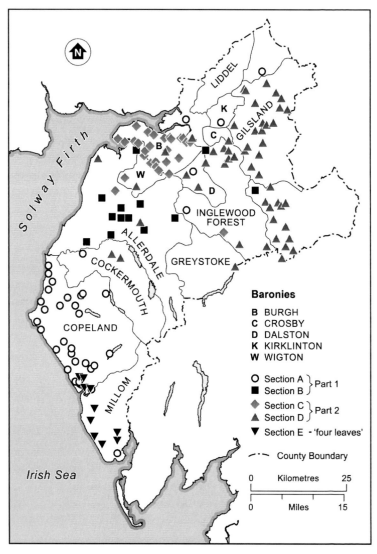

Cumberland: places included in John Denton's history.

INTRODUCTION

The manuscript history of Cumberland, compiled in the first decade of the seventeenth century and usually attributed to John Denton of Cardew, formed the basis of almost all antiquarian writing on the county until the nineteenth century and, in the absence of topographical volumes of the Victoria County History, continues to be cited. It is the earliest known attempt to write a history of Cumberland and one of the first generation of antiquarian accounts of an English shire. The original manuscript is lost but thirteen late seventeenth- or early eighteenth-century copies of the history are known (see Appendix I), one of which, a re-ordered copy known as the Gilpin MS (Appendix I, no. [11]), was used by Richard S. Ferguson as the basis of *An Accompt of the most considerable Estates and Families in the County of Cumberland* (Cumberland & Westmorland Antiquarian & Archaeological Society Tract Series 2, Kendal, 1887), hitherto the only published edition.

Ferguson made no attempt to collate the texts of the seven copies of the manuscript then known and included without comment additions to the text which had been made by Gilpin. His edition was thus some distance removed from Denton's original text. Nor did Ferguson check the factual accuracy of the text: indeed, as he produced his edition before the publication of most Public Record Office Lists and Indexes or the establishment of county record offices, to do so would have been a monumental task. The absence of a modern assessment of John Denton's work has been a longstanding gap in Cumbrian historiography and the difficulties presented by the lack of a detailed analysis of the manuscripts were highlighted recently when attempting to identify borrowings from John Denton's history in the perambulation of Cumberland compiled by his distant kinsman, Thomas Denton, in 1687–88.[1] Sections of Thomas Denton's text which were not in Ferguson's edition of the *Accompt* could

---

1   Denton, *Perambulation*, pp. 17–18.

nevertheless be found in other manuscripts of John Denton's text, demonstrating the inadequacy of the published edition.

John Denton's history has received a mixed press, largely because its validity has not hitherto been checked systematically against primary archival sources. Writing in 1859, Hodgson Hinde laid the blame for the perpetuation of misconceptions about the early history of Cumberland squarely at the door of 'two persons of the name of Denton [i.e. John Denton and Thomas Denton], whose manuscript collections have been the main source from whence the modern historians of the county have derived their information'.[2] In particular, John Denton's reliance on the erroneous account of the roots of the Norman pattern of landholding, contained in the 'Chronicon Cumbrie', was deemed to make his history unreliable and fatally flawed.[3] A much more sympathetic view came in 1911 from the pen of James Wilson, the learned vicar of Dalston and first editor of the Victoria County History of Cumberland. In exploring Denton's life and his high reputation among his contemporaries, Wilson concluded that John Denton's work, based as it was on extensive research in Crown and private muniments, was 'of the utmost historical value'.[4] Modern finding aids and a century and more of local historical research in Cumberland, published largely in the *Transactions of the Cumberland & Westmorland Antiquarian & Archaeological Society*, now make an assessment of Denton's work possible. The aim of this present volume is therefore to present a new, analytical edition of John Denton's history, attempting both to reconstruct as much as possible of the original text from surviving copies and, by identifying the sources from which it was drawn, to enable future historians to assess the history's accuracy.

THE MANUSCRIPTS

Known manuscript copies of the history attributed to John Denton are listed and described in Appendix I. Some are re-ordered copies or texts in which a later author has incorporated Denton's material into

---

2 J. H. Hinde, 'On the early history of Cumberland', *Archaeological Journal*, 16 (1859), pp. 217–35.

3 The 'Chronicon Cumbrie' and Denton's other sources are discussed below (pp. 19–21).

4 J. Wilson, 'The first historian of Cumberland', *Scottish Historical Review*, 8 (1911), pp. 5–21.

a fuller account of the county,[5] but most appear to be straightforward transcripts of an earlier text. The first task must be to examine the relationship between the surviving copies and to attempt an assessment of their relationship to Denton's lost original. David Mawson established over thirty years ago that most of the surviving copies of Denton's history may be grouped into two families, distinguished on the basis of the internal sequence of material.[6] In one, termed here Series A, the material is divided into two sections, 'Part 1' and 'Part 2'; in the other, Series B, there is no such distinction between two parts; the order of the entries is different; and an additional section, consisting of 'four leaves' said to have been 'stiched into the originall MSS',[7] is included. The structure and sequence of the two series can be summarised as show on page 4.

There is further evidence to suggest that the two series represent two families of transcripts in which individual copies are closely related to each other. Several of the Series A manuscripts can be shown to be copies of the Machell MS [1], since they contain additions and marginal entries made by Thomas Machell.[8] The seemingly independent but incomplete Series A manuscript Jackson A1114 [3] has identical pagination and layout to Machell MS, suggesting that their scribes were attempting to reproduce the layout of a source copy. In contrast, as David Mawson demonstrated, the Series B manuscripts are all associated with Hugh Todd (c. 1658–1728), vicar of Arthuret and Penrith, but whether Todd himself was responsible for the different ordering of the text is not clear.[9]

Which of the two series more closely reproduces the order of Denton's lost original manuscript? The answer appears to lie in the relationship between the four runs of entries, A, B, C and D, which

---

5   The Gilpin MS [11] may be classed as a re-ordered transcript, whereas the Queen's College MS [12] and Thomas Denton's 'Perambulation' [13b] incorporate Denton's material into fuller works. Another late seventeenth-century antiquary to reproduce sections of John Denton's text without acknowledgement was Sir Daniel Fleming in his description of Cumberland, dated to 1671, printed in *Fleming-Senhouse Papers*, ed. E. Hughes (Cumberland Record Series 2; Carlisle, 1961), pp. 34–61.

6   D. J. W. Mawson, 'Another important copy of John Denton's manuscript', *CW2*, 78 (1978), pp. 97–103.

7   As described in H (see below, Appendix I, no. [7]), p. 215.

8   The Holme [2], Jackson A177 [16] and Aglionby [19] manuscripts fall into this category.

9   D. Mawson, 'John Denton re-visited: a fresh appraisal of the manuscript transcripts of his "Accompt"', *CW3*, 4 (2004), pp. 165–6.

Series A	Series B
'Part 1'	
A1 [Cumberland bounds]	A1 [Cumberland bounds]
to	to
A44 [Linstock]	A44 [Linstock]
B1 [Ainstable]	D1 [Wetheral]
to	
	to
B14 [Caldbeck]	
'Part 2'	D55 [Waverton Parva]
	C1 [Crofton]
C1 [Crofton]	
	to
to	
	C15 [Langrigg]
C15 [Langrigg]*	B1 [Ainstable]
D1 [Wetheral]	
	to
to	
	B14 [Caldbeck]
	D56 [Waverton Magna]
D56 [Waverton Magna]	
	'Four leaves'
Series A manuscripts omit the account of Wiggonby [C10]	E1 [Millom]
	to
	E9 [Drigg]

are preserved in both series (that is, excluding the 'four leaves'). The lengths of these sections exhibit a striking pattern. In the Machell MS, 'Part 1' and 'Part 2' each contain 64 pages and are paginated separately. The length of sections A to D is as shown opposite.

In other words, two outer sections, each 46 pages in length, encase two inner sections (B and C), each 18 pages long. The symmetry may explain the different ordering of Series A and Series B manuscripts. In the Series B transcripts the two longer sections (A and D) precede the two shorter sections, the order of which is reversed (C, B). This can be explained by envisaging a central quire in the original, containing sections B and C, becoming detached, the leaves being folded back

Section	Pagination (Machell MS)	Length (pages)
Part 1		
A	1–46	46 pp.
B	46–64	18 pp.
Part 2		
C	1–18	18 pp.
D	18–64	46 pp.

on themselves so that the order was reversed (C preceding B), and then being copied after the surviving bound sections (A, D). If this explanation is correct, it follows that the arrangement of the Series A manuscripts is likely to be closer to the lost original.

Such a conclusion is supported by other evidence. Although there is little apparent method in the ordering of some individual entries, the order of the sections in the Series A manuscripts exhibits a broad geographical flow, across the county from south-west to north-east. Section A begins in the south-west corner and largely concerns places in the barony of Egremont; most of the entries in section B are for places in Allerdale; in section C the focus is on Burgh barony; and in section D on the east of the county in a sequence from Culgaith in the south to Stapleton in the north (see Map; Outline of Contents). Second, internal evidence for the date of compilation of Denton's text (see below) hints that section D was produced slightly later than sections A to C: it would seem more likely that those sections completed last would come at the end of original manuscript, as they do in Series A, rather than in the middle, as they do in the Series B arrangement. It is therefore suggested that the Series B transcripts were the result of merging 'Part 1' and 'Part 2' and re-arranging the order of the text.

However, if the order of the Series A transcripts is closer to Denton's original, the Series B manuscripts nevertheless include material missing from Series A (see Appendix II). Unlike the Series A copies, they include transcripts of the 'four leaves' (section E). These are described as being 'stiched into the originall' in Series B but as 'loose sheets' when Machell had them copied separately to accompany his Series A transcript. The Series B transcripts also capture more of the text in the latter pages of 'Part 1' (sections B11 to B14). Series A manuscripts carry a note following B11 (Newton) that 'The coppy whereout this transcript was taken is rent in the remainder of this title of Newton, as alsoe in the severall titles following'. The foot of that page (numbered p. 59 in the early Series A copies) and several of the following pages (pp. 60, 62 and 63) appear to have been decayed in the version from which the Series A manuscripts were derived.[10] In contrast, the Series B manuscripts do not contain a note about damage to the original and offer transcripts of material at the foot of these pages which is missing from the Series A transcripts. The Series B copies also include an account of Wiggonby (C10), which is missing from most Series A transcripts.

Conversely, some material in Series A transcripts is missing from Series B. This includes material in note form and in Latin, such as the name of Gilbert Curwen, adrift at the end of the account of Workington (A29); the three place-names similarly unattached at the end of the account of Burgh barony (A34); and Latin material in the accounts of Wampool (C5), Kirkbampton (C11) and Embleton (D51). These particular omissions might be explained by the Series B copyist concentrating on producing a transcript of the coherent prose. However, in one section, the source used by the Series B copyist was more damaged than that used for Series A: in Series B the bounds of Holm Cultram (D54) are incomplete and the copyist has noted that the source copy was torn, whereas the bounds are given in full in Series A versions.

As part of the work for this volume, a detailed analysis was made of the texts of seven Series A and Series B manuscripts,[11] comparing each copy in turn against Ferguson's printed edition to allow the pattern of textual variants to be captured and analysed. The Series A and Series B manuscripts differed from each other in detail: occasional phrases and some longer sections of text occur in one series but not in the other; and there are minor differences in wording between the two series (these are summarised in Appendix II). Perhaps the most significant variant is in the list of bishops of Carlisle (section A35): the last bishop named in Series B transcripts is Bishop Robinson (1598–1616) but in Series A copies the list ends with his successor Bishop Snowden (1616–1621). The implication is that Series B manuscripts are based on a source copy dating from before 1616, whereas the source copy of the Series A transcripts is of a later date.[12]

---

10 See below, pp. 104–10.
11 The manuscripts analysed are those numbered 1, 2, 3, 6, 7, 9 and 10 in Appendix I.
12 Such a conclusion is also consistent with the appearance of the Dalston genealogy in the account of Little Dalston (A36), where the Series B transcripts end with Sir George Dalston, who inherited in 1633 and died in 1657, but the

The weight of evidence suggests that the two series derived from different copies of the original, rather than being the work of different scribes transcribing an original text. The differences in the ordering of material might have been the result of different copyists working with the same original, but the distinction between the two series in terms of damaged pages and minor textual variations suggests that the two series had diverged at an earlier stage. The pattern of damaged pages is perhaps the clinching evidence: in the copy from which the Series A copyist was working, the bottom of the pages of sections B11 to B14 were 'rent' and could not be copied, whereas the page containing the bounds of Holm Cultram (D54) was intact. In Series B, by contrast, an attempt at transcribing the material in B11 to B14 could be made, whereas the page containing the Holm Cultram boundary description was 'torn'. Either one of the copyists was working from a transcript of the original made before the damage recorded by the other had occurred, or both were working from separate transcripts. One of the series, at least, must lie at least two removes from Denton's text.

Multiple copies were in existence when transcripts were made in the later seventeenth century, as is clear from the comment in the Machell MS that the final pages of Part 1 were 'rent' in 'the coppy whereout this transcript was taken' and expressing the hope that a 'faire(r) coppie may be comed by'.[13] However, it is possible that the original text did survive. William Gilpin's careful annotations in his re-ordered transcript [11], recording erasures and changes in ink in what he terms 'the originall' manuscript, show that the copy he was using bore the sort of modifications which might be expected to be found in an original text. It was clearly an early copy (Gilpin describes some of the amendments as having been made in an 'auncient hand'),[14] but he provided no information about its provenance. Both Gilpin's [11] and Thomas Denton's [13b] re-ordered transcripts contain most of the omissions listed in Appendix II, including the material omitted from both Series A and Series B transcripts. This, and Gilpin's belief that he was working from the original, strongly suggest that they both had access to a copy other than the source copies from which Series A and Series B manuscripts derived and that this may, indeed, have been the lost original.

Series A copies add his son Sir William and, in the case of MSS [2] and [3], the date '1670'.

13 Below, section B11.

14 Gilpin MS (CRO, DX 1915/1), pp. 8, 17, 66, 146, 185–6, 295, 298–9, 365–6, 374.

The only hints as to the possible whereabouts of an original text at the period from which the earliest surviving transcripts date lie in the references to collections of Denton's material in the hands of two separate individuals, 'Dr Denton' and James Bird of Brougham. Thomas Machell obtained access to material in the possession of 'Dr Denton': his transcript of the 'four leaves' (section E) derived from some loose sheets 'put in the ancient copy (penes Dr Denton)' but 'not part of the copy', and he also listed '3 Collections in Order to the Antiq[uities] of Cumb[erland]' which were likewise 'penes Dr Denton' and consisted of notes of escheats, fines and pleas from the Crown records.[15] The main clue to the identity of Dr Denton is provided by an addition to the sheet listing the latter '3 Collections' which locates him 'at the Corner house on your left hand as you goe into ...... [sic] streete towards Lincolns Inn fields'. The most likely candidate is Dr William Denton (1605–1691), the royal physician and a member of the Denton family of Hillesden, Hertfordshire, whose main residence was at Covent Garden.[16] It is not immediately clear why he should have been in possession of John Denton's history, though he was a scholarly man with an interest in history and the Hillesden Dentons claimed ultimate descent from the Dentons of Denton, Cumberland.[17]

A very similar assemblage of manuscripts associated with John Denton is recorded as being in the hands of James Bird (c. 1637 – c. 1714) of Brougham Hall, Westmorland, attorney and steward to Lord Tufton, in two independent sources, almost thirty years apart. In 1682 Bird lent Sir Daniel Fleming of Rydal, himself an antiquary, three of 'Mr Denton's' books, containing notes on charters, fines and pleas and the following year 'some loose sheets of Mr Jo. Denton's' which can be identified as the 'four leaves' (section E).[18] In 1708 Bird lent Bishop William Nicolson a copy of 'Mr Denton's MS', which, since Nicolson referred to its '2d part', may have been a Series A

15 CRO, Machell MSS, Vol. VI, pp. 525, 527.

16 See J. Broad, 'Denton, William', ODNB. See also Appendix I, no. [24]. The street directions referring to Lincoln's Inn Field are not incompatible with an address on the eastern side of Covent Garden, which is where William Denton dwelt: S. Whyman, Sociability and Power in Late-Stuart England: the cultural worlds of the Verneys 1660–1720 (Oxford, 1999), p. 68, Plate 16.

17 C. J. Denton, 'The Dentons of Cumberland: a pedigree', The Carlisle Patriot, 14 Nov. 1873, p. 3. I am grateful to Mary Wane for this reference. See also ODNB (as note 16).

18 See Appendix I, no. 4. Fleming's transcripts of the charters etc. are preserved in CRO, D/Lons/L12/2/11.

copy of Denton's history.[19] The descriptions suggest that the material in the possession of Dr Denton and James Bird was very similar. Questions such as whether there were two sets of copies or whether the manuscripts in Dr Denton's hands had passed to Bird before 1682; whether the copy or copies of the history were John Denton's original; and whether either Dr Denton or James Bird was the source of the manuscript that Gilpin considered to be 'the originall' when he transcribed it in 1687, remain tantalisingly unanswered.

AUTHORSHIP

Nowhere in the body of the text is the name of the author of the history stated, but the work was being attributed to John Denton of Cardew by the later seventeenth century. William Gilpin, in the preface to his re-ordered version [11], dated 1687, assigned authorship to 'an ancestor of Mr Denton's of Cardew';[20] to the transcriber of the Mawson MS [8] the author was 'One Mr Denton of Cardew near Carlisle, in the latter End of Queen Eliz's Reigne';[21] and both Sir Daniel Fleming, in his list of manuscripts, and William Nicolson, annotating the Machell MS [1] in the early eighteenth century, identified John Denton as the author.[22] Other transcripts do not assign authorship – Thomas Denton's transcripts of Part 2 [13a] are merely headed 'an Old Manuscript of the Etimoligies of divers Parishes, Townes, & houses in Cumberland, and also ye geneoligies, and and [sic] Pedigrees of many ancient Families, who were & are owners'.[23]

There seems little reason to doubt the attribution to John Denton of Cardew, who is known to have been an active antiquary and to have compiled materials towards a history of Cumberland.[24] He was born c. 1561, son of Henry Denton of Cardew in Dalston parish, the seat of the Dentons since the fourteenth century. Their estates

---

19 Nicolson transcribed a pedigree of the Dentons of Cardew and a note about the manor of Dalston magna which were to be found 'Before the 2d part of Mr Denton's MS. in a copy lent to me (W. Carliol.) by Mr Bird of Brougham, Jun. 3 1708': CRO, Machell MSS, Vol. VI, p. 81.

20 CRO, DX 1915/1.

21 This and the prefaces to the Gilpin and Craighall MSS (Appendix I, nos. [11] and [10]) are printed in Mawson, 'John Denton re-visited', pp. 169–71.

22 CRO, D/Lons/L12/2/15, f. 230; Carlisle Dean & Chapter muniments, Machell MSS, Vol. VI, p. 1.

23 Manx National Heritage Library, MS5A, p. 1.

24 The following biographical account is based on Wilson, 'First historian' and M. Wane and A. J. L. Winchester, 'Denton, John', ODNB.

were dispersed but not extensive: at his death in November 1617 John Denton held the manors of Cardew and Parton and a scatter of other properties in and around Carlisle, as well as lands in the vicinity of Wooler in north Northumberland (at Ingram, Heathpool, and Fawberry).[25] In 1587 the annual rental income from his estates had amounted to £107 8s. 7d.[26] The Dentons held their Cardew estate from the bishops of Carlisle and, in his youth, John Denton served as a page in the household of Bishop Richard Barnes (1570–1577). He trained in law and married Elizabeth, daughter of his neighbour, Sir John Dalston of Dalston, before 1585. After his wife's death in 1595, Denton was appointed as a Crown agent in Cumberland for the discovery of concealed lands, a role which almost certainly under-pinned his extensive knowledge of land-ownership in the county. He undertook a considerable search of public records in the Tower of London between January and April 1601.[27] It was later said that, under the 'pretence' of pursuing a claim that the Crown had an interest in the estates of Sir Wilfred Lawson of Isel, he obtained a warrant to search 'all the Records of the Crowne'.[28] Perhaps it is not surprising that Lawson was accused in 1608 of using 'Slanderous and hard speaches' against Denton.[29] Denton also gained access to Carlisle diocesan records through his kinsman Henry Robinson, bishop of Carlisle (1598–1616), which again led to an acrimonious dispute, during which Denton was accused of having 'embez-zled' charters; had 'the secrett fingering' of all the records of the church of Carlisle; 'insinuated' himself into private estate archives; and accumulated 'whole loads of old evidences gotten heere and there'. He ruffled the feathers of his neighbours in Cumberland and was said to be 'stored to fill his countrie full of broiles' as a result of his researches.[30] As James Wilson put it, Denton seems to have been 'a mischievous influence in Cumberland'.[31] A garbled memory of his dispute with the bishop probably lies behind the legend (almost certainly without foundation) reported by William Gilpin in the preface to his reordered transcript. The history, he said, was 'supposed to be writ by an ancestor of Mr Denton's of Cardew

---

25 PRO, C142/382/17.
26 CRO, D/Lons/L13/3/1, rental 1587.
27 The material he consulted is listed in PRO, SP12/279, ff. 124–5.
28 Wilson, 'First historian', p. 12.
29 PRO, SP14/32, f. 50 (modern numbering '62').
30 Wilson, 'First historian', p. 12.
31 Ibid., 8.

during the time of his imprisonment (as tis said) in the Tower, upon a contest that hapned to be betwixt him & Dr Robinson then Bp of Carliell'.[32] Rather than languishing in the Tower as a prisoner, Denton was, in all probability, assiduously working through the records there in connection with his work for the Crown.

It was, presumably, a short step from gathering historical evidence in an official capacity to organising his material into coherent histories of individual manors. Denton had apparently begun his antiquarian writing no later than 1600. Reginald Bainbrigg, the schoolmaster at Appleby, who was William Camden's correspondent in Cumbria, wrote of Denton's work in glowing terms. His letter to Camden, written in 1600 or 1602, is worth quoting at length:

> from thence I went to Mr John Denton of Cardew, with whome dyverse tymes I had bene verie earnest to further your work, being a man well reed in antiquities in his owne contrie, as anie one man in the northe. I found that he has taken great paines.

> To my comfort, and your credit, he haith wryt the antiquitie of Carelile, Holme Cultram and of the most ancient townes in Cumberland, the petegre and armes of the ancyent gentlemen of that countrie, you will find it a rare and worthie peace of work, we could have wished that Cumberland had bene omitted in this last impression, till you had receyved thes his notes, he told me that he wold bring them to you this next terme, he dailie traveleth from plaice to place about this busyness, till he have finished it with credit, he goes by no hearesaies but by ancient records, you will think yourself most bound unto him.[33]

It is highly probable that these antiquarian endeavours reported by Bainbrigg resulted in the texts which collectively came to be known as John Denton's history and are printed in this volume.

DATING

Several transcripts of Denton's manuscript had been made by the end of the seventeenth century, when William Nicolson could report that 'several of the Gentry' possessed copies.[34] None of the surviving transcripts can be placed earlier than c. 1670, the date on the title page of the Machell MS [1], probably the earliest of the early Series A copies. The Fleming 1 MS [4] appears to date from before 1683. The Holme [2], Jackson [3], Fleming 2 [5] and Hutton John [6] MSS do not

32 CRO, DX 1915/1, p. 1.
33 Printed in F. Haverfield, 'Cotton Iulius F. VI', *CW2*, 11 (1911), pp. 369–70.
34 W. Nicolson, *English Historical Library* (London, 1696), Vol. I, p. 30.

bear dates but the hands of [2], [3] and [5] and internal evidence of [6] suggest that all were produced before 1700. The Series B manuscripts may be slightly later. Only the Craighall MS [10] carries a date: the preface by Hugh Todd, offering the transcript to Viscount Preston of Netherby, is dated 29 August 1688. On internal evidence, the Mawson MS [8] can be dated to 1690x1694; its sister copy, the Holkham MS [7] is likely to be of similar date, though the hands of both these manuscripts would not be out of keeping with a date in the early eighteenth century. The text printed in this volume is drawn from Machell MS [1], transcribed in 1670, and Holkham MS [7], probably transcribed in the 1690s.

Arriving at a date for Denton's original compilation is problematic. It was suggested above that the surviving transcripts may be at least two steps removed from Denton's original text, so it is necessary to distinguish between the date of the 'original' and that of the intermediate copies from which the surviving manuscripts were taken. Further, it is clear from internal evidence that the lost original was itself of composite date: different sections appear to have been completed at different dates and in some individual entries there appear to be differences in date between the body of the text and marginal genealogies.

Both Series A and Series B manuscripts include amendments post-dating John Denton's death in 1617. The Series A manuscripts bring the list of bishops of Carlisle (A35) down to Robert Snowden, consecrated in November 1616; both series bring the Dalston genealogy (A36) forward beyond Sir John, who died in 1633, and two of the Series A copies include the date 1670. In the entry for Leathes (C6) the current owner is named in the text as Adam Leathes, who died in 1621, but the marginal genealogy, in the Series B Holkham MS, brings the descent forward to Thomas Leathes, with the date '3 Caro.' (i.e. 1627–28). It seems likely that additions continued to be made to the original or the copies derived from it.

Putting such additions aside, there can be no doubt that different sections of the original text attained the form in which they survive at different times. This is most immediately apparent in the case of manors in Crown hands: the accounts of those said to be 'in the queen's hand' must have been drafted before the death of Elizabeth I in March 1603; those said to be 'in the king's hand' must postdate the accession of James I. Extending the analysis of dating evidence to cover other current landowners and occasional dateable events, it appears that Parts 1 and 2 were drawn up at slightly different dates:

Part 1 (sections A1 to B14). The closest dating evidence is provided by the account of Workington (A29), which is described as the seat of 'Nicholas Curwen Esq.', placing it between December 1596, when Curwen inherited from his father, and 1603, when he was knighted.[35] Other evidence is consistent with a date within that seven-year range: a *terminus post quem* in the later 1590s is provided by the dates of inheritance of other landowners;[36] a *terminus ante quem* of March 1603 by the accounts of Crown manors, which are said to be in the queen's, rather than the king's, hand.[37] The Holme MS [2] has the date '43 Eliz.' (1600–01) in the margin beside the descent of the Hudleston family of Millom (A3), which may be the date at which these sections were compiled.[38]

Part 2 (sections C1 to D56). Such close dating is not possible for Part 2; rather there is evidence to suggest that some sections were revised later than others, and that the accounts in section C may be earlier than those in section D. Crown manors in section C are said to be in the queen's hand; those in section D to be in the king's.[39] While at least one account in section D, Skirwith (D15), appears to have a *terminus ante quem* of 1604,[40] several other sections have *termini post quem* later than this: the genealogy of the Aglionby family (D7) is brought forward to '2° Jac.' (1604–05);[41] the fire at Holm Cultram church in 1604 is recorded (D54), as is the sale of Wythop to Richard Fletcher in 1606 (D50).

The 'four leaves' (sections E1 to E9). The note prefacing the transcript of these sections in Machell MS [1] recognised that they were separate from the body of the text (Parts 1 and 2) and interpreted them as being 'a fair transcript collected out of it … being writt more compendiously & in a similar stile'. If that is correct, it is probably safe to assume that these sections post-date the accounts of the same estates included in Part 1 (A3 to A5) but internal dating evidence is sparse and does not allow close dating of these sections.

---

35 See C. B. Phillips, 'Curwen family (*per c.* 1500 – *c.* 1725)', *ODNB.*

36 William Hudleston (A3) inherited in 1598; Edward Musgrave (B11) in 1596; Christopher Perkins (B2) became dean of Carlisle in 1596.

37 These are Ennerdale (A20) and Kirklinton (A39).

38 Oxford, Bodleian Library, MS Top. Cumb. c.1, p. 9.

39 In the queen's hand: Aikton (C2); Gamblesby (C4); Grinsdale (C8); in the king's hand: Newby (D6); Holm Cultram (D54).

40 The account seems to date from after the death of Thomas Hutton in 1601 but before his son Lancelot sold Skirwith in 1604: *CFH*, p. 176.

41 It also includes the marriage of Edward Aglionby to Jane Brougham, which cannot be dated precisely but is thought to have taken place *c.* 1608: Summerson, *Aglionbys*, pp. 88–90.

In summary, therefore, John Denton's history is a composite text, parts dating from a few years either side of 1600, other sections having been completed (or revised) in the middle years of the first decade of the seventeenth century. It is very probable that the history was the work on which Denton was engaged *c.* 1600, when Reginald Bainbrigg wrote of his scholarship in such glowing terms. William Gilpin was therefore not far out in 1687, when he entitled his reordered transcript an account of estates and families 'from the Conquest unto the beginning of the Raign of K. James'.[42] The conventional date of *c.* 1610, assigned to the history by R. S. Ferguson, is almost certainly a few years too late for most of the text.[43]

JOHN DENTON'S HISTORY OF CUMBERLAND

Denton's collection of manorial histories of Cumberland was part of the flowering of antiquarian endeavour in the latter part of Elizabeth's reign, stimulated by the publication of William Camden's *Britannia* in 1586. The arrangement of Camden's work county by county, the publication of Christopher Saxton's county maps in 1579 and of William Harrison's 'Description of Britain' in Raphael Holinshed's *Chronicles* (1577) fostered an awareness of place and of county identity among the gentry, which generated an appetite for county histories. The first to appear in print was William Lambarde's *Perambulation of Kent* (1576).[44] Almost exactly contemporary with Denton's history were the manuscript *View of Staffordshire* by Sampson Erdeswicke (d. 1603); Richard Carew's *Survey of Cornwall* (published 1602); Robert Reyce's manuscript *Breviary of Suffolk* (1603); George Owen's manuscript *Description of Penbrokshire* (1603); and John Norden's published volumes for his intended series, *Speculum Britanniae* (Middlesex, 1593; Hertfordshire, 1598).[45] Although the scope of most

---

42 CRO, DX 1915/1.

43 Ferguson, *Accompt*, p. iii.

44 For the development of county history writing in the late sixteenth and early seventeenth centuries, see C. R. J. Currie and C. P. Lewis (eds), *A Guide to English County Histories* (Stroud, 1994); S. A. E. Mendyk, '*Speculum Britanniae*': *regional study, antiquarianism and science in Britain to 1700* (Toronto, 1989), and J. Broadway, '*No historie so meete*': *gentry culture and the development of local history in Elizabethan and early Stuart England* (Manchester, 2006).

45 For these authors see Broadway, '*No historie so meete*', pp. 33–6; D. Miles, ' "An exquisite antiquary": George Owen of Henllys (1552–1613)', *Transactions of the Honourable Society of Cymmrodorion*, new series 5 (1999 for 1998), pp. 5–23 and, with the exception of Reyce, entries in *ODNB*.

of these antiquarian accounts of other counties was generally wider than Denton's, parallels can be seen, most obviously in the focus on genealogy and gentry lineages and in the fascination with the meaning of place-names, seen particularly in Norden.

Structure

The surviving manuscripts of Denton's history provide only incomplete coverage of Cumberland (see Map). Although parts of the county are treated at the level of the individual manor or township, there are substantial gaps and large areas are missing. Denton's intention appears to have been to structure his account around the baronies and other major units of overlordship into which most of the county was divided. After a perambulation of the county boundary (A1), section A contains accounts of most of the baronies: Copeland or Egremont (A2), Allerdale (A30, A33), Burgh by Sands (A31, A34), Greystoke (A32), Dalston (A31, A35), Liddell (A37), Kirklinton (A39), Gilsland (A43) and Linstock (A44). The intended final structure is probably preserved in the account of Copeland, in which the descent of the barony (A2) is followed by accounts of its constituent manors (A3 to A13 and A15 to A29), arranged in more or less topographical order, from Millom (A3) in the south to Workington (A29) in the north. The 'four leaves' (section E), which probably represent the beginnings of a second recension of the treatment of Copeland, are again arranged topographically, from Millom (E1) to Drigg and Carleton (E9).

Most of sections B, C and D consist of accounts of individual manors and townships, though an entry for Wigton barony (B12) and a second account of Gilsland (C13) are also included. Some sections consist of topographical 'runs' of manorial accounts but the order of others appears to be random, as though a series of short individual texts has been gathered up and copied without attempting to place them in order. The most organised runs of text, apart from the accounts of manors in Copeland (A3–A13, A15–A29), are C1 to C8 (the Solway lowlands, consisting of a sweep of manors and townships from Crofton through the barony of Burgh to Grinsdale) and D13 to D45 (north-eastern Cumberland from Culgaith in the south, along the Pennine edge to the barony of Gilsland, ending in Laversdale). Other less systematic groupings include B3 to B11 (Allerdale manors from Uldale to Westnewton) and D1 to D9 (manors surrounding Carlisle, from Wetheral to Cardew). The overall result, as shown in the Map, is that the history provides good coverage of manors in the baronies of Copeland, Burgh by Sands and Gilsland and in the Carlisle and 'east of Eden' areas, but very little detail below the level of overlordship for the honour of Cockermouth, much of Allerdale, the baronies of Greystoke and Liddell, Inglewood forest and most of the honour of Penrith.

Although we cannot be sure of the exact order in which Denton intended to place his manorial descents, there is little evidence that he intended to structure his account of the county by following the course of rivers, as had become the convention among topographers following in the tradition of Leland and Camden.[46] Using the baronies as his framework, he tended to arrange the runs of manorial histories by reference to topographical features other than watercourses. The Copeland and Burgh barony sequences (A3–A13, A15–A29; C7–C8) trace settlements along the coast; the sequence for the 'east of Eden' manors (D13–D30) follows the villages along the foot of the Pennine scarp. Only the sequence following the east bank of the river Wampool from Parton to Whitrigg (C3–C7) uses a river as a route.

Content

Denton's accounts of each manor or township usually contain two elements, an interpretation of the meaning of the place-name and the descent of ownership from the earliest record he had found through, in many cases, to the time when he was writing. His approach was firmly in the tradition of what Jan Broadway has termed 'genealogical history', tracing the descent of property and the lineages of landowning families.[47] His focus was on documents, rather than antiquities, as he constructed a narrative of the descent of lordship, citing the evidence of deeds, inquisitions and fines, sometimes entering a summary list of owners in the margin of his pages. Like his contemporaries, he displayed an interest in heraldry but this was generally secondary to following the twists and turns of family fortune. Of the dozen coats of arms which he tricked, several were those of his own family and of his neighbours: Denton of Cardew and Lamplugh of Lamplugh (his mother's family); Brisco of Crofton, Orton of Orton and Raughton of Raughton.[48] The remainder are scattered and show little evidence of systematic collection, but references to armorial bearings become slightly more frequent in the sections which appear to have been completed later (sections D and E),

46 Broadway, *'No historie so meete'*, p. 222.
47 Ibid., p. 154.
48 See below: A23, C1, C9, D9, D49.

perhaps suggesting an evolving intention to include heraldic information more consistently.[49]

In general, Denton presented the factual information about each manor without comment but on a handful of occasions he allowed himself to express opinions, which, in their different ways, reflect the importance of lineage in the eyes of Elizabethan gentry. The concept of lineage, linking 'the inheritance of blood from one's ancestors inextricably with the maintenance of their ancient estate',[50] was strong. Millom castle provided him with an opportunity to offer a withering comment on the course of social change in the sixteenth century: the Hudlestons continued to live in the castle and, in Denton's view, the 'old manner of strong building ... doe better witness their ancient and present greatness & worth, than the painted vanityes of our times doe grace our new-upstartes.'[51] Lineage was also threatened by the passage of time and by human folly. Naworth Castle 'through negligence more then age begins now to decline and loose the beautye and strength which it lately had, as all such worldly things doe which are subject to tyme' and Millom Castle 'through length of time threatneth ruine.'[52] Of the early failure of Randulph Levington's male line, despite his name surviving in Randalinton, near Kirklinton, he commented 'soe much doth almighty God scorne that foolish ambitious desires of man, thinking to live by trust in himselfe and by his owne witt & strength to establish his name & succession'.[53]

A threat to Denton's own lineage seems to have lain behind his partisan attitude towards the Dacres, which appears to have had its origins in a deep-rooted sense of grievance over the loss of the manor of Ainstable, which Thomas Lord Dacre had, he claimed, 'extorted' from his forebear, John Denton, in the fifteenth century. In Denton's view this 'tyranny of the Dacres' did not go unpunished, as Dacre's son was killed at the battle of Towton in 1461.[54] His further comment that the Dacres had 'wrung out all the freeholders of Irthington and Brampton' also speaks of hostility towards the family[55] – a family

49 References to arms occur in sections A3, A23, A39, A43, C1, C9, C13, D9, D26, D39, D49, D53, E2 and E5.
50 Broadway, 'No historie so meete', p. 154.
51 Below, E1.
52 Below, D33, E1.
53 Below, A39.
54 Below, B1.
55 Below, B31.

which had notoriously lost its Cumberland estates as a consequence of Leonard Dacre's involvement in the Northern Rising of 1569/70.[56]

Stories concerning individual lords are woven into the narrative, such as that of the Muslim princess and the Christian captive (A3); the tradition about the tragedy which led to the founding of Bolton Priory, Yorkshire (A33); the story besmirching the name of Hugh Morvill's mother (B10); and the tradition about the slaying of Gilles-bueth, pre-Norman lord of Gilsland (repeated in A43, C13 and D35). Apart from the discussion of place-names, there is comparatively little topographical information or description of antiquities. The main exception is the account of Carlisle itself (B2), which describes the street layout of the medieval city, refers to the finding of a coin hoard and lists holy relics belonging to the priory. Little mention is made of Roman or other antiquities, the main exceptions being the fort at Bowness on Solway (C8) and Walls Castle at Ravenglass (B2 and E7), the latter of which is, however, interpreted variously as Arthurian or as a precursor of the lordly seat at Muncaster Castle.

The interpretation of place-names was also part of the standard fare of the late-Elizabethan antiquary. William Lambarde had started the tradition by prefacing the account of each place in his *Perambulation of Kent* (1577) with the meaning of the name, drawing on his knowledge of Old English, but the form of Denton's place-name interpretations owes more to John Norden's 'Speculum Britanniae', in which a Latin translation of the name is followed by an explanation.[57] Most of the interpretations offered by Denton and his contemporaries are wrong but they shed significant light on conceptions of the past.

Many of Denton's interpretations summon up the establishment of feudal landownership at the Norman Conquest, as in his – often correct – identification of twelfth-century landowners' names in -*by* compounds such as Moresby (A26) and Botcherby (D8), in which he noted that the place was named from the person who 'first seated

56 See H. Summerson, 'Dacre, Leonard', *ODNB* and K. J. Kesselring, *The Northern Rebellion of 1569: Faith, Politics and Protest in Elizabethan England* (Basingstoke, 2007), pp. 48–9, 88–9, 98–9.
57 Norden's explanation of Benington, Herts, provides a typical example: 'BENINGTON ... or BENIGNTON *villa Beningna*, eyther of the bountie of the inhabitants, or the pleasent and profitable scituation of the place. As *Blithe* in the North partes *de iucunditate* of myrth and good fellowship': J. Norden, *The Description of Hartfordshire* (London, 1598; Facsimile edition (The English Experience No. 403) Amsterdam, 1971), p. 13.

himself there'. Others demonstrate an awareness of the northern vernacular: Thwaites (E2) from 'thwaite', an enclosed clearing; Bigg-lands (C4), from 'bigg', barley; Laythes (C6) from 'leath', a corn barn, for example. He perpetuated one particular error of Lambarde's in assuming that the syllable *ing*, in *-ington* and *-ingham* compounds, represented the northern vernacular 'ing', a meadow.[58] One of the most striking aspects of Denton's place-name interpretations is the frequency with which he turned to the Celtic languages for explanations. A total of nineteen place-names are interpreted as being Celtic, the majority as deriving from Irish Gaelic (ten names are explicitly stated to be 'Irish').[59] His knowledge of Welsh and/or Gaelic is also evident in his suggestion that the arms of the Brisco family alluded to the Welsh *brysg* or Gaelic *brisg* ('lively').[60] How he acquired that knowledge is not known: it may be that Gaelic could be heard in Elizabethan Carlisle, as a result of contacts across the Irish Sea between Cumberland and Gaelic-speaking Scottish or Irish merchants. Certainly, some of his attempted explanations suggest oral rather than written transmission: he writes 'oan' or 'oon' for *abhann* (river); 'derig' for *darach* (oak); 'daen' for *domhain* (deep); 'fillough'/'flogh' for *fliuch* (wet).[61]

Sources

His etymological comments apart, Denton's history consists largely of a collection of manorial descents and genealogies. It is clear, both from internal evidence and from what is known of Denton's work as an antiquary, that his accounts are firmly grounded in archival sources. His starting point was the 'Chronicon Cumbrie' or

---

58 For example, in his explanations of Rottington (A16), Hensingham (A18) and Distington (A27). Discussing Kentish *-ingas* names (Malling, Yalding etc.), Lambarde wrote 'ing signifieth a lowe ground, or medow, and so remaineth knowen in the North countrie of England till this present daie': W. Lambarde, *Perambulation of Kent* (London, 1596 edition), p. 415.

59 He suggests Irish derivations for Arlecdon (A19), Calder (A12), Ennerdale (A20), Lamplugh (A23); Glasson (C8), Dundraw (C12), Glassonby (D11), Denton (D34), Ravenglass (E8), Drigg (E9) and British derivations for Torpenhow (B6), Cardurnock (C7), Croglin (D26). British or Irish derivations are suggested for Carlisle (B2) and Scarrowmanwick (D21), and Celtic derivations are implicit in his interpretations of Cargo (D12), Melmerby (D16), Castle Carrock (D28), and Kirkcambeck (D42).

60 Below, C1.

61 See C8 (Glasson); D11 (Glassonby); E9 (Drigg); D34 (Denton); A23 (Lamplugh); A19 (Arlecdon). I am grateful to Oliver Padel and Bernadette Cunningham for their comments on Denton's use of Celtic languages.

'Distributio Cumbirlandiae ad Conquestum Angliae', one of a group of documents drawn up in connection with a series of lawsuits concerning the Multon and Lucy families' claims to the honour of Cockermouth between 1275 and 1316. These describe the division of the county into baronies after the Conquest and trace the descent of the baronies of Copeland and Allerdale to the later thirteenth century.[62] Denton accepted without question the erroneous statement that it was William I who conquered Cumberland – and it was the heavy reliance of later antiquaries on Denton's history that ensured that the error was perpetuated until the nineteenth century. Despite this, the 'Chronicon Cumbrie' provided Denton with a valuable account of the descent of the two great western baronies.

The footnotes in this volume demonstrate that Denton's archival research was extensive and his use of his sources generally accurate: despite the distance of the surviving transcripts from Denton's original, errors of name and date are comparatively few. He appears to have undertaken systematic trawls of several major sources then in the Tower of London, notably the inquisitions *post mortem* and feet of fines. He also used the charter rolls and the 'Testa de Nevill'. The record of his thirteen visits to the Tower to consult public records in his capacity as Crown agent between 31 January and 18 April 1601 shows that he consulted *carta* (charters), *patentes* (letters patent), *fines* (final concords) and (by far the most numerous) *bundell'*, probably bundles of escheats, the inquisitions *post mortem* which feature so prominently in the history.[63]

He also had access to local records. He consulted monastic charters, almost certainly the full cartulary of Holm Cultram abbey and *inspeximus* charters, at least, for the priory of Carlisle and the houses of Lanercost, St Bees and Wetheral.[64] Whether he had access to Lord William Howard's library at Naworth is unclear: Howard possessed at least one of the surviving copies of the Holm Cultram cartulary as well as that of Wetheral.[65] The fact that Denton calendared in some

---

62 'Chronicon Cumbrie' is printed in *St Bees*, no. 498; the associated documents are printed ibid., Illustrative Documents VI and VII (pp. 530–3). These sources are discussed in *VCH Cumb., I*, pp. 297–8.

63 PRO, SP12/279, ff. 124–5.

64 James Wilson suggested that Denton did not have access to the St Bees cartulary but saw original charters relating to the priory in the private muniments of local gentry: *St Bees*, p. xxxvii.

65 G. R. C. Davis, *Medieval Cartularies of Great Britain: a Short Catalogue* (London, 1958), nos. 492–4, 1025.

detail the grants to Holm Cultram abbey suggests that he had free access to the cartulary of that house, perhaps to the copy that was later in the possession of members of the local gentry (including Thomas Denton of Warnell).[66] He also had access to the title deeds of some lay estates and his occasional references to seals show that he had looked at some original charters.[67] As has been noted, it was said that he had 'insinuated' himself into estate archives and some sections of his history suggest that he had consulted charters belonging to private landowners which no longer survive.[68]

Some of the collections of archival material which John Denton had gathered and which lay behind his history survived in the later seventeenth century. In 1682 Sir Daniel Fleming of Rydal borrowed and made transcripts of several volumes described as copies of 'Mr Denton's Book' from James Bird of Brougham. They included a 'Volume 1' (Cumberland and Westmorland fines levied in the reigns of John and Henry III), 'Volume 2' ('old pleas' from the reigns of Henry III and Edward I), and 'Volume 5' (copies of early charters, which Fleming did not transcribe), as well as copies of Denton's extracts from the 'escheats'.[69] Thomas Machell appears to have had access to similar material, which was then in the hands of 'Dr Denton', probably, as noted above, Dr William Denton, the London physician.[70] This consisted of three collections towards writing 'the Antiq[uities] of Cumb[erland]': first, 'The Sheat B' (presumably the 'escheats book'), containing *inter alia* escheats for Cumberland from 31 Henry III to 19 Edward IV; second, a volume containing 'fines levat' in com. Cumb. ab temp. H. 3 ad Hen. vii'; and thirdly 'old pleas' ('vetera placita Temp. R. H. 3 praecipiend' in Cumberland

---

66 The earliest copy of the Holm Cultram cartulary, which was given to Carlisle Cathedral Library by Joseph Nicolson in 1777, had previously been in the hands of 'Mr Blenerhasset' (owner of Flimby, one of Holm Cultram abbey's manors), Thomas Denton and Bishop William Nicolson: *Holm Cultram*, pp. viii–ix, 1.

67 He describes the seals of Henry of Little Dalston (A36), Hubert de Vaux (A43) and John de Crofton (C1).

68 Those of the Curwens of Workington (see section A29) and Hudlestons of Millom (E1), for example.

69 Volumes E, F, G and M of Fleming's antiquarian notebooks (CRO, D/Lons/L12/2/5–7 and 11) contain transcripts of Denton's material. Volumes E, F and G contain the 'escheats'; Volume M the transcripts described as Denton's 'Volume 2' (pp. 1–28) and 'Volume 1' (pp. 61–84). Hugh Todd copied a charter of Aethelwold, bishop of Carlisle, 'Ex Mss Denton': CRO, DX 1329/45, p. 661.

70 Broad, 'Denton, William'.

et alia').[71] The title of the third volume is strikingly similar to that of 'Volume 2' of Denton's books in James Bird's hands, perhaps suggesting that more than one copy of Denton's collected materials was then in existence.

One example survives of the method by which Denton organised his material when preparing his historical accounts. This is a descent of the manor of Gamelsby (in Aikton parish) of which Denton himself owned a moiety. Seemingly in Denton's hand, it consists of a series of abstracts taken from the 'bundles of escheats [Bondelles Escaetorum] remaining among the records in the Tower of London', arranged chronologically from 1305 to 1478 and tracing the descent of the two moieties, to demonstrate that Gamelsby was a manor in its own right, held in chief and therefore not owing suit to either Burgh or Aikton.[72] The entry for Gamelsby in Denton's history (below, section C4) is clearly based on these abstracts, summarising them into a succinct paragraph.

Had John Denton completed his manorial histories and succeeded in producing an organised account of the whole county, he would have left a remarkable and important text – manorial descents in the style of the Victoria County Histories, written three hundred years ahead of time. In the event, either Denton did not complete his work or parts of his manuscript history have been lost. What has survived is nevertheless an important and significant piece of antiquarian writing from the age of Camden. Its focus may be narrow and lacking when it comes to topography and physical antiquities – as Jan Broadway puts it, Denton's history is 'a county represented entirely through its landowning gentry'[73] – but, as this edition demonstrates, it is a history securely rooted in archival research and impressive in its accuracy. In the words of Reginald Bainbrigg, Denton's history of Cumberland is 'a rare and worthie peace of work',[74] which deserves recognition as the fount from which the writing of Cumbrian history has flowed for four hundred years.

---

71 CRO, Dean & Chapter Muniments, Machell MSS Vol. VI, p. 525.
72 CRO, D/Lons/L5/1/55, D.2. Although catalogued as 'W. Denton's account' of the manor, John Denton's authorship is made clear by the description of William Denton (*temp.* Henry VIII) as 'my great grandfather'.
73 Broadway, *'No historie so meete'*, p. 40.
74 Haverfield, 'Cotton Iulius F. VI', p. 369.

EDITORIAL METHOD

In the light of the analysis presented above, it is clear that a reconstruction of John Denton's history must take account of both Series A and Series B manuscripts. This edition is based on the Machell MS [1], the earliest complete surviving manuscript in Series A, incorporating additional material and noting textual variants from the Holkham MS [7], as representative of the Series B manuscripts. In his re-ordered copy of Denton's material, prepared in 1687 (Appendix I, no. [11]), William Gilpin noted those sections which had been erased or were in a different hand in 'the originall MS' from which he derived his text: those annotations are also noted in this edition.

The core of the text below is therefore that of the Machell MS [1] (hereafter 'M'): the order of the entries, the wording and the spelling are from that version. M contains numerous erasures and insertions, some identifiable as the work of Thomas Machell, for whom the transcript was made. Since the aim has been to present the text of M, shorn of Machell's additions and amendments, the incomplete Series A manuscript in Carlisle Library, Jackson A1114 [3] (hereafter 'J'), which appears to be of similar date to M, has been used as a guide when stripping out Thomas Machell's amendments. For the sections not covered by J, the text of the Holme MS [2] has been used.

The text presented below also incorporates variations found in the Series B Holkham Hall MS [7] (hereafter 'H'). Differences between H and M are treated thus:

- Material from H is shown between angled brackets, < thus >. Material which is additional to the text of M is presented without comment; replacement text from H, inserted where the wording of H appears more accurately to reflect the sense intended by Denton, is similarly treated but the wording in M is given in a footnote.
- Material in M which does not occur in H is underlined, thus.

Editorial changes

Since this edition is working with later copies of a manuscript in an attempt to reconstruct a lost original, I have felt free to modify the text of M and H in the interests of accessibility. The following method has been applied:

1. Original spelling has been retained.
2. Capitalisation and punctuation have been modernised. Punctuation differs considerably between M and H. In most cases the intended sense of the text is unproblematic but, where there is ambiguity in the placing of punctuation, this is explained in a footnote.
3. Some abbreviations have been expanded silently, including both standard English abbreviations (e.g. 'w^{ch}' for 'which'; 'y^t' for 'that') and abbreviated Latin ('fil' Radi' has been rendered 'filius Radulphi', for example). However, ampersands and abbreviated renderings of the names of kings and reigns (e.g. 'K. H. 3' for 'King Henry III') have been retained.
4. Other editorial material is given in square brackets.

Key to editorial conventions

Gilpin	Annotation in Gilpin MS [11]
H	Holkham Hall MS [7]
J	Jackson A1114 [3]
M	Machell MS [1]
< land >	material from H, either missing from or replacing material in M
<u>land</u>	material in M, missing from H
[*land*]	editorial material

OUTLINE OF CONTENTS

Second part

'Four leaves'

JOHN DENTON'S HISTORY OF CUMBERLAND

[*p. 1*]

[A Description of the Countey of Cumberland Booke the first.][1]

Cumberland

[**A1**] That country or countey now called Cumberland on the east side of the same is divided from Fournesse, a part of the countye of Lancaster, by the river of Dudden, which falleth into the Irish ocean at Milham-Castle, ascending by the banckes of that river upp to Uffay or Woolfhey-park,[2] Blakhall, & to the Shire-stones upon the mountaine Wryenose att the head of Dudden,[3] where it meeteth with the countye of Westmorland, first att Little Langdale in the fells, soe, leaving Great-Langdale and Gressmire on the east, it bordereth upon the same all the way from Langdale unto Dunmaile or Dunmaile-rase, a great heape or raise of stones at the head of Wythe-burne cast together in auncient time, either by King Dunmayle, sometime king or lord of that country, as a mark of the utmost border of his kingdome, or by some other in remembrance of his name, for some memorable act by him done there or some victorye against him;[4] and from thence on the back side of Helvelon or Hill-Belyne-hill by the

---

1 This marginal heading occurs in Holme MS [2] (Oxford, Bodleian Library, MS Top. Cumb. c.1, p. 1) but not in M, J or H.

2 Ulpha Park (SD 19 91).

3 The Three Shire Stone (at NY 277 027), where the counties of Cumberland, Westmorland and Lancashire met.

4 Dunmail Raise, the large cairn at NY 327 117, on the boundaries between the counties of Cumberland and Westmorland and the medieval dioceses of Carlisle and York, probably marked the southern edge of the kingdom of Strathclyde/Cumbria. It is named after Dunmail (Dufnal or Donald), king of Cumbria *c.* 940: see D. P. Kirby, 'Strathclyde and Cumbria: a survey of development to 1092', *CW2*, 62 (1962), pp. 87–9; C. Phythian-Adams, *Land of the Cumbrians: a study in British provincial origins AD 400–1120* (Aldershot, 1996), pp. 112–16.

head of Glenrhodden-beck[5] unto the head of Glenkewne-beck, by
that rill or little-beck Glenkewne-beck[6] < runneth > unto Ulswater,
a great laike; thence by the river Aymot,[7] which runneth forth of
Ulswater att Powley-stank,[8] descending by Dacre-Castle, Pearith,
& Carleton, falling till it be received of the great river of Eden; by
Eden unto the foote of Blenkarne Beck;[9] and thence by the sayd little
beck it is severed from Westmorland with that beck < that > springs
forth of the fells; it joyneth againe with Westmorland in the mountaines for the space of five or six miles. Then meeting with a little
corner of Yorkshire, it is boundred by the same untill the head of the
great river Teese, which divideth there Yorkshire from the county
of Duresme, and from thence to Kelloplaw- < hill >[10] by the same
countye Palatine of Duresme. From Kelloplaw-hill to the head of
Alneburne,[11] it adjoyneth to the countye of Northumberland, which
burne or little river untill Kirkhaugh (where it is received of the great
river South-Tyne) divideth two countyes, which in like manner on
the other side of Tyne are kept assunder by another little rill falling
into Tyne from the east side of the mountaines in Geltsdale Forrest;
from that little water untill the head of Hartley-burne, & thence
alongest the north east side of Geltsdale Forrest, and on Burntippelt
moore,[12] a great heath and waste, the said two countyes of Cumberland and Northumberland meete [p. 2] againe and are not severed
whilst[13] a little beck called Powtross[14] parts them, which falling into
the water of Irthing looseth its name, and then Irthing divides them;
ascending the same river, untill it receive a lesser water named Troutbeck, which in like sort falleth in beteewne them there they concurre
againe at the Horsehead, the Gele-cragg, and Christen-bury-cragg

---

5   Presumably Glenridding Beck is meant, but the county boundary followed the
    watershed from the summit of Helvellyn to Stybarrow Dodd (NY 343 189).
6   Glencoyne Beck (NY 37 18).
7   Altered to 'Eymot' in M; 'Aymot' in H. The modern form is Eamont.
8   Pooley Bridge (NY 470 243).
9   i.e. Crowdundle Beck (NY 65 30).
10 M reads 'Hall' but 'hill' is clearly meant. The modern form is Killhope Cross
    (NY 799 432).
11 i.e. Ayle Burn (NY 72 49).
12 This lost name presumably applied to the moorland where the Cumberland
    parishes of Denton and Farlam march with Northumberland (centred on
    NY 63 62). A memory of the name may survive in Tipalt Burn, Blenkinsopp,
    Northumberland (NY 669 643).
13 Crossed out; over-written 'till'. In margin: 'whels'. J reads 'whe'ls'; H reads
    'whels'.
14 Poltross Burn (NY 62 64).

unto Lamyford,[15] where Cumberland make a narrow poynt north-ward. There the river Lyddell on the north west side runns downe betweene Scottland and Cumberland, until Cannonbye holme where the water Esk entertaines it, & bereaves Liddell his name att the mote;[16] then ascending upp Esk towards Cannonbye it fetcheth in Kirkanders-Holmes, and there is parted from Scottland by a banck of earth & a ditch that reacheth from the side of Esk unto Sark,[17] a little Scottish brooke, which falling into Esk (and with Esk) soe into the river of Eden aforemencioned, are presently (together in one < channel >[18]) carried into the Irish Sea as the last bounder betweene them. From the foote of Eden Cumberland on the west side all along the coast bending southward like a bow is environed by the Irish Sea, until the foote of the river of Dudden, at Millam Castle aforesayd. Where it is broadest, from the Irish Sea on the west to Kelloplaw Hill, being there extended into a point on the east, it is betweene thirtye five and fortye miles over, and < from > Lamyford in the north to Millam-Castle in the south is scant fiftye and five miles in length.

[*p. 3*]

[A 2] The First Division of the County into Baronyes.[19] King William had given the whole countye of Cumberland unto Ranulph or Randolph de Meschiens and left him men and munition to defend the countrye from all hostilitye which might trouble the peace of the same, < either >[20] by tumult of thinhabitants or forreigne

---

15 The county boundary between Bewcastle Fells and North Tynedale, running via Horse Head (NY 617 808) and Christianbury Crags (NY 579 823) to Scotch Knowe (NY 562 885). 'Gele cragg' presumably appears on the modern map as either Sighty Crags (NY 605 818) or Burnt Tom Crags (NY 595 819); a memory of 'Lamyford', presumably in the vicinity of Scotch Knowe, may survive in the stream name Limy Sike (NY 560 889), as proposed by T. H. B. Graham (in *CW2*, 29 (1929), pp. 51–2).

16 i.e. Liddel Strength or 'the mote of Liddel' (NY 402 741).

17 This is the Scots Dike (which runs from NY 334 739 to NY 387 732), built in 1552 to divide the Debateable Land between the rivers Esk and Sark between the two kingdoms: see J. L. Mack, *The Border Line* (Edinburgh, 1926), pp. 85–97.

18 M: 'cannel' with a contraction mark.

19 Section A2 draws heavily on the 'Chronicon Cumbrie' (text in *St Bees*, no. 498), which erroneously credits William the Conqueror with granting Cumberland to Ranulph le Meschin (d. 1129). In reality, Ranulph's rule as 'lord of Cumberland' probably extended from *c.* 1100 to *c.* 1122: see E. King, 'Ranulph I, earl of Chester', *ODNB*; Sharpe, *Norman Rule*, pp. 43–52.

20 M: 'ither'.

invasion.[21] Randolph quietly possessed of every part of the same, presently surveighed the whole country, and gave all the frontyers bordering on Scottland, on Northumberland and alongst the sea coast, unto his friends and followers, retaineing still to himselfe the midle part betweene the east & west mountaines; a goodly great forrest (full of woods, red-deare and fallow, wyld-swine and all manner of wyld beasts) called the forrest of Englewood, which was sixteene miles long, and ten broad, and lyeth betweene the rivers of Shawk and Eden, extended in length from Carlisle to Penrythe. This Earle Randolph gave to his brother William Meschiens the great baronny of Cawpland, or Kopeland, which lyeth betweene the river Dudden and Darwent and the sea;[22] and soe much of the same as lyeth betweene the rivers of Cocker[23] and Derwent, the said William granted over to one Waldieve, the son of Gospatrick, earle of Dunbarr in Scottland; together with the five townes above Cocker (that is to say) Brigham, Egglesfield, Deane with Branthwaite, Craiksothen and Clifton, with the hambletts thereof, Little-Clifton and Stainburne.

The same Lord William Meschiens seated himselfe att Egremont, where he built a castle upon a sharpp topped hill, and thereupon called the same Egremont,[24] & all such lands as he or his successors (lords of Kopeland) granted to any knight or freeholder within the barony of Kopeland, they bound the same to be holden of that castle of Egremont, and caused the name of the barony to be changed from Kopeland, and to be called the barony of Egremont, which name it retaineth to this day.

This William Meschiens left noe issue att his death but a daughter, which was marryed to Robert Romly, lord of Skipton in Craven, by whom he had issue a daughter named Alice, whom the sayd Robert Romly gave in marriage to William Romly, then earle of Murrey in

---

21 The text of Gilpin MS, p. 8 (printed in *Accompt*, p. 4) differs substantially in the first part of this sentence. Gilpin notes 'this is rased in the originall MS' beside the whole of the sentence ending '… forreigne invasion'.

22 William le Meschin (d. 1129x1135) is stated in Testa de Nevill to have received Copeland from Henry I, but the possibility that he had already been granted it by his brother Ranulph cannot be ruled out: *Book of Fees*, p. 197; Sharpe, *Norman Rule*, p. 54.

23 Here and in subsequent references 'Cocker' has been altered to 'Kokar'.

24 Denton's suggested derivation of Egremont (French *aigre mont*, 'sharp pointed hill') is generally accepted (*PNC*, II, pp. 379–80) but the consistency of the form 'Egre' for the River Ehen in early documents perhaps suggests 'castle mound by the River Ehen' as an alternative explanation.

Scottland, the son of Doncanne, by which marriage the [*p. 4*] said William Fitz Duncanne became lord both of Skipton and Egremont, in the right of his wife, being sole heire of Skipton by her father, and of Egremont by her mother, the Lord Meschien's daughter.

William Fitz Doncane had issue by the said Alice, his wife, a son called William, which dyed an infant and was the first lord of Egremont and by her alsoe three daughters, co-heires. The eldest named Sibbell was wife to William le Gross, earle of Aumarle, and had issue onely a daughter, named Hawise, which was married to three husbands successively, to William de Mandevill, earle of Essex; Baldwin Beton; and to William de Fortibus, to whom the sayd Hawise bare a son named William de Fortibus, who had issue the third William de Fortibus, but his onely daughter and heire Aveline (wife to Edmond Crootchback, King Edward the first his brother) dying without children, the third part of William Fitz Duncanne's lands (which was Skipton in Craven), came to the king's hande, & by King Edward the second granted to Robert Clifford in exchange of the Clifford's lands in the countye of Munmouth, whose posteritye, now earles of Cumberland, enjoyeth the same.

Amabill Romley the second daughter of William Fitz Doncane, had for her part of the inheritance this barony of Egremont, and tooke to husband Reginald Lucy, by whom she had issue, Richard de Lucy, who had two daughters Amabil Lucy and Alice Lucy. [*In margin:*] This Reginald Lucy was captaine of Notingham anno 21 Henry second, 1175.[25]

[*p. 5*] Dame Alice Romley, the third daughter and coheire of William Fitz Doncane was married (by King Henrey the second) unto Gilbert Pippard. *This Gilbertt Pippard was justice iternerant into Wiltshire 23 Henr. 2;*[26] and after (by the Queene) unto Robert Courtney, but had

---

25 This marginal entry occurs in M, J and H. In M it is followed by a note in Machell's hand, subsequently crossed out: 'This is not in Denton's [*er*]go No original unless after added in a more correct copy.' The entry may be a reference to the Pipe Roll for 1174–5, which records a payment of 24s. by Reginald de Luci *ad tenend' servientes in cast' Regis de Notingeham*: Pipe Roll, 21 Hen. II: Pipe Roll Society Vol. XXII (London, 1897), p. 36.

26 Material between asterisks occurs in the margin of both M and H. Gilbert Pippard was one of the three justices on the south-west circuit in 1176–7: *Pleas before the King or his Justices 1198–1212*, Volume III, ed. D. M. Stenton (Selden Society Vol. 83, 1967), pp. lviii, lix; J. Boussard, *Le Gouvernement d'Henri II Plantegenêt* (Paris, 1956), pp. 335n, 506.

noe issue of her bodye; wherefore her part of her father's inheritance (which was the liberty of Cockermouth, Aspatrick, and the barony of Allerdale beneath the river Derwent), was divided betweene the earle of Albermarle and Richard de Lucy, her sisters' children, and soe continued divided untill the eldest sister's issue extinguished by the death of Avelina aforesaid, daughter to the last William de Fortibus; after whose death all the Romley's lands above Derwent and beneath (both the barony of Egremont and of Allerdale) came wholly to the heires of Reginald Lucy, and of Amabill Romley his wife, second daughter to the said William Fitz Duncanne.

Amabill Lucy and Alice Lucy, daughters & coheires to Richard de Lucy, son to Reginald Lucy and to Amabill Romley his wife, the daughter of William Fitz Duncane succeeded in the Lucye's lands in Cumberland.

Amabill Lucy for her moietye enjoyed the barony of Egremont, all save Lowswater (which was more by a great part[27] then the residue) and was marryed to Thomas Multon, by whom she had Lambert de Multon, who had issue Thomas de Multon, whose son John de Multon left the barony of Egremont to his three daughters and heires, Elizabeth marryed to Haverington of Haverington; Johan marryed to Robert Fitz-Water; and Margarett to the Lord Thomas Lucy.[28] Att which time that baronny was broken into parts, which from the conquest had continued entyre, except Loweswater & the lands between Cocker and Derwent, and the five townes granted to Waldieve, as afore is sayd. But now of late < it > is re-united by the earles of Northumberland, who are lords thereof, *by guift and purchase but not by discent from any of the sayd co-heires*.[29]

---

27 H reads 'tenth part'.

28 John de Multon's three heiresses were his sisters, not his daughters: see enrol-
    ment of the deed of partition of his estates in *Cal. Close (1337–9)*, pp. 468–96.

29 Gilpin, p. 17: 'This is a later addicion', referring to the phrase marked here
    by asterisks. The earls of Northumberland acquired the Lucy share of Egre-
    mont barony by gift of the Lucy heiress Maud d'Umfraville (d. 1398), who
    transferred her inheritance to her second husband, Henry Percy, 1st earl of
    Northumberland. The Fitzwalter share returned to the Percies in exchange for
    lands in Norfolk and Suffolk early in the reign of Henry VIII (see *L & P Hen.
    VIII*, vol. 12 (part 2), no. 398); the Harrington share was purchased by the 9th
    earl of Northumberland from Sir Edward Herbert and Mary his wife in 1594
    (CRO, D/Lec, box 302, exemplification of final concord, Michaelmas 1594).

This baronny of Egremont (or Cowpland) was first all demesne, but shortly after the Conquest granted [*p. 6*] away for services; all between Cocker & Darwent & the five townes were given by William Meschiens to Waldeiv lord of Allerdale; and to Kettell (filius Eldred filius Ivon Taylboyes baron of Kendall) were given Kelton, Salter, Workington and Salter by ....[30] The mannor of Beckermott, Frisington, Rottington, Weddekar & Arloghden to Fleming; Kirkby Segogh[31] to thabbey of York; Mulcaster to the Penningtons' ancestors; Dregg and Carleton to Stutevill; Millum to Godard Bevill; lastly Sainton, Boltone, Gosforth and < Hale >[32] to Thomas Multon of Gilsland.

[A3] < **Millum.** >[33] In the south-west corner of the said barony of Egremont lyes the lordshipp or seignory of Millum betweene the river of Dudden and Esk, reaching from the west sea, up into the mountaines above the mannor of Thwaites, which is holden of Millum and gave name to the gentleman's auncestors, Joseph Thwaites, now owner of the same. Itselfe being soe named by the great number of plaine-lands enclosed in the mountain woody country by the then inhabitants; as other places upon like occasion doe testifye in diverse parts of the country (viz) Micklethwaite, Sivythwaite, Moorthwaite, Kirkthwait, Lynthwait, Langthwaite, Branthwaite, < Brunthwaite >[34] & many other, for wee yett call a great plaine peece without bushes a thwaite of land, if it be severed by inclosure.[35]

Off this segniory < of > Millam the first possessors thereof were called de < Millum >[36] as I have seene them named in certaine old evidences belonging to the nunnes of Seaton in Millum, which doe report one William de Millum to have confirmed to the abbye of Holme Cultram a place called Leekley, which < Gunild >[37] his sister,

30 Both M and H have a dashed line, perhaps indicating that the original was defective here.
31 *Sic*, for Kirkby Begogh, i.e. St Bees.
32 M: 'Haw'.
33 Millom (SD 17 81). For Millom seigniory see also Denton's accounts in section E below (the 'four leaves').
34 'Brunthwaite' has been interlined in another hand in M and is not in J.
35 See also below, section E2. It is striking that the ON term *þveit* was still understood and in current use in Denton's time.
36 M: 'Mallam'.
37 M: 'Gimyld'; J 'Gunyld'. Here and subsequently the renderings in H are preferable and have been substituted. *Holm Cultram* (p. 31, nos. 83–5) confirms that Gunnilda is meant.

the daughter of Henry de Millum (son of Arthure de Millum) had given to the abbey, being widow & late wife to Henry filius Willelmi. Her father Henry filius Arthuri de Millum and his wife Godith gave Leekley to < Gunyld > in franck marriage which [*p. 7*] grant the sayd William de Millum filius Henrici filius Arthuri confirmed with certaine liberty in the fells and mountaines. And afterwards John Hudleston and Johan his wife, daughter and heire of Adam de Millum, son & heire of the said William confirmed Leekeley and the libertyes aforesaid soe granted by < Guinyld > unto the abbott's successors and the covent of Holme Cultram.[38]

This seginory [*sic*] of Millum was parcell of the auncient demesne of the barony of Egremont and was given by Ciciley (daughter of William Fitz Duncane) countess of Albemarle, to his brother or neer kinsman, as I have heard, upon this occasion. The baron of Egremont being taken prisoner beyond sea amongst the infidells could not be redeemed without a great ransom, & being farr of England entred his brother or kinsman for his surety, promiseing with all possible speed to send money to sett him free; but upon his returne home to Egremont, he changed his mind and most unnaturally and unthankfully suffered his brother to lye in prison, in great durance and extremitye untill the haire of his head was growne to an eccessive length, like to a woman's haire.

The panymes, out of hope of the ransome, in great rage most cruelly hang'd upp their pledge (his surety), binding the long haire of his head to a beame in the prison, and tyed his armes soe behind him that he could nott reach to the topp, where the knot was fastened, to loose himselfe. Dureing his imprisonment the panim's daughter became enamoured of him, and sought all good meanes for his deliverance but could not enlarge him; she understanding of this last cruelty (by meanes made to his keeper) entred the prison, and takeing her knife to cutt the haire, being haisted,[39] she cut the skin of his head soe as with the weight of his body, he rent away the rest, & fell downe to the earth halfe dead; but she presently tooke him up, causeing surgeons[40] to attend him secretly till he recovered his former health, beauty & strength, and soe intreated her father for him that he sett him att liberty. Then desirous to revenge his brother's

---

38 For these charters, see *Holm Cultram*, pp. 30–2 (nos. 78–86c). For further grants by the early lords of Millom, see below, section E1.

39 H: 'hastened'.

40 altered to read 'chirurgians'.

ingratitude he got leave to depart to his country, and tooke home with him the hatterell of his haire rent of<f> as aforesaid, and a bugle horne which he commonly used to carry about him when he was in England, where he shortly arrived and comeing towards Egremont Castle about noone-tyde of the day, when his brother was att dinner, he blew [*p. 8*] his bugle horne, which his brother the baron presently acknowledge<d> & thereby conjectured his brother's returne, and sending then his friends & servants to learne his brother's mind unto him, & how he had escaped, they brought back the report of all the miserable torment which he had endured for his unfaithfull brother the baron, which soe astonished the baron, halfe dead before with the shamefull remembrance of his owne disloyalty and breach of promise, that hee abandoned all company and would not looke on his brother, untill his just wrath was pacified by diligent intreaty of their friends, & to be sure of his brother's future kindness, he gave the lordshipp of Millam to him & his heires for ever. Whereupon the first lords of Millam gave for the<ir> armes the horne and the hatterell.[41]

This young gentleman seemes to me to be the very same Arthur before remembred whose sonne and heire Henry gave the lands in Seaton or Seaton itselfe (then called Leekley) unto the nunns of Seaton, which of late was granted unto Sir Hugh Askew, knight, when the nunnry was suppressed by King Henry the eight. But Seaton is now the inheritance of John Pennington gentleman; < second brother >.[42] The said deed of feoffment made by him to < Gunyld > his daughter approves the same Seaton soe to be called in these words: excepta terra < in > Leakleya quam dedi sanctis monialibus servientibus Deo et Sanctae Mariae in Lekeleya.[43] It takes the latter name Seaton of the sea, for that it stands nigh the same.[44]

---

41 This is a variant of the story of the enamoured Muslim maiden and the Christian captive, made popular by Orderic Vitalis' account of Bohemond's captivity during the first Crusade: see *The Ecclesiastical History of Orderic Vitalis*, 6 vols (Oxford Medieval Texts, 1969–80), ed. M. Chibnall, V (Oxford, 1975), pp. 358–73. I am grateful to Andrew Jotischky for this reference.

42 These words from H are entered in the margin of M with the note: 'in the marg. of the original.'

43 See *Holm Cultram*, p. 31, no. 83.

44 Modern place-name scholars note that Seaton nunnery's location, almost two miles inland, must cast some doubt on the name's significance. OE *sæ* might refer to a freshwater lake or even a marsh, rather than to the sea: *PNC*, II, pp. 319, 347; *Dict. LDPN*, p. 303.

The same Arthur and his successors gave diverse parts of Millam to their kinsmen and to their daughters and sisters in marriage, as Thwaites, Dalegarth, < & > Waybergh-thwaite, and some in mortmaine, as Leakley and Kirke-santon; all which places gave sirnames to the posterityes of the feoffies, as Thwaits of Thwaites, Wayberghthwaite of Wayberghthwaite and the rest, whereof some yet doe continue, and some names are worne out, but auncient records report and remember them.

[*p. 9*] Johan daughter and heire of Adam de Millum, last inheritor of that name, by marriage transferred the segniory of Millam to her husband John Hudleston, and the heires male of the said John Hudleston yet enjoy the same. And William Hudleston Esq. (filius Anthonii filii domini Johannis militis) filius Johannis militis[45] hath it at this present.[46]

To the said first named John Hudleston King Henry the third granted liberty to keepe a faire and markett in Millam in the 35th yeare of his reigne.[47] After the death of the first John Hudleston succeeded John his son, who had issue Radulphe father of Richard whose son John Hudleston < & successors. >[48]

and doe retaine that name till this time. Howbeit the right names are Penningtons, and all descended from one Gamell de Pennington the first of that name which I read of, which Gamell in like sort tooke his addicion of Pennington his chiefe seat about the time of the Conquest. They hold Mulcaster of Egremont immediately, and Ravenglass a towne soe named of the Irish, Ranigh a fearne or bracken and Glass greene, a fearne greene where now the towne stands att Esk side.[49]

[A 4] **Mulcaster.**[50] Next unto the north side of the seigniory of Millum stands Mulcaster, a faire mansion house of Joseph Pennington's Esq. He and his auncestors from the Conquest have enjoyed the same,

---

45 The last three words ('filius Johannis militis') are inserted in the margin of H; they are not in J.
46 For the Hudleston genealogy see H. S. Cowper, 'Millom Castle and the Hudle-stons', *CW2*, 24 (1924), pp. 200–1.
47 The charter was granted in 1251: *Cal. Charter Rolls Henry III*, I, p. 364.
48 In margin: 'great blanke'.
49 This paragraph occurs here in M, J and H, though it clearly refers to Muncaster. It has been crossed through in M, which has a note in the margin (in Machell's hand): 'This seems to belong to Mulcaster so I have placed it there'. For Ravenglass, see below, section E8.
50 Muncaster (SD 10 96).

sometimes collaterally but the most part lineally descending by theire issue male till this time.[51] The place is now corruptly named Moncaster. Howbeit the right name is Mulcaster or Meold-castre, of an old ruinous castle there towardes the water side nere unto Esk-meold, which was their auncient dwelling place; whereupon it was called the Meold or Mulecastre and hath ever beene soe written < Mulcastre > in all their evidence and records. [*p. 10*] Eskmeoll is a plaine dry low ground betweene the mountaines and the sea, every such place the old inhabitants tearmed the Mule or Meole, as Esk Meole, Kirksanton meale, Meol-holme, Cart-Meal in Furness, the Meil of Galloway, and many other such like.[52]

Though this mannor was alwayes the Penningtons, as aforesaid, yet some have greatly mistaken the same first to be the Mulcasters' patrimony and to come to the Penningtons from them by marriage or purchase. All the Mulcasters are descended from one David de Mulcastre filius Benedicti Pennington who lived in King John's tyme. He had two sonnes John and Adam, called both de Mulcaster, and soe their posterityes take that surname of the place where their first auncestor David dwelt.[53]

Carleton.[54] Betweene the water Myte and the river of Irt, towards the sea stands the village Carleton, now as of old time inhabited by carles or husbandmen and therefore soe called[55] and a little above, on the side of Irt, the mannor and towne of Irton and Irtondale, which are soe named of the water Irt.[56]

The auncient familye of the Irtons tooke their first surname of this towne and seate of Irton, which yet continue in their blood and name to this day. One of their younger sonnes named Radulphe, by his

51 The Pennington genealogy is reconstructed in J. Foster, *Penningtoniana: Pedigree of Sir Josslyn Pennington, fifth Baron Muncaster of Muncaster* (London: privately printed, 1878).

52 Here and in section E8 Denton is conflating two terms: ON *melr* ('sandbank', as in Eskmeals and, probably, Cartmel) and ON *muli* ('headland, promontory', as in Mull of Galloway). The first element of Muncaster is probably either *muli* or the ON personal name *Múli*: PNC, II, pp. 423–4; *Dict. LDPN*, p. 245.

53 The paragraph noted above at note 49 has been copied into the margin of M at this point.

54 Carleton in Drigg parish (SD 08 98). See also below, section E9.

55 Denton's interpretation is correct: Carleton is a compound of OE *ceorl* or ON *karl* ('peasant') and *tūn* ('farmstead, village'): *Dict. LDPN*, p. 67; PNC, II, p. 377.

56 Irton (NY 09 00), takes its name, as Denton states, from the river: see *PNC*, II, p. 402.

painefull diligence in studdy and learning became the 8th bishopp
of Carlisle in the begining of Edward the first's tyme.[57]

< Wasdale >[58] Above Irton (in the fells and mountaines) lyes a waste
forrest ground, full of red deere, which was called the Wast dale,
now Wasdale,[59] the inheritance of the earle of Northumberland; and
before, the Lucyes' land, being a parcell of their third part of the
baronny of Egremont, which Thomas Lucy got with his wife Margarett, one of the co-heires and daughters of John Multon, last of that
name, baron of Egremont.[60]

[*p. 11*]

[A 5] **Dregg.**[61] On the other side of the river Irt att the sea, is the
mannor of Dregg, which the Estutevills in King Henry the second's
tyme possessed, whose patrimonye descended by a daughter to the
Lord Baldwyne Wake, baron of Liddell, when King Henry the third
raigned, of which Baldwyne, William filius Thomae de Greystock,
and the Lady Adingham in Furness, in the tenth yeare of Edward the
first held a knight's fee betweene them in Dregg.[62] And in the 29th
of Edw. 1st th'abbott of Caldre, Patrick Culwen, the Lady Margarett
Multon, held Dregg of John de Greystock, and of John filius Robert
Harington, and they over of John Wake.[63]

[A 6] **Gosford.**[64] Above Dregg lyes the parish mannor & towne of
Gosford wherof the Gosfords an auncient family in those parts
tooke their surname. Robert Gosford the last of their house, left his
lands to be divided among five co-heires: Mariott, the wife of Alane
Caddy, eldest daughter & heire of Robert Gosford; Issabell, the wife
of Henry Huscock, second daughter; Johan, the wife of Adam Garth,
the third daughter; and Elline, the wife of William Kirkby, the 4th;

---

57 'tyme' crossed out; 'reigne' inserted. J reads 'tyme'; H: 'reign'. Ralph Irton
    (d. 1292), bishop of Carlisle from 1280, was probably associated with Irton
    near Harrogate, Yorkshire, rather than with Irton in Copeland: H. Summerson,
    'Irton, Ralph of', *ODNB*.
58 The Wasdale valley from Kidbeck (NY 11 04) to Wasdale Head (NY 18 08).
59 The first element of the name Wasdale is thought to be ON *vatn* ('lake'), rather
    than 'waste', as implied by Denton: *Dict. LDPN*, p. 359; *PNC*, II, p. 390.
60 For the partition of Egremont barony in 1338 see *Cal. Close (1337–9)*, p. 487.
61 Drigg (SD 07 99). See also below, section E9.
62 Inquisition, 1282: *Cal. IPM*, II, no. 439 (p. 258), which is discussed by James
    Wilson in *St Bees*, pp. 456–7n.
63 Extent of knights' fees on death of John Wake, 1301: *Cal. IPM*, III, no. 597 (pp.
    449–50).
64 Gosforth (NY 07 03).

and John Multon, the sonne of Agnes Estholme the 5th co-heire.[65] In the second yeare of Edward the third, Sara the < widow >[66] of Robert Leyburne held Caddye's part, John Penylton Kirkbye's part, & the said John Multon the residue.[67] But now Pennington, Kirkbye, and Senhouse of the Seaskale hold it.

[A7] **Hale.**[68] Hale in Henry the 3d's tyme was the lands of Alexander de Hale; Agnes and Constance his daughters and heires held it 23 Edw. 1 of Thomas Multon of Gilsland;[69] but in Edw. 2 tyme she is named Christian in John Multone's office.[70] The Ponconbyes[71] got Agnes part; and in Rich. 2 tyme William Bewchamp, Robert Harrington or Everington,[72] and Richard Meething,[73] and the heire of John Stanley the other part.[74] But now Punsonbye holdes it wholly.

[*p. 12*]

[A8] **Seascale.**[75] Towards the sea coast stands Seaskallhall, the now mansion house of John Senhouse,[76] which is soe called of this word Skale, drawne from the Latine (Scalinga ad mare) <u>a Skale or Sheele for cattle & sheep-cott att the sea</u>.[77] And nere it is Sealowfield (or the Sea-low-field) seated upon the brooke that falls from the mountaines by Cawdre Abbye.[78]

---

65 In 1316 Robert de Gosford's heirs were named as John son of Agnes de Estholm (who was under age); Mariota wife of Alan Bad alias Badde [*sic*] (aged 30); Isabel wife of Henry Hosecok alias Husecok (aged 26); Joan wife of Adam de Garth (aged 24); and Ellen, late wife of William de Kirkebi (aged 25), his daughters: *Cal. IPM*, V, no. 562.

66 M: 'wife' has been changed to read 'widow'.

67 2 Edw. III = 1328–9. The source of this statement has not been traced.

68 Haile (NY 03 08).

69 Inquisition, 1295: *Cal. IPM*, III, no. 285, p. 184.

70 In the inquisition after the death of John de Multon in 1334, the daughters' names are given as Agnes and Constance: *Cal. IPM*, VII, no. 628, pp. 433, 435.

71 Replaces 'Punsonbyes'. J: 'Punconbyes'.

72 Replaces 'of Heverington'. J: 'of Everington'.

73 In margin: 'rather Moothing or Morthing in the original'. H: 'Muthing'.

74 See inquisition, 1399: *Cal. IPM*, XVII, no. 1324, p. 517, where the tenants of lands in Haile are named as William Beauchamp, Robert de Echrengton, Richard Morthyng and the heir of John Scanlow [*sic*]. Robert de Ponsonby is also named as a tenant in Haile.

75 Seascale Hall (NY 039 028) in Gosforth parish.

76 M: altered to 'Seanos'; H: 'Senos'. For the Senhouse family of Seascale, see *CFH*, p. 300.

77 Denton's interpretation is correct: see *PNC*, II, p. 433.

78 Sellafield (NY 02 04) in St Bridget Beckermet parish. Modern place-name

[A 9] Punsonby.[79] Upon the said brooke stands Punsonby < habitatio Ponson >,[80] whereof that race of gentlemen (the Punsonbyes) tooke name, some of them yet remaine. Alexander the son of Richard Punsonby lived about the tyme of Edw. 2 and William in Edw. 3; Robert in Rich. 2. Butt the said Punson of whom the place tooke name, lived in King Stephen and Henry the first's time. His son John filius Ponson was fyned in Henry the 2 tyme because he wanted his pledge.[81] It is now the lands of .....

[A 10] Santon.[82] Santon was in Hen. 3 time the inheritance of one Alane de Cowpeland. His capitall mansion house was in the townshipp of Bootle where he held lands < & in Seaton of the lord of Millum. And his xx^{li} land >[83] in Santon, Irton, and Bolton, he held of Thomas Multon of Gilsland, who held over of the lord of Egremont.[84] After Alane and Richard his son succeeded Alane, John & Richard. And in the 22th of Rich. 2 one Alane son to Richard Copland held lands there in Retrantrell.[85] Att this present Mr. Irton, and one Wynder who bought his part of Latus, and he of one Lancaster.

[A 11] Bolton.[86] Bolton in Cowpland was the Wayberghthwaites' land in Edw. 1 tyme. One William de W< ayberghwait > held the 23 Edw. 1 x^{li} land there of Thomas Multon of Gilsland,[87] and his lands

---

scholars have been unable to offer an interpretation of the name, which is recorded only in post-medieval sources: *PNC*, II, p. 339.

79 Ponsonby (NY 05 05).

80 These words from H are interlined in Machell's hand in M and are omitted from J. The interpretation of the name is correct: 'the settlement (ON *by*) of Puncun', an Old French – and therefore post-Conquest – personal name. A John son of Puncun is recorded in the Cumberland Pipe Rolls from 1178 to 1185: *PNC*, II, pp. 426–7; *VCH Cumb.*, I, pp. 348–56.

81 Pipe Roll, 1177: *VCH Cumb.*, I, p. 347.

82 Santon (NY 10 01) was a township in Irton parish.

83 The section from H is in the margin of M in a later hand but is in the body of J.

84 Inquisition, undated [1294–5]: *Cal. IPM*, III, no. 285 (p. 184).

85 Inquisition, 1399: *Cal. IPM*, XVII, no. 1324 (p. 517). Denton's phrase 'lands there in Retrantrell' is almost certainly a misreading of his source, explained by the name 'Henry Tayntrell' following that of Alan de Coupland, heir of Richard de Coupland, in the list of free tenants on the estates of William Dacre in 1399.

86 Bolton was a township in Gosforth parish. The name is preserved in Hall Bolton (NY 087 025), Bolton Head (NY 087 039) and Bolton Wood (NY 10 04).

87 Inquisition, undated [1294–5]: *Cal. IPM*, III, no. 285 (p. 184).

in Wayb[erghthwaite] of the lord of Millam. It is at this day the lands of Senhouse[88] and Kirkby.

[*p. 13*]

[A 12] **Cawder** alias Caldre Abbey.[89] And at the other side of the beck is seated the Abbey of Cawder, alias Caldre, soe named of a rill or beck falling from the mountaines of .... into the dale where the abbey stands, and thence into the west ocean. The water had that name of the Irish inhabitants there, taken from the forme and nature of the place.[90]

The abbey (as I have read) was first founded in the year of grace 1134, about the last yeare of King Henry the first, when William Fitz Duncane was lord of Egremont baronny. Howbeit I thinke it was not perfected untill Thomas de Multon finished the worke and established a greater covent of monks there. Thomas Multon gave to the abbay halfe the mannor of Deerham in Cumberland, with the advowson of the church there, ad sustentationem unius convent' apud Caldram, preter convent' ibidem prius statutum. Ranulf Bonekill confirmed unto them their lands in Gilcruse. John Fleming gave Jollan, abbott, there the patronage of Arloughden with some land in Majore Beckermot.[91]

[*In margin:*] Jollanus 26 H. 3; Johannes 30 H. 3; Walter 40 H. 3.

Between Cawder Beck and Beckermott towards the sea stands St Brides.[92]

[A 13] Manerium de **Beckermit**.[93] A little above St Brides lyes the mannor of Beckermit, now (and of old tyme) the Flemings' lands of

---

88 M: altered to 'Seavenhowes'; H: 'Seavenhows'.

89 Calder Abbey (NY 051 064). The heading in J reads simply 'Cawder'.

90 Modern place-name scholars interpret Calder as a British, rather than an Irish, name, from the Welsh *caled* + *dwfr* ('swift or rapid stream'): *PNC*, I, p. 7; *Dict. LDPN*, p. 64.

91 For Calder Abbey see *VCH Cumb.*, II, pp. 174–8; for these grants, see J. Thorley, 'The estates of Calder abbey', *CW3*, 4 (2004), pp. 133–62. Jollan is recorded as abbot between 1241x1242 and 1246x1247: D. M. Smith and V. C. M. London (eds), *The Heads of Religious Houses: England and Wales*, II (Cambridge, 2001), p. 271.

92 A reference to the church of St Bridget Beckermet (NY 015 061), which stands in fields on the seaward side of the village of Beckermet.

93 The Flemings' manor of Beckermet formed the southern part of the parish of St John Beckermet (NY 018 067). H has the marginal heading 'Beckermit.' There is no catchword in J.

Rydall, who as mesne lords between the baron of Egremont and the possessors and land tennants of Rotington, Frisington, Arloughden and Weddikar, did hold them as fees of Beckermitt, and itselfe as a demeasne of the baron (as a fee) of Egremont-baronny. The first Fleming I read of was Rayginer Fleming whose son John was seized of the same in King Edw. the second's tyme[94] and his son Thomas filius Johannis in Edward the third's raigne.[95]

[p. 14][96]

[A14] **Brigham**[97] villa ad pontem[98] was one of the five townes which William Meschiens, lord of Cowpland, gave to Waldieff, lord of Allerdale, at the Conqest. Waldieff gave Brigham to Dolphin the sonne of Aleward, together with Little Crosbye, Applethwaite and Langrigg, in franck marriage with Matild his sister.[99] After some few descents it fell to sisters, for in the 40th yeare of H. 3[100] Beatrice de Lowther and Thomas de Huthwaite gave the part of the rectorye of Brigham to Issabell countesse of Albemarle, then < lord >[101] paramount of Allerdale,[102] who in the 7th yeare of Edw. 1[103] impleaded Robert de Yenwith and Alice his wife for the rectory. But after they agreed by fine levied, that the countess and the heires of Issabell the wife of Walter Twinham, the daughter of the said Alice uxor Yenwith, should present alternis vicibus.[104] In the 8 of Edw. the first Gilbert Huthwaite held the moiety of Brigham,[105] and after them the Swinburnes of Huthwaite ever enjoyed that part, which at this day is in the possession of John Swinburne. The other moietye descended from Walter Twinham to Adam Twinham his sonne, who dyed seized

94 John Fleming held the fee in 1322 and 1334: *Cal. IPM*, VI, no. 331 (p. 200); VII, no. 628 (p. 433).
95 For the Fleming family and their estates in west Cumberland, see *The Memoirs of Sir Daniel Fleming*, ed. R. E. Porter and W. G. Collingwood, CWAAS Tract Series XI (Kendal, 1928).
96 At head of p. 14 in J and M (but not in H): 'Cowpland Forrest', in a different hand.
97 Brigham (NY 08 30).
98 Denton's interpretation is accepted by modern scholars: *PNC*, II, p. 355.
99 See 'Chronicon Cumbrie': *St Bees*, p. 493.
100 40 Hen. III = 1255–6.
101 M: 'lord' erased and replaced by 'lady'. J: 'lord.'
102 See FF Cumb. 51 Hen. III [1266–7] (*CW2*, 7 (1907), p. 227, no. 110).
103 7 Edw. I = 1278–9. The source has not been traced.
104 FF Cumb. 9 Edw. I [1280–1] (*CW2*, 7 (1907), p. 229, no. 139).
105 8 Ed I = 1279–80. Robert of Yanwith and Gilbert of Huthwaite had held the vill of Brigham *c.* 1269: PRO, SC11/730, m. 14v.

thereof 35 Ed. 1.[106] And Walter the son of that Adam < Twinham > gave the rectory by fyne unto John Harcla and his heires 13 Ed. 2.[107] And by the attainder of Andrew Harcla, earle of Carlisle, the rectory was seized to the king, though he stood seized in trust to the use of Henry Harcla son and heir to John[108] Harcla.[109]

[*p. 15*]

[**A 15**] **Bega or Bees.**[110] The church of St Begh was aunciently a parish church erected and dedicated in honour of an Irish woman named by some writers Begogh some tyme there and of great sanctimonye, whereupon the towne was first called Kirkby-Begogh, id est, villa sive habitatio ad fanum Begae,[111] and by that name of Kirkby-Begogh the church, rectory, and towne, conteining then seaven great carracats of lands, were given to the abbey of St Marye's in York by William de Meschiens, then lord of Egremont barony or Coupeland, and by the said William made a cell of York abbey.[112] He layd the first foundacion of the priory, and that church which now standeth and endowed it. And his son Randall Meschiens gave his lands in Annerdale, or Annanderdale, and halfe a carrucate of land in Egremont, and other nobles, barons, and gentlemen of the country did afterward contribute unto the same, untill it became, of a small foundation, to be a priory of good revenue; able to support a prior and < six monks >[113] there at all tymes and to defrey the charges of buildings and other necessaryes of the house, yet alwayes as a cell of York untill it was dissolved by K. Henry the 8th.

The name Begogh is Irish, derived of two words Beg-og, which by interpretacion are Englished little-young.[114]

---

106 Inquisition, 1307: *Cal. IPM*, IV, no. 421.
107 FF Cumb. 13 Edw. II [1319–20] (*CW2*, 7 (1907), p. 233, no. 192).
108 Replaced by 'Geo.' H and J: 'John'.
109 Andrew Harcla or Harclay (*c.* 1270–1323), created earl of Carlisle in 1322, was executed for treason in 1323: H. Summerson 'Harclay, Andrew', *ODNB*.
110 St Bees (NX 968 121).
111 Denton's interpretation is correct: Kirkby is ON *kirkja* + *by* ('settlement with a church'); Beghóc is the Irish diminutive of the name of St Begu: *PNC*, II, p. 431.
112 In margin: 'Anno domini 1140'. For the history of the priory of St Bees, see *VCH Cumb.*, II, pp. 178–83 and *St Bees*, pp. i–xxxv. The date of foundation was probably before 1140, but after 1120, perhaps *c.* 1125: *VCH Cumb.*, II, p. 179; *St Bees*, p. v.
113 M and J have a blank in the text and '6 monks' in margin.
114 Denton interprets the name as Gaelic *beag* ('little') + *og* ('young'). Modern interpretations see 'Beghóc' as the Irish diminutive of the saint's name, Begu

The boundes of William Meschiens aforesaid which he gave to the priory were in these words: tota terra et totum feodum inter has devisas (videlicet): a pede de Whitofthauen ad Kekell et per Kekell donec cadit in Egre et per Egre quousque cadit in mare.[115] Kekell runneth from of Whillymore by Cleator & Egremont and soe into Eyne att Egremont: Egre is the foote of Eyne which falleth out of Eynerdale. Aenanderdale is that which now is called Eynederdale, a towne and chappelry in the fells above Egremont.

To this priory & abbey of St Marye's att York, Waldeofus, lord of Allerdale (filius Gosp\<atricii> comitis) gave Staineburne, that prayers should be said there for the souls [*p. 16*] and health of King Henry the first, Matild his wife, the donor, his wife, children, auncestors & sucessors. The charter was made to Thurstane, archbishopp of York.[116]

[A 16] Rotington,[117] villa ad prata Rot-inges, soe called because it was usueally haunted with barnacles (rott-geese) and wild fowle before it was inhabited.[118] It is now the mansion house of Henry Sands, the .... lord or owner thereof of that name according to the pedegree in the margent;[119] whose auncestor ...... Sands in the .... year of King

---

(see *PNC*, II, p. 431) but there is a possibility that the name may be Old English and refer not to a person but to the holy bracelet, recorded at St Bees as the only known relic of the supposed saint. As James Wilson put it, 'Sancta Bega is good ecclesiastical Latin for the Anglo-Saxon *halgan beage* or its English equivalent *holy bracelet*': *St Bees*, p. xxxiv. See J. M. Todd, 'St Bega: cult, fact and legend', *CW2*, 80 (1980), pp. 23–35.

115 The wording of these bounds in the charters of William Meschin differs in detail but not in substance from the wording given here: *St Bees*, nos. 2, 3, 5, 6.

116 Waldeof's grant of Stainburn is recorded in William Meschin's confirmation charter but the original does not appear to have survived: *St Bees*, no. 2 and p. 29n.

117 Rottington (NX 96 13), a township in St Bees parish, on the southern slopes of St Bees Head.

118 Denton's interpretation of the name assumes wrongly that the element 'ing' is ON *eng* ('meadow'). The Barnacle goose (*Branta leucopsis*), or its close relation the Brent goose (*Branta bernicla*), was believed to grow vegetatively, one of the myths being that it was produced from rotting timbers (hence, presumably, its vernacular name 'rot goose'). Writing in 1653, Izaak Walton referred to: 'The Barnacles and young Goslings bred by the Sun's heat and the rotten planks of an old Ship, and hatched of trees' (cited in *OED*). The place-name Rottington is an OE *-ingtūn* compound, the first element probably being an OE personal name, *Rota*: *PNC*, II, p. 429.

119 Neither M, J nor H contain a pedigree in the margin here.

...... had by ..... from ..... Rottingtons. But of what house or name the Rottingtons came I cannott say, unless some younger brothers of the Flemings, for it is a fee of Beckermitt. I read in a deed in K. John's time Robert de Rotingtona to be a wittness, and one Regenold de Rottington in H. 2 tyme.

[A 17] Whitthaven.[120] Whitthaven or Whitttofthaven is a creek in the sea at the north end of a great bergh or riseing hill there, which is washed with the flood on the west side, where it is a great rock or quarry of hard white stone which gives name to the village and haven.[121] A very little rill falls there into the sea which makes that harbour where small barkes may enter & be defended by the hill from the tempest & winds. It was belonging to St Beghes of auncient tyme, for the abbott of York (in Edw. 1 tyme) was impleaded for wreck, and his libertyes there by the King which he claimed from the foundation and to be confirmed by Richard Lucy in King John's tyme to his predicessors.[122] It is now ....

[*p. 17*]

[A 18] Hensingham.[123] Hensingham alias Hansingham (villa ad pratum Johannis)[124] is a mannor and towne there now purchased by Thomas Salkeld of Saltre, from Thomas Skelton of Branthwait, whose auncestors had the same from the lords of Branthwaite. It was holden of the abbott of St Marye's at York, per quartam partem feodi militis by the Skeltons in the tyme of King Henry the 6th. But Mr Robert de Branthwait (4th Ed. primi) held a moiety thereof of Adam de Moresbye, together with the mannor of Branthwaite, per servicium 1d. per annum ad Natale Domini pro omnibus serviciis.[125] It descended from the Branthwaites to the lords of Banton, & from them to the Skeltons, who married the coheire of Thomas de Whittrigg, lord of Little Banton. Att the conquest one Gillesby, Gilleby or rather Gillesbued held the same, whose sonnes Roger and William

120 Whitehaven (NX 97 18).
121 The name Whitehaven is, indeed, 'the harbour (haven) by the white headland (ON *hvít* + *hofuð*)': *PNC*, II, pp. 450–1.
122 *Placita de Quo Warranto* (London: Record Commission, 1818), p. 122.
123 Hensingham (NX 98 16). Gilpin notes (p. 66): 'This paragraph in the MS is all in another (but auncient[)] hand'.
124 Denton again makes the mistake of assuming that 'ing' represents ON *eng* ('meadow') and offers an ingenious interpretation of 'Hens-' as being a variant of 'Hans', i.e. John. The name is an early OE *-ingahām* compound, with an uncertain first element: *PNC*, II, p. 401.
125 FF Cumb. 4 Edw. I [1275–6] (*CW2*, 7 (1907), p. 227, no. 117).

granted to the abbott of York duas bovatas in Hensingham et terram de Snartheved.[126] Hence gave the tenor to the abbott. Also Alanus filius Ketelli amonicione[127] Christianae uxoris ejus gave milnestones to the abbot Holme Cultram infra divisas terrae de Hensingham.[128]

[A 19] **Arloghden.**[129] Ar-flogh-den (now corruptly called Arlokenden, Arnaden and Arladen) is percell of the signiory of Beckermitt, a fee thereof. The place was so named by the Irish,[130] and gives name to the parish, towne and to a family of gentlemen called Harlakenden, of whose issue male there are yet remaining some in the south parts. John de Fleming gave the patronage of the rectory to Jollan abbott of Caldre in 26th H. 3.[131] The lay fee was thinheritance of ..... whose 3 daughters & coheires transferred that patrimony to the Haringtons, Lamploughes and ...... in King John's tyme.

[A 20] **Enerdale**[132] (vallis ad Eyn) is soe called now by thinhabitants, both the towne & parish. The Irish named it Lough-Eanheh (lacus volucrum) of the fowles that breed there in the islands; & the river Ooinh-Eanheh and the dale Eaner or Ar-ean.[133] The Saxons retaining still the Irish name called the bottome and valley Enerdall. It was att the Conquest demeasne land of Cowpland in William Meschien's tyme, but his son Randall Meschienes gave it to the abbye of York,[134] and halfe a carrucat in Egremont or (as I think) but some part of Enerdall, for it was Harrington's part of the demeasnes of Egremont in the particion of John Multon's three coheires,[135] & descended to the Barnvills, and to the Greys and Parrs, marquesses Dowcett & now to the Q. Elizabeth as escheat for want of issue of Parr.[136]

---

126 *St Bees*, nos. 11, 223–4, 233 record the grant of the vill of Hensingham by Roger son of Gilbert and of 'Swarthof' by William son of Gilbert of Lancaster.

127 *Sic*: 'admonitu' is probably meant.

128 See *Holm Cultram*, p. 69, no. 196.

129 Arlecdon (NY 05 19). In the margin, M offers an interpretation of the name ('*ad humidum profundum vall*') but this occurs in neither J nor H.

130 Modern scholars prefer an OE derivation: *earn-lāce-denu* ('eagle stream valley'): *PNC*, II, p. 335.

131 FF Cumb. 26 Hen. III [1241–2] (*CW2*, 7 (1907), p. 222, no. 56).

132 Ennerdale, upstream from Ennerdale Bridge (NY 070 159), was part of the forest of Copeland.

133 Modern scholarship prefers an ON derivation, initially *Anundar-dal* ('Anund's valley'), later becoming 'valley of the Ehen': *PNC*, II, p. 385.

134 See *St Bees*, no. 10.

135 See *Cal. Close (1337–9)*, p. 495.

136 For this descent, see below A22 (Kelton), note 145.

[*p. 18*]

[A 21] Frisington.[137] Frisington was aunciently a gentlemen's seate of that name, whose last heire male in H. 4 tyme left 3 daughters and coheires: Johan, uxor Richard Gaitfald; Agnes, uxor John Lowcon; and Margrett uxor John Atkinson, who sold it to William Lighe[138] with whose posteritye it continued till Henry (filius Thomae filii Willelmi) sold the same to Anthony Patrickson, now owner thereof.[139] It is a fee of Beckermett and holden of Fleming.

[A 22] Kelton alias Ketell-ton and Saltre.[140] villa Ketteli, Kettell's-towne, now called Kelton was first a parcell of Lamplughe, and made a village by Kettellus filius Eldredi;[141] and Saltre the capitall messuage or demeasne there was afterwards given by Gospatrick, filius Orme filii Kettelli, to the abbey of York in franck-almes.[142] The abbotts made Saltre a part of the cell of [*St Bees*].[143] But Kelton continued alwayes a lay fee and is the inheritance of one Moore-house, grandchild to ..... wife to ..... Moorehouse, laundress some-tyme to Q. .... who gave them Kelton & to their heires male.[144] It escheated to the crowne for want of issue in the Lord Marquesse of Northampton, W. Parr, heire to the barons of Kendall, and to the Harringtons of Harrington and Addingham. Parr was heire to the Marquess Dorcett (Gray) who had right thereunto by Cicilie the

---

137 Frizington (NY 03 16), a township in Arlecdon parish.

138 FF Cumb. 11 Hen. IV [1409–10] (*CW2*, 7 (1907), p. 245, no. 329). The vendors names are given as Richard Gaytesaweld and Johanna his wife; John Lowcowe and Agnes his wife; and John Atkynson of Neweton and Margaret his wife.

139 Patrickson's purchases of Frizington took place between 1580 and 1590: R. P Littledale, 'Some notes on the Patricksons of Ennerdale', *CW2*, 25 (1925), pp. 186–7.

140 Kelton township, centred on the village of Kirkland (NY 07 17), and Salter with Eskett (NY 05 16).

141 Despite the attractiveness of a derivation from the name of Ketel son of Eldred, the major twelfth-century landholder in this part of Cumberland, Kelton is thought more likely to derive from ON *kelda* ('spring or well'): *PNC*, II, p. 405.

142 See *St Bees*, no. 32.

143 The manuscripts leave a blank here. Salter was a grange of St Bees priory: *St Bees*, p. 598.

144 Christopher Morys (i.e. Moorhouse), described in 1555 as one of the grooms of the Privy Chamber, was granted the manor of Kelton in 1557. John Moor-house was lord of Kelton in 1578; by 1616 the manor was in the hands of Francis Kay, who had married Moorhouse's daughter, Elizabeth: see Littledale, 'Patricksons of Ennerdale,' pp. 177, 187–9.

Lord William Bonvill's daughter & heire; her grandmother daughter
& heire to the Harringtons of Harrington.[145] Kelton was holden as
a fee of Beckermitt until the lord paramount's heire and iii[i] coparcener, Elizabeth filia < Thomae > Multon[146] transferred the segniory
to Robert Harrington, and thereby extinguished the messnaltye of
the lords of Beckermett. At the suppression of abbeyes Doctor Lighe
bought Saltre,[147] and now Thomas Salkeld brother to Lanclot Salkeld
of the Whitehall, enjoyeth the same, by purchase from Henry Lighe,
son to Thomas, son to William, brother to the doctor.

[p. 19]
[A 23] **Lamplughe.**[148] Lampleughe in the fells is that mannor house
and segniory in the baronny of Egremont which gave name to the
auncient familie of the Lampleughes, a race of valourous gentlemen
successively for their worthyness knighted in the field all or the most
part of them. They beare for armes a sable corss batuny flurie in a
field d'ore. There issue male enjoyeth the same from the Conquest
(or nere that tyme) to this day. The first lord of Lamplughe that I
read of was William de Lancaster, who exchanged Workington &
Lamplugh with Gospatrick the son of Orme, lord of Seaton beneath
Derwent, for Midleton in Lonsdale.[149] This William de Lancaster was
a great baron, his lands lay about Kendall in Westmorland. He was a
great commander under King Henry the second in the warrs against
King David of Scottland and Earle Henry his son, in these parts;
& helped to recover the counties of Cumberland and Northumberland from the Scotts, which King Stephen had given them.[150] By that

145 William Parr (d. 1571), marquis of Northampton, acquired the Harrington
estates after the execution of Henry Grey, marquis of Dorset and duke of
Suffolk, in 1544. Grey's grandfather, Thomas Grey (1451–1501), marquis of
Dorset, had married Cicely, daughter and heir of William Bonville (d. 1460),
lord Harrington, whose mother was Elisabeth, daughter and heir of William,
lord Harrington (d. 1458): *Complete Peerage*, IV, pp. 418–21; VI, pp. 318–21; IX,
pp. 669–74.
146 M: 'Johannis'. H is correct: Elizabeth daughter of Thomas Multon (d. 1322)
inherited one-third of the barony of Egremont from her brother John (d. 1334)
in the partition of 1338: see *Cal. Close 1337–9*, pp. 494–6.
147 The possessions of St Bees priory, including the grange of Salter, were leased
to Sir Thomas Legh (d. 1545), whose family came from Calder and was probably a cadet of the Leghs of Isel, in 1540: *St Bees*, pp. 598–600; A. N. Shaw,
'Legh, Sir Thomas', *ODNB*.
148 Lamplugh (NY 08 20).
149 The charter is printed in *VCH Cumb.*, I, p. 323n and *St Bees*, pp. 539–40.
150 William de Lancaster otherwise called William fitz Gilbert (d. before 1170)

exchange of lands Lamploughe became the lord of Seaton's lands. The said Gospatrick held it all his tyme, but after his death, his son Thomas filius Gospatricii gave it to one Robert de Lamplughe and his heires for paying yearly a paire of gilt spurrs to the lords of Workington. This Robert held it in Hen. 2 tyme and when Richard the first raigned. After Robert's death it descended to Adam his sonn in King John's tyme; to which Adam Richard de Lucy (then lord of Egremont & all Copeland) as lord paramount of Lamploughe, confirmed the same & other things, as Murton & Arlocden, unto him and his heires, with diverse immunityes. After Adam it descended according to the pedegree in the margent unto John Lamplugh Esq., now lord of the same. It was named Glan-flough or Glanfillough of the Irish inhabitants before the Conquest whereof is formed this present name Lamplughe, which Irish word signifies the dale-wett, vallis humida.[151]

[*In margin:*] Wm. de Lancastre; Gospatr filius Orme; Tho filius Gospatr; Rob de Lampl. H. 2; Adam [*temp.*] John; Rob [*temp.*] 3 H., Meliora ux'; Wm; Rob; John; Radulf; Thom; John; John; Thomas; John; John; John; John.[152]

[*p. 20*]

[A 24] Murton.[153] Moor-towne (villa ad ericetum)[154] is next unto Lamplughe westward, and is now the inheriance of John Lamplugh Esq. Of old his auncestors enjoyed the same, & enjoyed great libertyes thereby, to attest and hold plea of greater nature then debt and

---

was the progenitor of the barons of Kendal. His lordship of the barony originated in a grant of lands in Kendal, Lonsdale and Horton-in-Ribblesdale from Roger de Mowbray *c.* 1150: see W. Farrer, *Records Relating to the Barony of Kendale* (ed. J. F. Curwen), 3 vols (CWAAS Record Series IV–VI; Kendal 1923–1926), I, pp. xi–xii, 377–8.

151 Place-name scholars agree that Lamplugh is probably a Celtic name but a British, rather than a Gaelic one. The first element may be *landa* ('enclosure') or the whole name may derive from *nant bluch* ('bare valley'): *PNC*, II, p. 405; *Dict. LDPN*, pp. 204–5.

152 Denton's pedigree ends with Sir John Lamplugh (d. 1604). The descent agrees with the attempt to reconstruct the Lamplugh genealogy made by S. Taylor ('The Lamplugh family in Cumberland', *CW2*, 38 (1938), pp. 71–137), though there is some uncertainty about the number of generations in the fourteenth century: see Taylor's pedigrees, *op. cit.*, p. 82, and between pp. 118 and 119.

153 Murton, an area of scattered settlement on the skirts of Murton Fell (NY 09 19), was a township in Lamplugh parish.

154 Denton's interpretation of the name is correct: see *PNC*, II, p. 406; *Dict. LDPN*, p. 246.

detynnue. Sir John Lamplughe held the same in Edw. 2 tyme[155] and before him I read of three of another family successively, grandfather, father and sonne, Gerrard, Roger and Adam de Murton, which have taken their surnames of the place. Moorton is within the parish of Lamplughe, and is holden of Egremont immediately; but Lamplughe itselfe of the lord of Workington.

[A 25] **Lacus in valle sive profundo. Lowswater**[156] is the name of a great lake in the next dale to Lamplughe on the east side. It gives name to the towne and parish church & was the lands of Randall Lindsey in Hen. 2 tyme. In the 4 of R. 1 William Lindsey sued a writt of right against Henry Clerk of Apulby, the countess of Albermarle and Nicholas Stutvile, for Lowswater & other lands.[157] And in the 16 of Edw. 1 Lowswater was auncient demeasne of Egremont, & by the partition betweene the two daughters and coheires of Richard Lucy, it was allotted to the moiety of Alane Multon & < Alice >[158] his wife as the xx[th] part of the baronny of Egremont.[159] Thomas Multon, calling himselfe Lucy after his mother's name, seated himselfe there. He bought of the Moresbyes, Brakenthwaite, in exchange of the moietye of Distington, < also >[160] Thackthwait, of one Agnes Dundraw the wife of Roger Lindsey, which he gave in marriage to his sister Margrett the wife of Thomas Stanley, and her heires.[161] Howbeit it reverted to the heires of Thomas Lucy & descended to Maud Lucy, who gave it and the rest of her patrimony to her second husband the earle of Northumberland, in whose blood it continued till his posteritye gave the same to K. Hen. the 8th, who sold it to one Robinson, a priest, whose heir did aliene it to .....

---

155 He held it at the death of Thomas de Multon of Egremont in 1322: *Cal. IPM*, VI, no. 331, p. 200.

156 Loweswater (NY 12 21) is thought to derive from ON *laufsaer* ('leafy lake'), rather than the adjective 'low' as Denton appears to imply: *PNC*, I, p. 34; *Dict. LDPN*, pp. 223–4.

157 Pipe Roll, 1192: *VCH Cumb.*, I, p. 371. The payment can be traced back to 1188 (ibid., p. 364).

158 Altered from 'Agnes' in M.

159 16 Edw. I = 1287–8. The partition, dated 29 Oct. 1230, is recorded in CRO, D/Lec, Lucy Cartulary, no. 162.

160 M and J: 'of' but 'also' is clearly meant.

161 For the exchange of Distington for Brackenthwaite, see inquisition *ad quod damnum* 1 May 1300: PRO, C143/313/2. Thomas Stanley and Margery his wife were in possession of Thackthwaite by 1306: PRO, C143/63/13. The descent of Thackthwaite in the thirteenth century is rehearsed in PRO, SC8/334/E1187.

Stanley, master of the mint. Sir Edward Herbert and ..... his wife, daughter & heire to Stanley, sold it to Anthony Patrickson now lord thereof.[162]

[*p. 21*]

[A 26] **Moresby.**[163] Morisceby (or Mauriceby) tooke name first of Maurice, who first seated himselfe there, the ruines of whose mansion house yet appearing approves the same.[164] In that tyme when a gentleman placed his capitall messuage (or mannor house) foorth of a towne or auncient village he named the same after his owne name, as this demaine of Mauricebye (and such others in the countrye (viz): Gamelsby of Gamell, Etardby of Etard, Ormesby of Orme, Corsbye, Cannonbye, Richardby, Botcherby, Scotby, Terriby, Hubertby, Alanby), one part of the word remembring his name and the word Bee or By his being or building there.[165] And as the said Maurice gave name to that place, soe in success of tyme the same gave surname to his successors there who were called Moresbyes or de Morescby, the eldest of which family that I have yett read of was one Ucknan,[166] who gave land in Harrays & common in Moresby, to the abbey of Holme Cultram.[167]

[A 27] **Distington**[168] (villa ad pratum Disting)[169] lies betweene Harrington & Moresby. It is soe called of the low-wett-meadow-grounds there & was the inheritance of Sir Gilbert filius Gilberti de

---

162 The manors of Brackenthwaite, Loweswater and Thackthwaite were released by John Robinson to Thomas Stanley, Master of the Mint, in 1562. Between 1583 and 1593 Sir Edward Herbert and Mary his wife, daughter and heir to Stanley, sold Loweswater and Thackthwaite to Anthony Patrickson: Littledale, 'Patricksons of Ennerdale', p. 185.

163 Moresby (NX 98 20).

164 This is probably a reference to the remains of the Roman fort at Moresby (NX 983 210), for which see E. Birley, 'The Roman fort at Moresby', *CW2*, 48 (1948), pp. 42–72 and J. Bennett *et al.*, 'A watching-brief south-east of Moresby fort, 1980', *CW2*, 87 (1987), pp. 256–8.

165 For place-names in -*by* see Gillian Fellows-Jensen, *Scandinavian Settlement Names in the North West* (Copenhagen, 1985), pp. 10–43, which notes the significant number of names in Cumberland where -*by* is preceded by a Norman personal name, of which Maurice (in Moresby) is one.

166 'Ucknan' is in the margin of M and J and interlined in H.

167 But Adam de Harrais (fl. 1220s) is named as the grantor of land in Harras and common in Moresby to Holm Cultram: *Holm Cultram*, p. 32, no. 87.

168 Distington (NY 00 23).

169 Denton's explanation again suggests that he interpreted 'ing' as ON *eng* ('meadow'). It is, however, an OE -*ingtūn* compound: *PNC*, II, p. 375.

Dundraw, knight (which was son to Odardus lord of Wigton-baronny, called Odardus de Logis). He lived in King Rich. the first's tyme and K. John's, and was lord of Distington, Dundraw & Crofton. He gave lands to the Abbey-holme & the priory of Karlisle in Distington and Crofton.[170] He had issue Isolda wife to Adam de Tinmow. They gave the fourth part of Distington and th'advowson of the rectory to Thomas filius Lambert de Multon, anno 42 H. 3.[171] And he had issue, Ada the wife of Stephen de Crofton, who gave their part of Distington to Thomas de Moresby and Margarett Lucye his wife, anno 6 Ed. 1.[172] Margerett did exchange it with her brother Thomas Lucy, for lands in Thackthwaite, and Thomas < sold >[173] the same with the Moresbyes, for Brackenthwaite in Lowswater.

[*p. 22*]

[A 28] **Haverington**[174] lyes betweene Distington and Workington & was at the Conquest parcelle of the inheritance of ..... lord of ..... and is holden of Workington. This place gave name to the first of that auncient familie of the Harringtons alias Haveringtons, of which house there have sprung divers families, as of Wetherslack, of Adingham in Furness & Lancashire, of Beamont in Cumberland, & one in Rutlandshire.[175] The eldest were lords of Harrington, and married the heire de sanguine of Seaton, and therefore confirmed Flemingby to th'abbey of Holme-Cultram,[176] but got not the lord of Seaton's land, for his wife dyed in the grandfather's tymes who gave the land to her unckle Patrick de Culwen. Afterwards they married Elena the sister & heire of William Cansfield, whose father Richard Cansfield married Alice the daughter and heire of William (and sister and heire to Michaell) Fleminge of Adingham, in H. 3 tyme. In Edw. 3 tyme they marryed with the third coheire of John Multon, lord of Egremont, and at last a daughter transferred their inheritance to the Bonvills, whose daughter Cicilie in like sort [transmitted][177] the same (with the Bonvills' < lands >) to Thomas Gray, filius Johannis, marquess Dorcett. They held it three descents and lastly it fell to

---

170 See *Holm Cultram*, p. 33 (nos. 89–90).
171 FF Cumb. 42 Hen. III [1258–9] (*CW2*, 7 (1907), p. 226, no. 103).
172 Ibid., 6 Edw. I [1277–8] (*CW2*, 7 (1907), p. 228, no. 122).
173 M and J: 'so'. M has the marginal comment 'for chang'd'.
174 Harrington (NX 99 25).
175 See R. Horrox, 'Harrington family (*per* c.1300–1512), magnates', *ODNB*; *Complete Peerage*, VI, pp. 314–19.
176 See *Holm Cultram*, pp. 24–5 (nos. 59–60).
177 This word is interlined in M but is not in J or H.

the crowne by escheat from the death of William Parr, marquess of Northumbr'.[178] Another Harrington marryed the daughter and one of the < two >[179] coheires of Bastingthwaite, whose last rebelled with Martin < Swarth >;[180] another marryed the < 3d > coheire of Robert Brune of Bothell & had her purpartye.

[*p. 23*]

[A 29] Workington.[181] Next unto Harrington, betweene it & the foote of the river Derwent towards the sea, stands Workington-hall, now the mansion house and chiefe seate of Nicholas Curwen Esq. (lord of the manor of Workington in the baronny of Egremont, and of the manor of Seaton on the other side of Derwent in the baronny of Allerdale), a gentleman descended of honourable and great parentage continually in the issue male from one Ketellus < or >[182] Ketell his first auncestor (that I read of),[183] who lived in King William the Conqueror's tyme or in the dayes of William Rufus his son the next king of England, about which tyme I read of this Kettellus, without any certaintye of his father or from whom he descended or in what place or country he was seated. There was one Kettellus, lord of Newton, and another Ketellus filius Ulff, a wittness to diverse auncient evidences and deeds of feoffment made nere that tyme, which neither in respect of the tyme nor place I may probably think to be the same.[184] Kettellus filius Eldred gave the rectory of Morland to the abbey of York & the parsonage of Workington.[185]

The first lord of Workington after the Conquest was William de Lancaster, who by the consent of William his son and heire, gave

---

178 *Sic*, for 'Northampton'. H: 'Nhland'. For the descent from the Harringtons to William Parr, see above, note 145.

179 M: 'second'.

180 M: 'Thwarth.' Martin Schwartz (d. 1487) was a mercenary, born in Augsburg, who supported the Yorkist pretender, Lambert Simnel: I. Arthurson, 'Schwartz, Martin', *ODNB*.

181 Workington (NX 99 28).

182 M: 'of' but 'or' is clearly meant.

183 For the Curwen family see J. F. Curwen, *A History of the Ancient House of Curwen* (Kendal, 1928) and C. B. Phillips, 'Curwen family (*per c. 1500–c. 1725*)', *ODNB*. Nicholas Curwen (1550–1605), knighted 1603, inherited Workington on his father's death in 1596.

184 Ketel son of Ulf (fl. late 12th century), also known as Ketel de Cauplandia, was ancestor of the Copeland family (see *St Bees*, pp. 251n, 290n). Ketel, lord of Newton, has not been identified.

185 The last sentence is written in the margin of M, J and H. The charter of Ketel son of Eldred is in *St Bees*, no. 212.

the townes of Workington and Lamplugh to Gospatrick filius Ormi filii Ketell, in exchange for the towne of Midleton in Lonsdale in Westmorland, where the sayd William de Lancaster had other large possessions. And he reserved to him & his heires a yearely rent of vi^d ad nundinas Karlioli or a paire of gilt spurrs, and bound Gospatrick and his heires to doe him homage and to discharge his forreine service for the same to the baronny or castle of Egremont. To this deed of exchange was witness the fore remembred Ketell filius Ulffi.[186]

To this Orme the son of Ketell, one Waldieff (the son of Gospatrick, earle of Dunbarr in Scottland), then being lord of the baronny of Allerdale, by the guift of therle Randolph Meschiens gave the mannor of Seaton beneath Derwent (parcell of the said baronny) in franck marriage with < Gynold >[187] his sister, and the townes of [p. 24] < Camberton >,[188] Crayksothen, and Flemingby.[189] So became Seaton < a mannor >[190] and the said Orme first lord after the Conquest of the said mannor. The walls and ruines of this mansion house are yet to be seene there att Seaton to this day.

The said Orme filius Ketelli had issue a son & heire by his wife < Ginuld > (the lord Waldieff's sister), whom he named Gospatrick after the name of < Ginuld's > father.

To this Gospatrick filius Orme & his heires, his cousen germaine Alane, second lord of Allerdale, sonne and heire to the said Waldieff gave High Ireby, which continued the Curwens' lands < untill Sir Henry Curwin, Nich[olas'] father, sold the same to Anthony Barwis >. Sir Ralph Vane sold Ireby to Richard Orpheur & he the same to Antho. Barwis.[191]

---

186 The charter is printed in *VCH Cumb.*, I, p. 323n and *St Bees*, pp. 539–40.
187 M: 'Gimyld' here and throughout. The readings from H, while still erroneous, are closer to the intended name, Gunild.
188 M: 'Cambmerton'.
189 This sentence derives from the 'Chronicon Cumbrie', where the name of Waldeof's sister is given variously as 'Gravelda' or 'Gurwelda': *St Bees*, p. 493. The places listed are Seaton (NY 02 30), Camerton (NY 04 31), Greysouthen (NY 07 29) and Flimby (NY 02 33).
190 M and J: 'almainer' but the wording in H is clearly meant.
191 The last sentence is in the margin of M, J and H. Gilpin, pp. 90–1, marks it in square brackets, which, as stated in his preface, he usually used to indicate material that he had added to Denton's text. It appears to contradict the previous statement, found in H but in neither M nor J. The manor of High Ireby passed from Richard Orfeur, junior, of Plumbland to Anthony Barwis of Islekirk in 1546: CRO, D/Van, Acc. 2543, larger deed box 2.

The said Gospatrick filius Ormi, was the first of his house that was lord of Workington, by the aforesaid exchange made with William de Lancaster, the second lord of the manor of Seaton. He had issue Thomas, Gilbertt, Adam, Orme & Alexander, which took their surnames (as the mannor was in that age) of their father's name & were called Thomas filius Gospatri, Gilbert filius Gospatri and Alexander filius Gospatri.

Gospatrick their father gave 2 parts of the fishing in Derwent < and Flemingby > to the abbey of Holme Cultram, withall thappendices except Waytcroft,[192] which he gave to the priory of Carlile, which Waytcroft John then prior of Carlile regranted to Thomas filius Gospatricii his heire, to be holden of the priory freely, paying yearly vii[s] rent at Penticost & Martinmas.[193]

Thomas filius Gospatricii, eldest son & heire of Gospatrick, succeeded his father in the inheritance and had issue Thomas filius Thomae filii Gospatrii; Patrick; Alane.

To this Thomas filius Gospatricii, one Rowland filius Ughtredi filius Fargus, sometyme lord of Galloway, gave the great lordshipp of Culwen in Galloway in Scottland, in which grant the brethren of the said Thomas, Alex. & Gilbert sonns of Gospatr', & Thomas and William sonnes of the said Gilbert, are mencioned as wittnesses.[194]
[p. 25] The said Thomas filius Gospatrick, confirmed his father's grant of Flemingby to the abbott and convent of Holme Cultram, and gave them the whole fishings of Derwent, which fishings Thomas filius Thomae, his eldest son, confirmed unto them.[195]

And the said Thomas filius Gospater' gave Lampleughe to Robert de Lampleugh and his heires to be holden of him by paying yearely two guilt spurrs.

And he gave to Patrick his second sonne Culwen in Galloway.

---

192 See *Holm Cultram*, p. 18, no. 49 (grant of Flimby); p. 22, no. 52 (confirmation of grant of fishery).
193 See *Holm Cultram*, p. 21 (no. 50).
194 The grant of Colvend (NX 87 53), near Rockcliffe, Kirkcudbright, does not appear to have survived, though the detail Denton gives suggests that he had seen it or a copy. It must date from towards the end of the twelfth century: the grantor Roland son of Uctred died in December 1200 and Thomas son of Gospatrick was dead by 1201: *St Bees*, pp. 64n, 91n.
195 See *Holm Cultram*, p. 22, nos. 51, 52.

The said Patrick filius Thomae filii Gospatrii, by the death of his elder
brother Thomas filius Thomae succeeded as next heire to Thomas his
father, & was called Patrick Culwen de Workington. He pull'd down
the mannor house of Seaton & dwelt thenceforth at Workington.
From him all his posteritye were surnamed Culwen.

He gave Camberton to his brother Alane which was before as
parcell of Seaton & boundred furth Camberton. From that Alane the
Cambertons tooke their name.

Gilbert Culwen filius Patricii de Workington.

[p. 26]
[A 30] The Catalogue of the Barons of Allerdall[196]

1. Waldeof the first baron of Allerdall, son of Gospatrick, earle of
Dunbarr in Scotland, to him the earle Randolph Meschiens gave
the baronny of Allerdall beneath Derwent and the lord William
Meschiens, baron of Egremont, gave him all the lands betweene the
rivers of Cocker and Derwent, and the five townes, Brigham, Egglesfield, Deane, Crakesothen, Branthwaite, & the two Cliftons and Stainburne.[197] His first seat or mansion house was at Papcastle and afterwards att Cockermouth. He gave divers mannors within Allerdall
to his kinsmen and followers (viz:) to Odard de Logis he gave the
baronny of Wigdon, Kirkbride and Ulton, Waverton, Dundraw, and
Blencogow; to Odard filius Lyolf, Tallentire & Castlerigg with the
forrest betweene Gretey and Calter; to Adam the son of Lyolf, Ulnedale & Gilcruce; to < Gamell the son of Brun >,[198] he gave Bothil; to
the priory of Gisburne, Appleton and Bridekirk with the patronage
of the church of Bridekirk; to Melbeth his phisicion he gave Brumfield towne, excepting the patronage of the church there; to Walldieff
the son of Gilmin with his sister Ochtred, he gave Brochton, Ribton

---

196 Section A30 draws substantially on the early fourteenth-century account of
the descent of the baronies of Allerdale and Copeland, known as the 'Chronicon Cumbrie', which is printed in *St Bees*, pp. 491–6 and discussed in *VCH
Cumb.*, I, pp. 297–8.

197 The 'five towns' were the *villae integrae* of Brigham (NY 08 30), Clifton
(comprising Great and Little Clifton (NY 04 29 and NY 05 28) and Stain-
burn (NY 02 29)), Dean (NY 07 25) (which included Branthwaite (NY 06 24)),
Eaglesfield (NY 09 28) and Greysouthen (NY 07 29): see A. J. L. Winchester,
'The medieval vill in the western Lake District: some problems of definition',
CW2, 78 (1978), pp. 55–69.

198 M: 'Gimald the son of Brime' J: 'son of Brim'. 'Chronicon Cumbrie' reads
'Gamello filio Brun': *St Bees*, p. 492.

and Little Brochton, and Bewalldre, ad unum logum; to Orme the son of Kettell, he gave Seaton, Camberton, Flemingbye and Craksothen, with < Gunild >[199] his sister; and to Dolphin filium Dillward,[200] he gave Applethwaite, Little Crosbye, Langrigg, and Brigham, with the patronage of Brigham. He went to Jerusalem & brought thence a peice of the holy cross.

2. Alane, second baron, had issue a son named Walldeoff, who dyed in his father's life tyme, and therefore he gave to the priory of Carliell the bodye of his said son Walldeoff, and Crosbye, now called Crosscannonby, with the patronage of the church there & the service of Uchtred. To which Uchtred the said Alane gave a carracut of land in Aspatrick to be summoner in Allerdall, which is called att this day Uchtredsett;[201] the patronage of Aspatrick-church with the services of Alane of Branton, the patronage of the church of Irebye with the services [*p. 27*] of Waldeoff de Langthwaite and the peice of the holye cross which his father Waldeoff brought from Jerusalem.

He gave to King Hen. 2 the forrest ground of Allerdall now called the Westward and Holme Cultram. To the priory of St. Bega he gave Staineburne; to Ranall de Lindsey with his sister Octred[202] he gave Blennerhassett and Uckmanby; to Uchtred the son of Fergus, lord of Galloway, with his sister < Gunild >,[203] he gave Turpenhow and the rectory there; to his steward Kettelus he gave Threepland; to Gospatrick the son of Orme aforesaid, his cousen germane, he gave High Ireby pro tertia parte unius villae; to Gamell < Brun >[204] aforesaid he gave < Issall >[205] & Ruthwait pro tertia parte unius villae; to Odard he gave Newton < cum pertinenciis; to Radulph Eggayne he gave Issall cum pertinenciis, Blencrake > with the services of Newton; to Gospatrick, his bastard brother, he gave Bolton, Bastenwaite & Eastholme; to Simon Sheftling, half of Deerham & to Dolphin filius Gospatrick, the other half of Deerham; to Waldeoff filius Dolfinii he

---

199 M: 'Gimyld'. The name is rendered 'Gravelda' and 'Gurwelda' in 'Chronicon Cumbrie': *St Bees*, p. 493.

200 'Dulfino filio Alwardi' in 'Chronicon Cumbrie': *St Bees*, p. 493.

201 i.e. Oughterside (NY 11 40).

202 'Ethereda' in 'Chronicon Cumbrie': *St Bees*, p. 493.

203 M: 'Gimald'. The name is rendered 'Gornella' and 'Gurnelda' in 'Chronicon Cumbrie': *St Bees*, p. 493.

204 M: 'Brim'.

205 M: 'Issuell'. The inclusion of Isel here appears to be an error: in 'Chronicon Cumbrie' this grant to Gamell le Brun consisted solely of Ruthwaite: *St Bees*, p. 493.

gave Brackenwaite, & to Herbart, the third part of Thursbye; and to Dolphin, six oxgang of land in High Crosbye, to be the king's serjeant or baliffe in Allerdall. And he gave to his three huntsmen Seliff[206] and his fellowes, Hayton. He dyed without issue male, therefore his nephew William Fitz Duncane, earle of Murrey, succeeded him in the inheritance.

The said Randalphe Meschienes gave to the lord Waldief (the son of Gospatrick, earle of Dunbar in Scotland) the great barronny of Allerdall, which lyeth betweene the rivers of Derwent and Wathempoll on the south & north parts, and upon the west side is compassed by the sea, abutting on the east side upon Dalston baronny and Seburgham, where it is from them devided by the brook called Shawk, which falleth downe northward into Wathempoll from Caldbeck, & on the other side of the hill by Bowland Beck, which falleth southward into Caldbeck beck; then by the same rill running eastward untill it falleth into Cawdey, which river descending betweene it and Castle Sowerby & the baronny of Greystock keepes them assunder there on the east side of the mountaine Carrocke and Grisedall fells.[207]

It is called Allerdall of the river Alne, < it was anciently named Alner-dall (viz.) the dale upon Aln >, this sillable (er) being interposed betweene Alne and Dale which signifies ad or apud, [*p. 28*] at or upon, as in other names of places in that country, < as > Miterdale, the dale upon Mite; Enyerdale, the dale upon Eyne; Annerdale, the dale upon Anand; Dudden-er-dale, corruptly Dunerdale, the dale upon Dudden. <u>Aln-er-dale contractly Allerdaile. Annand-er-dale, contractly Annerdale.</u>[208]

[A31] Upon the northside of the River Wathempoll lyes the baronny of Burgh by Sand, environed by the sea and the River Eden on the west and north sides and towards Carlisle and from thence unto Thursbye, on the east side it abutteth upon Dalston as the common high way leadeth from Carlisle to Thursbye. The earle Randolph Meschienes gave this baronny unto Robert de Estrivers or Trivers.[209]

---

206 'Sleth' in 'Chronicon Cumbrie': *St Bees*, p. 493.

207 The streams demarcating the eastern boundary of Allerdale are as follows: 'Shawk': Chalk Beck (NY 32 44); 'Bowland Beck': Bowten Beck (NY 32 40); 'Caldbeck Beck': Cald Beck (NY 33 39); and 'Cawdey': the River Caldew.

208 The '-er' element in these names represents the ON genitive, *ar*: *PNC*, III, p. xxv.

209 As stated in 'Testa de Nevill' of 1212: *Book of Fees*, p. 198.

And he gave the said barony of Dalston unto one Robert (brother of Hubbart de Vallibus, first baron of Gilsland) and his heires; which baronny of Dalston is extended in length from Carlisle to Welton in Seburgham, where it is devided from Sowerby by the River Cawdey. Att the foote of Sowerby it reacheth over Cawdey and taketh in little Rawghton field until the foot of Raugh, where Cawdey bounders it againe alongst great Raughton field.

[A 32] Greystock. On the east side of Allerdall att the mountaine Carrock and Grisedale fells & adjoyning to the south side of the forrest of Englewood lyes the baronny of Greystock, which containes all that part of the countye above the said forrest betweene the segniory of Penreath and the mannor of Castlerigg towards Keswick. This baronny the earle Randolph Meschienes gave to one Syolf or Lyulphe,[210] and King Henry the 1st confirmed the same unto Phorne the son of the said Syolf or Lyulphe, whose posteritye took their surname of the place and were called de Greystock.[211]

There issue male continued barons untill K. Henry the 8th tyme, when by a daughter named Elizabeth the Lord Thomas Dacre became baron in her right, being his wife.[212]
[*p. 29*] It is holden of the king by knight service in capite by homage and cornage paying yearely iiii^{li} att the faires of Carlisle, and suit att the countye monthly and serve the king in person against Scottland.

A Catalogue of the Barons of Greystock
1. Syolf[213] or Lyulph was the first baron of Greystock.
2. Phorne filius Syolf the second baron in the tyme of K. H. 1
3. Ranulph filius < Phor' >[214] lived in the tyme of K. Steph. & H. 2
William filius Radulphi lived in Ric.1 & K. John's tyme.[215]
4. Robert filius Willelmi dyed in the 38 yeare of Hen. 3.[216]

---

210 H: 'Syolf br' to Liuliph'.
211 Forne son of Sigulf (d. *c.* 1130) was named in the Wetheral Priory foundation charter of 1101x1112, suggesting that he already held Greystoke then. Charles Phythian-Adams has suggested that Greystoke may have been granted to Sigulf before the Conquest: *Land of the Cumbrians*, pp. 30, 178–80; Richard Sharpe is more cautious: Sharpe, *Norman Rule*, p. 54.
212 Elizabeth (d. 1516), daughter and heir of Sir Robert Greystoke, married *c.* 1488 Thomas Lord Dacre of Gilsland (1467–1525): *Complete Peerage*, IV, p. 21.
213 H: 'Sigolf'.
214 M and J name him Ralph son of Ralph.
215 This line is in the margin of M but in the body of the text in H.
216 Denton's descent is confused here. The lord who died 38 Hen. III (1254) was Robert son of Thomas de Greystoke (not son of William as stated by Denton).

Thomas frater Roberti
William filius Thomae dyed in the 17 y. of K. E. 1.[217]
John filius Willelmi dyed in the 34 y. of E. 1.[218]
Radulphus frater Johannis
Robertt filius Radulphi dyed in the 10 y. of Ed. 2.[219]
Radulphus filius Roberti
Willielmus filius Radulphi
Radulphus filius Willelmi
John filius Radulphi
Radulphus.

[A 33] Allerdale

3. < The third baron of Allerdall, > William Romley, called alsoe
William Fitz Duncane, earle of Murrey, marryed Alice the daughter
& heire of Robert Romley, lord of Skipton in Craven, begotten by the
said Robert of his wife, the Lord William Meschiens his daughter
and heire, sometyme baron of Egremont or of Copeland, and the
Earle Randall Meschiens brother, was the third baron of Allerdall
and of Egremond, and lord of Skipton. He had issue William, first
lord of Egremont, which dyed under age, and thre daughters – Cibell
or Cicilie, marryed to William le Gross, earle of Albemarle with the
honour of Skipton by King Henry the second; Amabill marryed to
Regnald Lucye, with the segniory of Egremont, by the sayd king;
and Alice Romley, first married to Gilbertt Pippard, with the honour
of Cockermouth, Aspatrick and the baronny of Allerdale, by the said
Henry, and afterwards to Robert Courtney by the queene.[220]

[*p. 30*] 4. Because the baronny of Egremont was lesser in value then
Allerdale, Reginold Lucy had some part of the baronny of Allerdale
after the death of William Fitz Duncane, but Dame Alice Romley his
wife's sister was cheife lady of the signiory. She dyed without children and therefore gave away divers mannors and lands to houses
of religion and to her freindes and kinsmen. She had a son named
William, who was drowned in Craven comeing home from hawking

He was succeeded by his brother William son of Thomas, then aged 30, who
died 17 Edw. I (1289): *Cal. IPM*, I, no. 314; II, no. 714. Denton's 'Thomas frater
Roberti' appears to be spurious.
217 Inquisition, 1289: *Cal. IPM*, II, no. 714.
218 Inquisition, 1306: *Cal. IPM*, IV, no. 375.
219 Inquisition, 1317: *Cal. IPM*, VI, no. 51.
220 This paragraph derives from 'Chronicon Cumbrie': *St Bees*, p. 494.

or hunting. His hound or spaniell, being tyed to his < girdle >[221] by a lyne as they crossed the water near Barden Tower in Craven, pull'd his master from off his horse and drowned him. When the report of the mischance came to his mother, she answered bootless baile brings endless sorrow.[222] She had three daughters Alice, Avice and Mavice, which dyed all unmarryed and without children, wherefore thinheritance was after her death parted betweene the house of Albemarle and Reginald Lucy baron of Egremont, discending to her sisters' children and their posteritye.

A moietye of the barony of Allerdale came to William de Fortibus, earle of Albemarle, as sonne and heire to Hawiss, daughter and heire to Cibell or Cicilie the sister of Dame Alice Romley; after his death to William de Fortibus his son, whose sole daughter and heire Avelina (wife to Edmund King Ed. 1 brother) dyed without issue, & thereupon that moietye came to Thomas Lucy and his heires.[223]

---

221 M: 'girld'.
222 'bootless baile': pain without relief. The story of this tragedy was immortalised by William Wordsworth in 'The Force of Prayer or, the founding of Bolton, a tradition' (*Shorter Poems 1807–1820*, ed. C. H. Ketcham (Ithaca, 1989), pp. 43–6). It can be traced back to Oxford, Bodleian Library, MS Dodsworth 125, f. 144, which records an unprovenanced 'report of the occasion of the foundacion of Bolton Abbey' thus (interlineations are printed between angled brackets): 'Alice de Rumelli having only one sone, who on a tyme being ou conting [*sic*, for 'out hunting'] had his Greyhoundes fastned in a slipp att his girdle & coming to a place called the stride (being a place over the river of Wharfe betweene Bolton & Berden Towre) wher the said river of Wharfe is so narrow that a man may easily stride over itt. he having < forgotten that > his dogges < were > tyed to his girdle offred to stepp over the river was hindered & drawne backe by the dogges & most untymely drowned. The Huntsman coming to his mother to acquaint her with this mischance questioned with her after this manner – asking her What was good for booteless Bale. She dening [*sic*; for 'denying' or 'divining'?] her sonnes deathe answered Endles sorrow. he replied itt was her owne Case & therupon acquainted her with the manner of her sonnes death, which she for certayne understanding said that she would make many a poore mans child her heires & thereupon founded the Nunnes of Eumsey afterward removed to Bolton by ..... [*sic*] for a priory. I have seene in Bolton Abbey the picture of the la: with her sonne & Dogges.' The account is undated but the account of Beamsley Hospital on f. 144v appears to date from 1618. Denton's may thus be the earliest known reference to the story.
223 The younger William de Forz d. 1260; his daughter Aveline d. 1274. The Forz moiety of the barony remained in the hands of William's widow Countess Isabella until her death in 1293, when it escheated to the crown. It was granted to Anthony de Lucy, heir of the other moiety of the barony, in 1323: B.

That moiety was Cockermouth and Papcastle & the fees holden of them, viz., of Cockermouth: Brigham, Eglesfield, Deane, Clifton, Crakesothen, Huthwait, Collanland, Ullaike, Branthwaite, Emelton, Pardshaw and other lands [*above*] Derwent.[224] < And of Papcastle were holden Threpeland, Hames, Castlerigg, Tallentyre, Broghton, Ribton, Ireby Bast, Bolton & Wigton, with their appurtenancies. >

[*p. 31*] **Allerdale.** Th'other moiety descended to Amabill and Alice Lucyes, daughters and coheires to Reginald Lucy and Amabill his wife, sister to the said Dame Alice Romley. To Amabill Lucy succeeded Lambert Multon filiusThomae. Lambart had issue Thomas. Thomas had issue John Multon, Lord Egremont, whose three daughters parted his lands amongst them and one of them named Margarett marryed to the last Thomas Lucy, united againe that moiety of Allerdale.

Alice Lucy, th'other daughter of Reginald Lucye, had issue Thomas Lucy, who had issue another Thomas Lucy, to whom th'other half and moiety of Allerdale descended by the death of Avelina, countess of Albemarle, & dyed without issue.

Anthony Lord Lucy, brother and heire to the last Thomas Lucy, succeeded in th'inheritance. He marryed Elizabeth the daughter of Robert Tilliolff, lord of Skalebye. He arreasted Andrew Harcla, earle of Carlisle, in King Edw. 2 tyme, and gave judgement for his treason; had issue Thomas, and dyed.[225]

Thomas marryed Margarett, one of the daughters of John Multon of Egremont, and by her brought in againe the fourth part of Allerdall; soe became he sole lord of Allerdale. He dyed the 39th of Ed. 3. Anthony succeeded Thomas; hee dyed in the 42 of Ed. 3.[226]

[A34] Burgh Barony super sabulones. Next unto Allerdale and beneath the river of Wampole on the north side of the same, lyes

---

English, 'Forz [Fortibus], William de (d. 1260)' and 'Forz [Fortibus], Isabella de'; H. Summerson 'Lucy, Anthony', *ODNB*.

224 M reads 'about Derwent' but 'above Derwent' (i.e. in Copeland, otherwise known as Allerdale ward above Derwent) is meant. H reads 'about' but has 've' written above the last two letters.

225 For Anthony Lucy (*c.* 1283–1343) and Andrew Harclay, earl of Carlisle, executed for treason in 1323, see Summerson 'Lucy, Anthony' and 'Harclay, Andrew'.

226 Thomas de Lucy died 1365; his son Anthony died 1368: *Cal. IPM*, XII, nos. 17, 233.

Brugh barony, which towards the north-west is washed by the sea
flowing upp into the foote of the river Eden, and by the sayd river
towards the north-east untill Carlisle is boundred in. And from Carlisle unto the said river Wampole towards the south east it is devided
from the baronny of Dalston by the beaten high street that leadeth
through Thursbye to Wigdon. In this baronny are divers mannors
holden of Burgh, and some within the bounder, yett no part of the
baronny (as Orton and < Gamelsby >[227]) nor holden of the same.

[*p. 32*] This seigniory of Burgh was given by the earle Randolph
Meschiens to one Robert de Estrivers, whose daughter Ibria Trevers
(wife of < Randolph >[228] Engayne, lord of Issell) translated the same
to the Engaynes.[229] Radulphe Engayne had issue William Engayne.
The said Radulphe and Ibria & William their son gave Henrikby
alias Herribye beside Carlile unto the priory of Carlile, which gift
Hugh Morvill confirmed. The sayd Earle Randolph gave also to the
said Robert Trivers the chiefe forrester's office in the forrest of Englewood; which office with great and many liberties to the same all
the lords of Burgh enjoyed successively untill Thomas de Multon de
Gilsland forfeited the same by treason committed against the king
.... the .... in the insurreccion made by Symon de Mounsford, earle
of Leceister.[230]

After Robert Trivers, Radulph Engayne, William Engayne successively lords of Burgh, Sir Hugh Morvill enjoyed the same as fourth
lord thereof, in the tyme of King Henry the second, as next heire unto
the said William Engayne by Ada .... his daughter & heire, mother
to Sir Hugh Morvill. This Sir Hugh Morvill was of great possessions
in Cumberland. He was lord of Burgh baronny, Lazonby & Issell;
in Westmorland of Temple Sowerbye, Hoff Lun & about Wharton
he held divers lands. The great mountaine Hugh Seat Morvill took
name of him.[231] He was one of the foure knights that kild Thomas

---

227 M and J: 'Gennetsby'.
228 M and J: 'Robert'.
229 For the descent of the barony, see R. L. Storey, 'The manor of Burgh by Sands',
     CW2, 54 (1955 for 1954), pp. 119–30.
230 The privileges of Thomas de Multon, forester of Inglewood, which embraced a
     range of rights, including underwood, retro-pannage, birds of prey, charcoal-
     making and non-royal game rights, and the right to appoint under-foresters,
     are described in *Calendar of Inquisitions Miscellaneous*, 7 vols (London, 1916–),
     I, no. 471.
231 Hugh Seat Morvill (SD 809 991), on the boundary between Mallerstang
     (Westmorland) and Swaledale (Yorkshire North Riding).

Beckett, archbishopp of Canterbury, after which deed he came to great misery.[232] He gave therefore the abbey of Holm Cultrum the rectory of Burgh, which the bishopps of Carlisle, Hugh, Bernard and Walter did appropriate to the monkes.[233]

The sword that kild St Thomas was att Issell in my father's tyme, and since remaineth with the house of Arrundell.[234] He was hated greatly of the churchmen of his tyme; therefore they write many things to his disgrace hardly to be credited, which I omitt. After great repentance he dyed & left two daughters his heires, one named Johan wife to Richard Werin or Gern; another named Ada wife first to Richard Lucy, 2[ly] to Thomas Multon, and thirdly to William Lord Furnivall.

[p. 33] After Sir Hugh Morvill, succeeded Richard Lucy and Richard Werne, with the two daughters of Sir Hugh in the inheritance of Burgh. Richard Lucy had by his wife two daughters, Amabill and Alice. By Ada her death the whole moiety of Burgh, which Richard Lucye had, fell to the second Thomas Multon aforesaid (brother to Lambert < Multon >[235] of Egremont). < [In margin:] Thos de Multon had issue Lambert Multon and Alane. >

Richard Werne had by his wife Johan Morvill, Sara a daughter marryed to Richard Boyvill, baron of Kirklevington, who had issue Hawiss uxor Eustachii Balioll.[236] She dyed without issue; thereupon that moiety alsoe descended to Thomas filius Thomae de Multon aforesaid, or to Thomas Multon de Gilsland his sonne, the third of that name.

---

232 Hugh de Morville (d. 1202), lord of Burgh barony, has been confused with his namesake (d. 1173–4), the murderer of Becket, for whom see R. M. Franklin, 'Morville, Hugh de', *ODNB*.

233 See *Holm Cultram*, pp. 4–6, nos. 12, 15, 16, 19, 20. The episcopal confirmations are printed in *EEA 30: Carlisle*, nos. 22–3, 47–8 and 88.

234 The sword, first recorded in 1297, when Robert Bruce swore allegiance on it, was apparently in Carlisle in 1307, when Edward I made offering to it. It was still at Carlisle Priory in 1535: H. Summerson, 'Medieval Carlisle: cathedral and city from foundation to Dissolution', in *Carlisle and Cumbria: Roman and medieval architecture, art and archaeology*, ed. M. McCarthy and D. Weston (Leeds, 2004), pp. 32, 36. Denton's statement that it was 'with the house of Arrundell' is confirmed by Camden, who stated that the sword had been kept at Kirkoswald (*Britannia*, p. 777), which passed to Philip Howard (1557–1595), earl of Arundel, in 1571 on his marriage to Anne, the heiress to the Dacre estates: *CFH*, p. 81.

235 M: 'Multum'.

236 See below, section A39.

The second Thomas de Multon marryed Matild Vaulx the sole daughter and heire of .... Vaulx, baron of Gilsland, and by her had issue Thomas de Multon de Gilsland, and dyed in the 55th of Hen. 3.[237] He forfeited the chief forrest office of the forrest of Englewood by insurrecion with Symon de Montford.

Thomas de Multon de Gilsland was baron of Burgh and Gilsland. He marryed Issabell, daughter ...... [*In margin:*] This Issabell was afterwards marryed to John de Castre, knight], and had issue Thomas de Multon de Gilsland < and dyed in the > 23 Ed. 1.[238]

Thomas de Molton de Gilsland had issue a daughter and heire named Margarett marryed to Ranulph Dacre filius Willelmi, soe became the Dacres first to be barons of Burghe and of Gilsland. This Thomas Multon dyed the 7 Ed. 2.[239]

Ranulph Dacre and Margarett Multon his < wife >[240] succeeded her father Thomas Multon and had issue William Dacre. Ranulph dyed 13 Ed. 3 and Margarett 36th of the same King.[241]
William Dacre dyed in his mother's life tyme 35 Ed. 3,[242] and had issue Ranulph the second.
Ranulph dyed.
Hugh dyed 7 Ric. 2.[243]
< William died the 22th Ric. 2nd >[244]
Thomas dyed
Thomas
Randolph
Humphrid'
Thomas
William
Thomas
George & three sisters coheires.[245]

Rocliff parcell

237 Inquisition, 1271: *Cal. IPM*, I, no. 758.
238 Inquisition, 1295: *Cal. IPM*, III, no. 285.
239 Inquisition, 1313: *Cal. IPM*, V, no. 452.
240 Both M and J read 'next', which is presumably a transcription error.
241 Inquisitions, 1339, 1362: *Cal. IPM*, VIII, no. 229; XI, no. 317.
242 35 Edw. III = 1361–2.
243 Inquisition, 1384: *Cal. IPM*, XV, no. 972.
244 Inquisition, 1399: *Cal. IPM*, XVII, no. 1324.
245 George, Lord Dacre, died as a child in 1569. His three sisters and coheirs were Anne, who married Philip Howard, earl of Arundel, Mary who died young,

Lazenby
Kirkoswald.

[*p. 34*]

[A 35] Dalston. Betweene Burgh barony and the forrest of Englewood lyes the barony of Great Dalston, which is devided from the
great forrest by the river of Cawdey on th'east side and reacheth
from Carliell to Welton. This segniory was given first to one Robert
that was second brother to the first baron of Gilsland, whereupon he
was called Robert de Dalston. The earle Randolph Meschiens gave
it to him. This Robert & his issue enjoyed it till King Stephen gave
Cumberland to David, king of Scotts. And then or presently after
King Hen. of England the 2 of that name, banishing the Scotts, seized
that barony amongst other things and united them to the forrest of
Englewood when Allan de Nevell was chief forrester ultra Trentum.
It continued forrest from that tyme dureing all the raignes of the
said K. Hen. 2, R. 1 and John his sons, and of H. 3, John's son, untill
the 14 year of his raigne, who first disforrested the same & granted
Dalston with great priviledges to Walter Malclerk, then lord treasurer of England and bishopp of Carliell, and to his successors, bishopps there.[246] And at this day Henry Robinson, bishopp of Carliell,
enjoyeth the same by that grant,[247] being the 35th bishopp of that sea
< as > appeareth by this cattalogue of the bishopps' names ensueing:

1. Athelwold or Athulf, first bishopp of Carliell. He was K. Hen. 1 his chaplaine
& prior of St Botolphes; & after him:

2. Bernard	13. Thomas Appleby	24. Edward Storrey
3. Hugh	14. Robert Reed	25. Richard Bell
4. Walter Malclerk[248]	15. Thomas Mark	26. Roger Leyburne[249]
5. Sylvester de Eversden[250]	16. William Strickland	27. William Senos
6. Thomas	17. Roger Welpdale	28. John Penny

---

and Elizabeth, who married Lord William Howard: *Complete Peerage*, IV, p.
23.

246 For this grant of 1230, see *Cal. Charter R 1226–57*, p. 115; *Cal. Close (1227–31)*,
p. 391.

247 Henry Robinson was bishop 1598–1616.

248 H adds 'L[or]d Treasurer'. Walter Mauclerk, bishop of Carlisle 1223–1246,
was appointed treasurer of England in 1228, a position he was forced to
surrender in 1233: N. Vincent, 'Mauclerk, Walter', *ODNB*.

249 The order of bishops Leyburn and Senhouse is reversed: William Senhouse
was bishop 1495–1502; Roger Leyburn, 1503–1508.

250 H adds 'L[or]d Chan[cello]r'. Sylvester of Everdon, bishop of Carlisle 1246–
1254, was appointed keeper of the great seal in 1242, 1244 and again in 1246

7. Robert Chorry	18. William Barrow	29. John Kite
8. Randolph Irton	19. Marmaduke Lumley	30. Robert Aldridge
9. John Halton	20. Nicholas Close	31.< Owen >[251] Oglethorpp
10. John Rose	21. William Peircye	32. John Best
11. John Kirkby	22. John Kingscot	33. Richard Barnes
12. Gilbert Welton	23. Richard Scroope	34. John May
		35. Henry Robinson
		36. Richard Snowdell.[252]

[*p. 35*] Robert de Dalston, brother of Hubbert de Gilsland aforesaid, had another brother named Reginold, to whom Randolphe Meschiens, the earl, gave the mannor of Castle-Sowerby, Carleton[253] and Hubbartby, as appeareth in the title of Sowerby hereafter.[254]

The said Robert de Dalston had issue a son whose posterity in the eldest lyne transferred the right of the segniory of Dalston to the Harcleyes, wherefore after that King Hen. 3 had granted away the barony to the bishopp of Carliell, which his grandfather King Hen. 2 had seized as an escheat taken from the Scotts, yet one Michael de Harckley, father to Andrew Harckley sometyme earle of Carlisle, did implead Robert Chorry, bishop of Carlisle in the 1 yeare of K. Ed. filius Henrici in Mich. terme for the said baronny in a writt of right.[255]

[A 36] Little Dalston.[256] The said Robert de Dalston or some of his posterity granted to a younger brother named ...... the manor of Little Dalston, lying in the baronny of Great Dalston, whose posterity and issue male yett enjoy the same to this day, lineally for the most part descended from father to son and sometyme collaterally from brother to brother as appearethe by this true pedegree gathered by survey

---

but was not formally made chancellor: H. Summerson, 'Everdon, Silvester of', *ODNB*.

251 M, erroneously, names him 'Robert'.

252 Henry Robinson was bishop 1598–1616; Richard Snowden 1616–1621.

253 H: 'Karlatton'.

254 No account of Castle Sowerby survives in the manuscripts. It is conceivable that the account of the descent of the manor in Denton, *Perambulation*, p. 298 was drawn from a lost draft by John Denton.

255 The documents concerning this dispute, from 1274 to 1281, are printed in J. Wilson, *Rose Castle* (Carlisle, 1912), pp. 203–4.

256 The estate focused on Dalston Hall (NY 376 515).

of divers auncient evidences yet extant that may < approve >[257] the same.

Reginald de parva Dalston had issue Henry filius Reginald, who gave Brownelston to the priory of Carlile; his seale was a quarter-foile. He had issue Adam.

Adam de parva Dalston, filius Henricii

Henricus filius Adae

Symon filius Henricii

Henricus filius Simonis

Johannes filius Henricii

< Johannes filius Johannis >[258] had issue a daughter marryed to Ribton.

Henricus frater Johannes as heire male recovered the land by entayle

Robertus filius Henricii marryed .... Sowthaike daughter

Johannes filius Roberti marryed one of Kirkbride's daughters & heires

Thom. filius Johannis marryed Mabell Denton of Cardew

Johannes filius Thomae marryed Katherine Tolson

Johannes filius Johannis marryed Anne Tirell & Fran. Warcop < inheritours >.[259] Georgius filius

Gulielmus filius.[260]

[p. 36]

[A37] **Lydall Baronia nunc Esk.** The baronny of Lydall, now called Esk, inhabited by the Grahames bordereth upon Scottland lying on the north side of the river Eden betweene the river of Leven & Scottland. It containeth Esk, Lydall, Arthurett, Stubhill, Carwendlow, Speersykes, Randolph Levington, Eston, Northeaston, Solpart[261] and Brakenhill. [In margin: Solpart and all that forrest called Nichol forrest until Liddisdale.] The freeholders of this baronny defrayed the charges of < the > baron's eldest son when he was to be made

---

257 M: 'appeare' which is clearly a transcription error. Both H and J read 'approve'.

258 John son of John is omitted in J and the name is an insertion (in Machell's hand?) in M.

259 M: 'enherit.' The detail of this pedigree no doubt reflects the fact that Denton's wife was Elizabeth, daughter of Sir John Dalston.

260 In J this name is inserted in a different hand, which adds 'in anno 1670'. Sir William Dalston (d. 1683), MP for Carlisle 1640–44, was the son of Sir George (d. 1657), son of Sir John (1557–1633) by his second wife Frances, daughter and coheir of Thomas Warcop of Smardale, Westmorland (CFH, p. 83).

261 Solport is an interlineation in J.

knight & payd his daughters' dowryes. The great wast forrest called aunciently Nicholl forrest of Nicholas Stutvill, sometyme lord thereof, is parcell of the baronny. It was given first after the Conquest to Turgrus Brundas, a Fleming, by the earle Randolph Meschienes, and to him confirmed by King Henry the first.[262] In King John's tyme the Lord Nicholas Stutvill enjoyed it.[263] His daughter and heire married to Sir Hugh Bigott, by a daughter transferred it from the Stutevills to the Bigotts, and from them to the Lord Baldwyne Wake.[264] The said Baldwyne, John and Thomas Wake held the same successively, and after them Prince Edw. surnamed the Black Prince, Ed. 3 < his > eldest son, in the right of his wife, the earle of Kent's daughter, and after her death, she dying without issue, King Edw. bought it for money of the earle of Kent and gave it to the duke of Lancaster, his sonne John of Gaunt. It is now holden by lease as of the dutchy of Lancaster.[265]

[A 38] **Sebergham.**[266] Sebergham, soe called of the place where it stands which is a hill or riseing ground in the forrest of Englewood, whereof the west side was woodland & dry ground, but the north-east side a wett springy earth covered with rushes which the country people call seeves, and therupon the place was called Seevy-bergh.[267] Before it was inhabitted it was forrest and a great waste & wilder-nesse at the Conquest. After in the latter end of King Hen. 2 tyme one William Wastall or de le Wast-dale, begun to enclose some part of it. He was an hermitt and had lived there to an extream age, by the labours of his owne hands and fruite trees which he used.[268] He

---

262 For Turgis Brundos, also known as Turgis de Rossedale, see T. H. B. Graham, 'Turgis Brundos', *CW2*, 29 (1929), pp. 49–56.

263 See *Book of Fees*, p. 198.

264 Joan de Stutevill, who held the barony on her death in 1276, had been married to Hugh le Bigot, who predeceased her. Her son, Sir Baldwin de Wake, was her heir and of full age: *Cal. IPM*, II, no. 195.

265 Liddel barony descended from the Wake family to the Crown through the marriage in 1325 of Margaret, sister and heir of Thomas Wake (d. 1349), to Edmund Plantagenet (1301–1330), earl of Kent. Their daughter, Joan (c. 1328–1385) married Edward, the 'Black Prince' (1330–1376), father of Richard II: W. Ormrod, 'Wake, Thomas' and R. Barber, 'Joan, suo jure Countess of Kent', *ODNB*.

266 Sebergham (NY 36 41).

267 The derivation of the place-name Sebergham remains unclear but Denton's suggestion that it contains the dialect term 'seave' ('rush') is almost certainly wrong: *PNC*, II, p. 151.

268 H: 'planted'.

came thither in Henry the first's tyme and dyed about the end of King John's raigne or in the begining of Henry the third's. King John granted him the hill Sebergham and he left it to the priory of Carlile. The hermite's grant was afterwards < to the successors confirmed by certain bounds >[269] under the seale of the king of Scotts, to whom the king of England had given divers parts of the country in franck-marriage. William Wastall had a chappell there where the church now standeth & a little cell, but after his death the prior lett all forth to tenants and farmers and enlarged the church and made it paro-chiall and the place and village now called villa de Sebergham and Langholme which is a long dale and low holme by [*p. 37*] the river of Cawdey now also inhabitted and parcell of the forrest,[270] and first enclosed as purprestures by the forresters the Raughtons and others sith the Conquest, and are now and of long tyme beene soe named and used as one towneshipp whereof the Kirthwaits are parcells.

[A 39] **Levington.**[271] Upon the east side of the baronny of Lydell lyes the barony of Levington, which King Henry the first confirmed and the Earle Randolph gave unto Richard Boyvill, a commander in the armie royall under the Earle Randolph.[272] His posteritye changed their surname from Boyvill into Levington, soe many of them as did reside there, viz. the lords of the chiefe seignory att Kirklevington; a younger brother named Reginold, lord of the mannor of capitall messuage att West Levington,[273] & his posteritye, Adam, Hugh, Hugh, John, John, whose daughter transferred the inheritance of West Levington to Alexander Highmoore of Harby brow and his heires < by >[274] marriage in Ed. 4th tyme; and in Hen. 8th tyme one of the heires of the said Alexander sold the same to the ..... Lord Dacres, whose patrimony is now in the queene's hands by attainder. And another brother also of the Boyvills named Randolph seated himself att Randolph Levington in Lyddall baronny, so nameing the place of his dwelling,[275] which by his daughter in the next descent

---

269 M and J: 'The hermitt's grant was afterwards called, the sucesors confirmed it by certaine bonds'. The reading in H is to be preferred.
270 The location of 'Langholme', a name recorded frequently in medieval and early modern sources (see *PNC*, I, p. 151), is not known.
271 Kirklinton (NY 43 67).
272 For the origins of the Boyville family, see G. W. S. Barrow, *The Anglo-Norman Era in Scottish History* (Oxford, 1980), pp. 81, 176.
273 Westlinton (NY 39 64).
274 M: 'of'.
275 i.e. Randalinton (NY 401 657).

became the Kirkbride's lands, soe much doth almighty God scorne that foolish ambitious desires of man, thinking to live by trust in himselfe and by his owne witt & strength to establish his name & succession. Another brother named Robert was placed of a carracut of land in Bothcastre & thereupon was called Robert de Bothcastre. Another brother marryed the daughter and heire of Thuresbyes, lords of Thurseby and of Waverton; his name was Guydo Boyvill. He gave to his armes argent a fret vert, whereunto was added a canton in the right corner or quarter of the field, of what colour or content I cannott report. I have seene his seale of his armes att divers evidences, & the colours in glass in St Marie's church in Carliell on the south side of the quire, the canton defaced and broken out.[276] This Guydo had issue William, John & they two were both knights & forresters in Allerdale from Shawk to Elne, which was the west ward of the forrest of Englewood, which office descended unto them from Herbert de Thursbye, first lord of Thursbye, by the guift of Alane, second lord of Allerdale, the son of Waldeof.[277]

[*p. 38*] Richard de Levington, the last of that name baron of Levington, dyed the 34 of Hen. 3 his raigne, had issue Hawiss his only daughter and heire, who was wife to Eustace Balioll and was heire to Richard de Levington.[278] She dying without issue left her inheritance of the barony of Levington to < iii > coheires, her father's sisters and their children;[279] and her moiety of Burgh, Aicton, Kirkoswald & < Lazonby >[280] to her cousen germaine, Thomas filius Thomae de Multon; and her moietye of Glassenby and Gamelsby to Adam de Crookdakes; her lands in Stapleton to ..... and her lands in Bothcastre to Adam Swinburne.[281]

---

276 Heraldry answering this description does not appear to survive in the frag-ments of ancient glass which were gathered and placed in a north window of the nave in 1925: F. C. Eeles, 'Ancient glass at Carlisle cathedral', *CW2*, 26 (1926), pp. 312–17.

277 In H there follows the final sentence from the account of Rockcliffe, clearly misplaced.

278 Richard de Levinton (d. 1248) was succeeded by his brother Ralph (d. 1253), the father of Helewise (d. 1272), wife of Eustace de Baliol: see T. H. B. Graham, 'The de Levingtons of Kirklinton', *CW2*, 12 (1912), pp. 59–75; *Cal. IPM*, I, no. 199.

279 See below, note 283. The number of coheirs was six, not three.

280 M and J read 'Lessingba'. *Cal. IPM*, I, no. 811 has 'Laysingby', confirming that Lazonby is meant.

281 The account of the dower of Sara, late wife of Richard de Levinton, in 1299 lists the holders of the Levington estates: *Cal. IPM*, III, no. 583.

The coheires of Levington were Richard Kirkbride, William Lokard, Eufemia uxor Jo' Seaton, Walter Twinham knight, Gilbert < Suthaik >,[282] Matild uxor Nich' Aghenlocks, Matild Carik, Patrick Tromp, Walter filius Walter Cary, and Margarett uxor Henry Malton.[283]

[A40] **Rothcliff.**[284] Rothcliff is a parish, towne and mannor lying beneath the river Eden on the north side thereof, abutteth on Cargo on the east, on Levington on the north, is boundred by the foot of the river ..... on the west. The mannor was aunciently the inheritance of Radulph de Bray, who gave the same to William filius Johannis de Rocliff in the 6 yeare of K. John,[285] and in the 5 yeare of the same king one Adam de Bray gave the rectory to John, prior of St Marie's in Carlile, who did appropriate the same to their church of Carlisle.[286] In the 4 yeare of King John Radulff Bray farmed the rectory for corne for terme of life granted by William, then priest of Rocliff.[287] In the 33 yeare of King Henry the third William de Hardrighall and Matild his wife (whom I take to be the said William de Rocliff, and Matild to be a daughter of the Brayes), did give the mannor < to John Francys > to be holden of them and their heires paying five pounds per annum in rent.[288] The same yeare John Francis redeemed of John Ludbrook & Johan his wife.[289] The land was holden as fee of Burgh per ii[s] vel unum esperuarium. 54 H. 3 Gilbertt Frances held the same by the sayd services and dyed 6[to] Edw. 1.[290] His son Richard Frances being under age, one Michael de Harcla took him & married him to his daughter, wherefore the king seized Michaell<'s> lands & fined him. In the 22th yeare of his raigne the said king gave the mannor [p. 39] of Rocliff to Richard Wernon or Gernon for his life and to remaine after

282 M: 'Suthait'.
283 In 1272 the heirs of Helewise de Levyngton, wife of Eustace de Baylioll, were the heirs of Euphemia de Kirkbride, Isabel de Twinham, Agnes de Corri, Margery de Hampton, Juliana de Carrig and Eva de Sutheayt. All were in Scotland, except Robert de Hampton, heir of Margery and Richard de Kirkbride, heir of Euphemia: *Cal. IPM*, I, no. 811. Denton traces the descent of these shares in the account of Skelton (below, C14). The division of the barony between the six co-parcenors in 1274 is discussed in Graham, 'De Levingtons of Kirklinton', pp. 62–70.
284 Rockcliffe (NY 35 61).
285 6 John = 1204–5.
286 FF Cumb. 6 John [1204–5] (*CW2*, 7 (1907), p. 219, nos. 14, 15).
287 4 John = 1202–3.
288 FF Cumb. 33 Hen. III [1248–9] (*CW2*, 7 (1907), p. 224, no. 84).
289 Ibid., (no. 85).
290 54 Hen. III = 1269–70. Inquisition, 1278: *Cal. IPM*, II, no. 246.

him to Richard his son, and to Elioner daughter of Gyles Fyennes, Rich. wife, and to the heires of their bodyes, which mannors the king had of Richard Vernon the father's guift.[291] The Frances are named in evidence Francoys and Francegena, which I think was soe for that the first soe named < was born in France. It may be therefore their surname was Vernon. Afterwards > in the 23th yeare of K. Ed. 3 Thomas Daniell dyed seized of Rocliff,[292] whose daughter Margarett uxor Jo' Ratcliff entailed the same & her lands to all the Ratcliffes and their heires male of their kindred, anno 40 and dyed in the 44 yeare.[293] After her posterity sold it to the < lord > Dacres.[294]

[*In margin:*] Reginald de Rocliffe

John de Rocl'

Willm' filius

Randolf Bray

Adam Bray

Randolff Bray

Matild uxor Willelmi de Hardred hall

John Francis

Gilbt Francis

Rich. Francis

Rich. Vernon

Thomas Daniell

Margarett uxor John < Ratcliff >.[295]

[A41] Boothcastre alias Bewcastle.[296] Northward above Levington towards the waists betweene Nichol Forrest and a part of Lyddall lyes Bewcastle dale, which tooke that name first of the castle there built by one named Bueth and the castle soe called Bothcastre upon this occasion.[297] The place where it stands (aunciently) was a waste forrest ground where the barons of Burghe and their tennants in

---

291 For Edward I's grant in 1294, see *Cal. Pat. Edward I*, III (1292–1301), p. 84.

292 Inquisition, 1349: *Cal. IPM*, IX, no. 193.

293 FF Cumb. 40 Edw. III [1366–7] (*CW2*, 7 (1907), p. 240, no. 278). No inquisition after the death of Margaret Daniell, which Denton dates to 1370–1, has been located.

294 The final section, from 'in the 23th yeare of K. Ed. 3 …' occurs in the middle of the previous entry (re Kirklinton barony) in H.

295 M: 'John Rocl'.

296 Bewcastle (NY 56 74).

297 Place-name scholars now reject the suggestion that the name derived from the personal name Bueth. The modern interpretation is that it is a compound of ON *búð* ('booth; temporary dwelling') and OE *caester* (referring to the Roman fort there): *PNC*, I, pp. 60–1.

summer tyme yearely keept their goods, haveing noe other pasture for them, because the baronny itselfe was very populus and well inhabitted, fitting better for corne & meadow then for pasture. And therupon it is alwayes found in auncient inquisicions as parcell of that baronny and to be holden of the same. But it is not within the said baronny, for the two segniories of Lyddall and Levington lye in betweene Burgh and it. It was a place greatly infested by the Scotts then, as att this day it is; and therefore none durst inhabitt there till the barons of Burgh-baronny tooke upon them to summer their cattell there and made themselves sheales and cabynes for their people, dwelling themselves in tents and boothes for defence of their goods. That castle which now is there standing was first called Boothcastre[298] and after corruptly Bew Castle. It became to be inhabitted long before Henry the third's tyme. Upon the building of that castle and in that king's dayes Richard, baron of Levington (by his right in Burgh) held < there >[299] demayne lands and other lands, rents & services as parcell of Burgh.[300] In Ed. 2 tyme Adam de Swinburne held the same of the lord of Burghe, Ranulph Dacre & Margrett his wife; < & > after him Adam Swinburne his son.[301] In Ed. 3 tyme Sir John Strivelin, knight, in the right of his wife Jacoba, Swinburne's daughter, < held it. >[302]

[p. 40]
[A 42] **Scalby.**[303] Next unto the barony of Levington eastward untill Brunsketh Beck lyes the mannor of Scaleby and the castle, which tooke name first of the buildings there which they call scheales or skales, more properly of the Latine word Scalinga, a cabban or cottage.[304] And when King Henry the first had established Carliel he gave that lordshipp unto one Richard the Ryder, whose <sur>

---

298 In margin of M: 'of Bueth the first founder. After Bueth Addock.'
299 M: 'three'.
300 Inquisition, 1250: *Cal. IPM*, I, no. 199.
301 See *Cal. IPM*, VI, nos. 164 (Adam de Swynburne, 1318); 751 (Adam de Swynburn, 1326, whose heirs were his daughters and their descendants).
302 Sir John de Swinburne, sheriff of Cumberland 1277, bought the manor, which passed to his son, Sir Adam (d. before 1327), who forfeited Bewcastle as a result of his support for John Balliol. Sir Adam's daughter and coheir, Barnaba, married Sir John de Strivelyn (d. 1378). In 1357 Edward III restored her lands in Cumberland, in recognition of her husband's good services: *CFH*, pp. 328, 331.
303 Scaleby (NY 44 63).
304 Denton's interpretation of the name is broadly correct: it represents ON *skali* ('shieling') + *by* ('settlement'): *PNC*, I, p. 106.

name was Tyliolffe, who first planted their habitations.[305] From him
it descended by one or two degrees unto Symon Tyliolff, in the latter
end of Hen. the 2 tyme. His son Pieres Tyllliolff (or Peter) was ward
to Jeoffrey de Lucy by the king's grant about the tyme of King John
and dyed the 31 of King Hen. 3.[306] This Jeoffrey did < bear >[307] the
cap of maintenance before K. Rich. the first at his coronacion.[308] They
held (as their posteritye now doe), the said castle and mannor of the
crowne, all save a carracute of land which is holden of the baron of
Gilsland. It containeth Scaleby, Haughton, and Eatardby. They were
lords of Solpart which they held of Lyddall and of Richardby in the
baronny of Lynstock nere Carlisle, which they hold of the bishopp
of Carlisle. Att this Richardby, the sayd Richard, their first auncestor,
seated himselfe; whereupon it was so called after his name, & the
gate, port and street in Carliell leading thither soe called Richard gate
or Richardby gate, in old evidence vicus Richardii; as in like sort the
port and street leading toward Bochardby, where the first inhabitant
named Bochardus had a place of dwelling, is called Botchardgate,
both within the port and without. And the other gate Caldew gate
of the river Cawdey towards the west running by the same. Att that
tyme the Scotts did tyrannize the country adjoyning them, which
enforced the gentlemen to dwell in Carlisle, and therefore every man
provided himselfe to be served with corne, soile and hay, as nigh
the citty as they might; as this Richard att Richardby, Botchard att
Bochardby, Hubbert the baron of Gilsland att Hubbertby, Henricus
father [*p. 41*] to Radulf Engayne (or grandfather to his wife Ibria) att
Henrikby, Agillon att Agillonbye (now called corruptly Aglionby),
Pavya the widdow of Robert de Grinsdale in the territory called
Pavifeild, Avery < filius >[309] Roberti in Haversholme, Albert filius
Yervan (or Harvey) in Hervy-holme (now called Denton holme), and
diverse others.[310]

---

305 See *Book of Fees*, I, p. 199, where Simon de Tilliol's lands are said to have been
    granted by Henry I to his ancestor Richard 'Ridere'. Richard appears in the
    Pipe Roll for 1130 as *Ricardus Miles*, collector of royal revenues in Carlisle
    1125–9: Sharpe, *Norman Rule*, pp. 13–14. For the Tilliol family, see J. Wilson,
    'Some extinct Cumberland families, III: the Tilliols,' *The Ancestor*, 4 (1903), pp.
    88–100.

306 Inquisition, 1246: *Cal. IPM*, I, no. 115.

307 M: 'weare'. J appears to read 'beare' rather than 'weare'.

308 This sentence is in the margin. The cap of maintenance was a symbol of high
    rank, carried before the sovereign in processions (*OED*).

309 M: 'fillys'.

310 The frequency of post-Conquest continental personal names incorporated

The said Pieres < Tylliolf >[311] marryed the daughter of the sayd Jeoffrey Lucy (his tutor and guardian) and had issue two sonnes, one named Jeoffrey after her father's name, who succeeded in the inheritance and dyed the 23th of Edward the first,[312] and another named Adam that marryed the daughter of Henry de Cormaunce of Houghton, and by her he gott the inheritance of the 6th part of Houghtons. This Adam had Richardby for tearme of life and was therefore called Adam de Richardby; of that familie are descended all the Richardbyes.

Jeoffrey had issue Robert < Tylliolffe > who dyed the 18th of K. Ed. 2.[313] He purchased the third of Levington, and had issue Peter or Pieres and Elizabeth uxor Anthony de Lucye. Piers the son of Jeffrey < Tylliolfe > dyed the 23 Ed. < 3 >.[314] He added to his living < dimidium >[315] de Newbiggin parcell of Croglin, which he held of Hugh de Wharton, and had issue Robert Tylliolff.[316]

Robert filius Petri dyed 41 Ed. 3 and had issue Pieres and Jeoffrey, lord of Emmelton, by his wife Alice daughter of [........].[317] Piers Tilliolff filius Roberti dyed 13 Hen. 6.[318] He marryed Robert Mulcaster's daughter of Hayton, and his heire, and gott with her Hayton, Turpenhow, Rothland, Bleamire; and had issue Margrett his second daughter uxor Thom. Crackenthrop, and < first of Christopher

---

into the -by place-names clustered around Carlisle is striking. They include Aglionby, Botcherby, Etterby, Harraby, Rickerby and Tarraby. As Denton notes, some of the landowners recorded in these names appear in the documentary record in the twelfth century: *PNC*, III, pp. xxxi–xxxiii; Fellows-Jensen, *Scandinavian Settlement Names*, pp. 13, 15, 288, 329–31. Pavyfield may be connected with later individuals called Pavie, recorded in the thirteenth and fourteenth centuries: *PNC*, I, p. 50.

311 Here and subsequently, M renders the name 'Talliolff'.
312 Inquisition, 1295: *Cal. IPM*, III, no. 227.
313 *recte* 14 Edward II [1321]: *Cal. IPM*, VI, no. 279.
314 23 Edw. III = 1349–50. M, erroneously, gives the date as 23 Edw. II.
315 This word is an interlineation in H. It is omitted in M and J.
316 Inquisition, 1349: *Cal. IPM*, IX, no. 189, which does not, however, mention Scaleby.
317 Text runs on here but the name of Alice's [*recte* Felicia's] father is presumably missing. Robert Tilliol died in 1367; his heir was his son Peter, then aged 11 years. Robert's widow was Felicia, who died in 1369: *Cal. IPM*, XII, nos. 170, 417.
318 Inquisition, 1435: *Calendarium inquisitionum post mortem sive escaetarum*, 4 vols (London, 1806–28), IV, p. 159. His son Robert died the following year: ibid., p. 164.

Morresby >[319] by whom she had issue Christopher. And his 4th daughter Issabell marryed to John Colvyll, to whom they transferred that inheritance. Piers had issue Robert < Tylliolfe > (the foole), which dyed without issue.[320]

[*p. 42*]

[A 43] **Gilsland.** The great baronny of Gilsland lyeth on the east side of the river all alongst the river side from the border of Linstock and Crosbye baronny unto Northskeugh beck, a rill that divideth Ainstableh from the same. Above that beck toward the mountaines the bounder of Gilsland compasseth in Croglin up eastward into the fells, where the bounder of the countye divides the baronny from Northumberland untill the head of a rill called Powtross. Then the Powtross untill it be received of Irthing; and from thence the river Irthing itselfe till it receive Troutbeck; and thence Troutbeck untill the head thereof on the north east side of the same att the utmost lymitts both of the baronny and countye.

It is called Gilsland of many little < narrow > valleys in the same, which th'inhabitants call gills, in Latin valles, in French vaulx; and therefore that same Hubbart and his posterity are named Vaus and in the old muniments de Vallibus.[321]

This baronny th'earle Randolph Meschiens gave unto one Hubbertus, to be holden of him by two knights fees and by cornage, which K. Hen. 1 confirmed unto him to be holden of the king in capite,[322] when th'earle Randolph resigned the countye of Cumberland to the king and obteined the earledome of Chester < after the death of Richard the 2d earl of Chester[323] > who with the said king's children (comeing forth of Normandy) was drowned in the sea on the coast

---

319 In H this has been changed to 'afterwards of Christopher Moresby'. M, erroneously, reads 'first heire of Christopher Moresby'. Margaret (1410–1459), daughter of Sir Piers Tilliol (d. 1435), married (1) Sir Christopher Moresby; (2) Thomas Crackenthorpe: *CFH*, p. 341.
320 Robert Tilliol, aged over 30 on his father's death in 1435, was said to be an incurable lunatic (*fatuus ideotus et fatuetate detentus*): Wilson, 'Extinct Cumberland families III: Tilliols', p. 98.
321 Denton's attempt to draw a connection between the name of the barons and that of the barony is fanciful: Gilsland ('Gille's land') is thought to preserve the name of the pre-Norman lord, Gille son of Bueth: *PNC*, I, pp. 2–3.
322 Denton's account is incorrect here: Gilsland remained in the hands of a native lord, Gille son of Bueth, after whose death Henry II granted it to Hubert de Vallibus in 1158: *VCH Cumb.*, I, p. 306 and n.
323 This phrase is an insertion in the margin of H.

of England; to which Richard the sayd Randolph was next heire & cousen germaine, the son of John Bohun by his wife Margarett the sister of Hugh Lupus, first earle of Chester.[324] The said Hubbert did beare his armes < chequer >[325] d'or et guels. His seale was a griffin eating a < lizzard. >[326]

This Hubbart gave Denton in Gilsland to one Westcopp, by his deed of feoffement in these words: Omnibus Cumbrensibus Francigenis Alienigenis, Dannes, Normans, Hubbartus de Vallibus < salut' > &c., which makes < probably >[327] to prove his antiquitie and what people did then or late before inhabitt that countrye.[328] He had two brethren Robert de Dalston & Reginald de Sowerby; to this Reginald he gave Carlatton in Gilsland & Hubartby beside Carlisle, which guift Randolph Meschiens confirmed.

[*p. 43*] King Hen. 2 gave all the land which was Gilbartt's the son of Beweth to the first Hubbart de Vallibus; et de incremento he gave him Kirkby,[329] which was Westcouthbreight the son of William the son of Stephen; and Catterleying (with the mill) which Villtred the sonne of Adam sometyme held.[330]

After Hubbert succeeded Robert de Vallibus which founded the priory of Lanercost.[331] This Robert was justice itenerant into Cumberland together with Ranulph Glanvill and Robert Pickiet his associats

---

324 The *White Ship* tragedy in November 1120, after which Ranulf le Meschin was made earl of Chester: King, 'Ranulf I, earl of Chester'. See also Sharpe, *Norman Rule*, pp. 51–2.

325 M: 'cheq.'.

326 M: 'lacert'.

327 M: 'probally'.

328 This deed, which would be dated to April 1158 x May 1165, is not known to have survived. Wescop, son of Gille Bueth, subsequently granted Nether Denton to Bueth Barn, a feoffment confirmed by Robert de Vaux (1165x1177): see *Lanercost*, pp. 403, 406. The address clause of the deed cited by Denton, like that of Wescop's grant to Bueth Barn, reflects the ethnic diversity of twelfth-century Cumberland. I am grateful to Hugh Doherty for sharing with me his understanding of these grants.

329 *recte* 'Korkebi', i.e. Corby.

330 In H this paragraph occurs at the end of this section on Gilsland barony. The charter to Hubert de Vallibus in 1158 is reproduced in *VCH Cumb.*, I, plate opp. p. 306.

331 Lanercost priory was founded *c.* 1169 [1165x1174]: *Lanercost*, p. 4; H. Summerson and S. Harrison, *Lanercost Priory, Cumbria: a survey and documentary history* (CWAAS Research Series 10; Kendal, 2000), pp. 2–7.

in the 23 H. 2,[332] which Ranulf Glanvill succeeded Richard Lucy in the office of lord chiefe justice of England in the 26th yeare of that king, when Richard became a monck in the abbey of Lenois or Westwood, resigneing that office for age and debillitye.[333]

King Hen. the second rather confirmed Gilsland to Hubbert < Vaulx >[334] then first gave it for < if > Hubbert lived till he was of extreame age; yet the coppie of inquisicion returned by the sheriff of Cumberland into the Exchequer saith Robertus de Vallibus tenet terram suam de Domino Rege per servicium duorum militum quam R. Hen. pater domini Regis dedit Hughoni de vallibus antecessori suo per predictum servicium. This inquisicion was taken in K. John's tyme.[335]

I read of one Beweth a Cumberland man, about the tyme of the conquest. He builded Bewcastle and was lord of Bewcastledale. His son Gillesbeweth had (or pretended) right to all (or part of) the baronny of Gilsland, or that part of the same which adjoyneth to Bewcastle.[336] He was kinsman to the auncient lords of Burgh-barony which were before the conquest, either by consanguinitye or affinitye. His son Gillesbeweth stood with Hubbart de Vallibus and before him with William de Meschiens (when he lay there in garrison by commandment of his brother, the earle Randolff) as his father Beweth had done in the Conqueror's tyme, being then a follower of Gospatrick the great. They wasted that country, male content and disinherited, till either the said Hubbart himselfe (or Robert de Vallibus his son) slew the said Gillesbeweth at a meeting for agreement appointed betweene them under trust and assurance, which

---

332 Robert de Vallibus was justice itinerant in the northern counties with Ranulf de Glanville and Robert Pikenot in 1176 (i.e. 22 Hen. II). He was also a justice in 1178 (24 Hen. II) but with different companions: *Pleas Before the King or his Justices 1198–1212*, ed. D. M. Stenton, Vol. III (Selden Society Vol. 83, 1967), pp. lvii, lx.

333 For Richard de Lucy (d. 1179), chief justiciar 1168–78 and his successor, Ranulf de Glanville (d. 1190), chief justiciar 1180–9, see E. Amt, 'Lucy, Richard de (d. 1179)' and J. Hudson, 'Glanville, Ranulph de', *ODNB*.

334 M: 'Valux'.

335 i.e. Testa de Nevill of 1212 (*Book of Fees*, p. 197). Denton's comment on Hubert's age is the result of his erroneous belief that he had originally been granted Gilsland by Ranulf le Meschin.

336 Gille son of Bueth, the pre-Norman lord of Gilsland, who was dead by 1158, is named as one of four *Cumbrenses judices* in an inquest of *c.* 1120, ordered by Earl David, brother of the king of Scots: *Lanercost*, p. 1 (citing A. C. Lawrie, *Early Scottish Charters* (Glasgow, 1905), p. 46).

shamefull treason made Robert Vaulx [*p. 44*] leave armes and betake himself to his booke att the innes of court, wherein he soe profitted that he became justice of Assize, and to great honour and account with his prince; yet could not his conscience be att quiett untill he had made satisfaction with endowing the holy church with that patrimony which occasioned the murther and therefore he founded the said abbey of Lanner-coast.[337] This Gillesbeweth, < is that >[338] Gill filius Beweth, which the register booke of Lannercoast reports to be lord of Gilsland, yett < he > never possessed < a > foote in the same; for his father was banished before this Gilesbeweth became a man. This man therefore seated himselfe in Scottland, where he dwelt untill he was slaine. His children & posterstye were called after his name Gilesbeweth or lords Gillesbeweth corruptly Gilsbies < or lords of Gillsbie >, of the place where they dwelt, which place was first soe called of the said Gildesbeweth (after his name) because he first builded there his father's house att Boothcastle or Buecastle or Bewethcastle soe called after his name,[339] was afterwards possessed by one Addock who married with the lord of Denton in Gilsland, which Denton the sayd Hubbart de Vallibus had lately given to one Westcopp, his follower or kinsman. But whether the said Addock was kinsman, friend or enemye to Beweth's posterity I find nott.

[A 44] **Linstock and Crosbye.**[340] Betweene the river Eden and Brunskeweth-beck lyes the baronny of Lynstock and Crosbye, which is now a segniory of the bishopp of Carlisle's. King Hen. 1 gave Lynstock and Carleton to one Walter his chaplein, to be holden of the king of England by cornage silver to be payd yearely. The said Walter voluntarily of himselfe and by the said king's lycence, tooke upon him a religious habitt of a regular chanon in the priory of St Marie's in Carlisle, and by the king's consent he gave Linstock and Carleton to that house of religion in pure almes for ever.[341] Whereupon the king released and acquitted the rent and services to the channons there and they made the said Walter their prior. He was

---

337 There is no evidence to support this tradition, which has been rejected by modern historians: Summerson and Harrison, *Lanercost Priory*, p. 4.

338 M: 'that's'.

339 For the derivation of the name Bewcastle, see above, section A41, note 297.

340 Linstock (NY 42 58) and Crosby on Eden (NY 44 59).

341 As recorded in Testa de Nevill (*Book of Fees*, p. 199). For Walter the priest, see J. C. Dickinson, 'Walter the priest and St Mary's, Carlisle', *CW2*, 69 (1969), pp. 102–14; H. Summerson, 'Athelwold the bishop and Walter the priest: a new source for the early history of Carlisle Priory', *CW2*, 95 (1995), pp. 85–91.

the second prior of that < house > of St Marie's in [*p. 45*] Carlisle. After they were possessed of Lynstock baronny they made a grainge att Crosbye which was soe called Crosbye, for that it was church lands,[342] & sometyme the baronny of Linstock is soe called Crosby baronny of that grainge or cheife seat, Crosby, which is now become a towne of many inhabitants. At the first foundation of that house of channons by K. H. 1 and of the bishopp's sea att Carlisle, both their lands were holden pro indiviso < as in common >. After the first particion therof made by the Pope's legat Gualo scti Martini presb'r cardinall,[343] this barony of Lynstock fell to the bishopp & his successors, and Carleton to the prior and covent and < so >[344] the bishopps remained still undevided untill Pandolph another legate in K. H. 3 tyme by the second distribucion assigned them to the bishopp's part of Carleton and other things in Cumberland for their moietye of the appropriate church of < Werkworth >[345] in Northumberland.[346] The aforesaid Walter the prior and Athelwold the first bishopp of that sea were wittnesses to the grant of confirmacion of Holme Cultrum made < to > the abbott there by Malcolumb filius Henricii comitis, filii David K. of Scottland, which Malcolumb lived in the begining of the reigne of K. H. 2 & was king 12 yeares.[347]

This barony conteyned Lynstock, Crosby, Walbye, Richarby, and Newbye. Walby was soe named of the Pights-wall whereunto it adjoyneth, and Newby as a latter building, yet now an auncient towne. For King Hen. 1 gave the same Newby to one Hyld to be holden of the king by cornage, and one Trute succeeded Hyld, and

---

342 Crosby is ON *krossabýr*, 'settlement marked by crosses' (*PNC*, I, p. 76), rather than church land as such, though the root of the name implies religious associations; see Fellows-Jensen, *Scandinavian Settlement Names*, pp. 28, 391.

343 In M and J there is a space after 'Gualo' and the marginal note 'in K. Jo. tyme'. The initial division of the revenues by Guala the papal legate was confirmed in 1219: see below, note 346.

344 M: 'to'.

345 Corrupted to 'Werkinmerth' in M and J.

346 For the division of endowments between the bishop and the priory, which was finally settled in 1249, see *EEA 30: Carlisle*, no. 41 and discussion on pp. 32–3; H. Summerson, *Medieval Carlisle: the city and the Borders from the late eleventh to the mid-sixteenth century* (CWAAS Extra Series XXV; Kendal, 1993), I, pp. 71–2, 156–7; *Calendar of Entries in the Papal Registers relating to Great Britain and Ireland. Papal Letters*, 20 vols (London, Dublin 1893–), I, pp. 81, 91, 112, 256.

347 The confirmation by Malcolm IV, king of Scots 1153–1165, can be dated to 1153x1156: *Holm Cultram*, p. 92, no. 262.

Rich. filius Trute succeeded his father. In K. John's tyme < one >[348] Wm filius Bernardi held that land as guardian to Richard the son of Richard the son of Trute aforesaid.[349] Shortly after the said last Richard filius Rich' confirmed Newby to Reginald de Carlisle and his heires, to be holden of him by paying x^s yearely rent service to him, and xvi^d cornage.[350] The said Reginald de Carlisle gave the same to the abbott & covent of Holme Cultram, reserving the like rents. And after [*p. 46*] the death of Richard filius Richardi, his sister Margarett uxor Roberti de < Wathempole >[351] filia et heres Richardii filii Trute released her right to the same Newbye unto the moncks of Holme Cultram saveing the said rents reserved. Bishopp Walter himselfe, Thomas and Robert Chorry his successors, acquitted the abbott and his men there of all services except cornage, common ayds & < 10^s >[352] rent to the lord of the fee.[353]

[*p. 46 contd.*]

[B 1] Ainstaplight[354] is a mannor and townshipp < on >[355] the south side of Gilsland devided from the baronny by Northskeugh-beck aforesaid, and reacheth from the river Eden on the west upp east-ward into the mountaynes and bordereth upon Staffole lordshipp towards the south. It conteyneth Ainstaplewgh, Ruccroft, and the Nunry, which nunry was founded by William Rufus.[356]

This segniory and other lands in Cumberland[357] K. H. 1 gave to one Adam the son of Swene, from whom it descended in K. H. 2 tyme to William de Nevill, whose lands in Cumberland, in the tyme of K. John, were in the holding of Roger de Monte Begon, Symon filius Walter, and Alexander de Nevill.[358] In K. Hen. 3 tyme Ainstable

---

348 M and J: 'of', presumably a transcription error.
349 *Book of Fees*, p. 198, where the tenant is named as Walter son of Bernard, guardian of Richard son of Truite.
350 H adds in margin '& forens service'.
351 M and J: 'Mathempole', presumably a transcription error.
352 M, erroneously, reads 'xx^s'.
353 For these charters see *Holm Cultram*, p. 11, nos. 30–35.
354 Ainstable (NY 53 46). H renders the name 'Ainstapligh'; J as 'Ainstaplighe'.
355 M: 'of'.
356 For the religious house at Nunnery (NY 53 42), usually termed the nunnery of Armathwaite, see *VCH Cumb.*, II, pp. 189–92. Denton's statement that it was founded by William Rufus derives from the confirmation, in the Patent Roll for 1480, of a charter which has long been regarded as a forgery.
357 In margin: 'vide Culgaith'.
358 Confirmed by 'Testa de Nevill', which does not, however, identify these lands as being in Ainstable: *Book of Fees*, p. 199.

lordshipp became the inheritance of John Murry and Henry Terriby, Michael de Vallibus filius David, and others; about the yeare of our lord God 1239 and in the latter end of that king's tyme William Boyvill of Thursbye, knight, was lord thereof and held the same of Richard Nevill. When he dyed it fell to his son John Boyvill, whose brother Edmund sold Ainstaplighe to Andrew Harcla, who forfeited to the king,[359] < who gave it and others to > to Sir Richard Denton and from him to John Denton of Cardew, whose posteritye William and John Denton enjoyed it as lords thereof successively from father to son untill Thomas Lord Dacres extorted it from the said last John Denton in the tyme of King Hen. 6, for that the said John Denton was towards the partye of King Edward the fourth.[360] Which tyranny of the Dacres God seemed to take revenge, for, shortly after, the said Lord Dacre and Randall his sonne were both slaine att Towton feild or drowned in the river att Ferrybridge in Yorkshire, when K. Edw. gott the victory against Henry the sixth and thereby the crowne of England.[361] Afterwards the Lord Humphrid Dacre, by marrying of Dame Mabell Parr, the daughter of the king's favorite, recovered the Dacres' lands < and right > and keept still Ainstiplighe by his father's pretended right, & so to his posteritye untill all their lands fell to the crowne by attainder.[362]

---

359 Andrew de Harclay or Harcla, earl of Carlisle (*c.* 1270–1323) entered into secret negotiations with the Scots, for which he was executed as a traitor: Summerson, 'Harclay, Andrew'. Edward II granted to Richard de Denton all the lands de Harcla had acquired from Edmund Boyvill: see *Cal. Pat. 1334–8*, p. 111.

360 In 1446 John de Denton granted the manor of Ainstable to William de More, vicar of Ainstable, who, the following year, settled the manor on Thomas Dacre and Philippa his wife, William Marshall, rector of Kirkoswald, and John Hussher. The conveyance had been challenged and a certificate of execution of the charters, taken at Ainstable on 9 January 1448, includes a sworn affadavit from de More confirming that it had been Denton's intention that he should convey the manor to Dacre: DUL, Howard of Naworth, C1/1. After the siege of Carlisle in 1461, John Denton petitioned Edward IV for recognition of his service, especially the part he played in 'kepyng of youre towne of Carlell' during the siege. Among the grants he sought was the manor of Ainstable, late of Humphrey Dacre, the king's enemy: CRO, D/Lons/L5/1/55, D.62.

361 Denton's account appears to be confused: Thomas, Lord Dacre died in 1458; his son Ralph was slain at the battle of Towton, 29 Mar. 1461, and was buried at Saxton, Yorks: *Complete Peerage*, IV, pp. 7, 18.

362 Humphrey Lord Dacre (d. 1485) married Mabel (d. 1508), daughter of Sir Thomas Parr of Kendal: *Complete Peerage*, IV, p. 20. For the confiscation of the

[*In margin:*] Wm. Boyvill; John; Edm' qui vendidit Andra Harcla < temp > Ed. 2 R & Rich. Denton; John Denton.

[*p. 47*]

[B2] Carlisle. In the northwest corner of the forrest of Englewood stands that auncient cittye of Carliell, environed with the rivers of Eden on the northeast side, Pettrell on the south-east, and Cawdey on the southwest, and enclosed with strong walls of squarred stones, fortified with a castle rampired in the west end and the cittidell in the east. It was before the Saxons tyme called Lugu-vildun or Lugub-allum and by some Luguballia, whereupon the Saxons called it Luell and Lu-wall, the last Brittons there inhabitants and the Irish of that word Luell named it Carrluell or Leyll.[363] It lay waste for the most part two hundred yeares before the last Conquest, saveing a few cottages among the ruines inhabitted by the Irish Scotts, after the Danes had wasted the < country >[364] with sword and fire.[365] William Rufus returning that way from Alnwick < about the latter end of his raigne >[366] when he had made peace with ......, king of Scotts, seeing the place of strength convenient to entertaine his forces att any tyme against Scottland, commanded the same to be reedified and to be soe fortified with walls & the castle;[367] but he was prevented by untimely death before he could performe all that which he intended for the good of the cittye. He placed there a collony of Dutchmen which were shortly thence translated into the Ile of Anglsey by him or his next successor Henry Bewclark, his brother, first of that name after the Conquest king of England. And in steed of them a new regiment of southern men out of Essex, Kent, Midlesex and other parts of the realme were brought to supply the place, and to inhabitt the counties of Cumberland and Westmorland, under the leading of Ranulff de

---

Dacre estates see K. J. Kesselring, *The Northern Rebellion of 1569* (Basingstoke, 2007), pp. 49, 88–9, 98–9.

363 Denton's account of the development of the place-name is broadly correct, though the 'Car-' element is Brittonic *caer* ('fortified place') rather than Irish: *PNC*, I, pp. 41–2.

364 M: 'countey'.

365 The source of this statement is probably John of Worcester: see *The Chronicle of John of Worcester*, ed. P. McGurk (Oxford, 1998), III, pp. 62–3.

366 In margin of M but in body of text in H.

367 In the aftermath of his unsuccessful invasion of Scotland in 1091, William Rufus returned north to Carlisle in 1092 and drove out Dolfin, the ruler of Cumbria under the suzerainty of the king of Scots. For the events leading up to the Norman occupation of Cumbria see Summerson, *Medieval Carlisle*, pp. 14–16, 47–9; Phythian-Adams, *Land of the Cumbrians*, pp. 24–5, 152–62.

Meschiens, sister son to Hugh Lupus or Lou, first earle of Chester.[368]
When the cittey was replenished with people, for to maintaine better
policye in the same and to enforme the people, < K. H. founded >
insteed of < a nunnery >[369] (which had aunciently beene there
before and which William Rufus had translated thence and established att Ainstaplighe, or rather in recompence of the lands to that
nunry belonging had founded another att Ainstapligh, endowing the
same with other revenues there),[370] K. Hen. 1 founded a colledge
or priory of secular priests in the second yeare of his raigne and
made Athelwood, his confessor or chaplaine, prior of St Botolphes,
first prior [p. 48] of Carliell, dedicating the church for the honour of
the blessed Virgin Mary, and endowed them with the tythes of the
churches then founded in the forrest of Englewood. But hindered by
the tumults and troubles of his tyme, hee could not perfect all things
before the 33th yeare of his raigne, and then striken with griefe for
the loss of his children that were drowned as aforesaid, the king by
the councell of the prior Adelwal, to please God for his sinnes (as
he thought), erected a bishopp sea at Carlisle and made the said
Athelwold first bishopp there, whom th'archbishopp of York named
Thurstane did consecrate in the yeare of grace 1133. And in his stead
another chaplaine of the said K. Henrie's named Walter was made the
second prior of that house, who a little before his election had taken
upon him by the king's lycence a religious habite of a regular chanon
there, which order of channons the king and Bishopp Athelwold had
placed in that house, banishing the secular priests immediately upon
his consecration.[371] The said Walter gave to the church of Carlisle in
pure almes for ever his lands in Lynstock, Richarby, Crosbye, Little
Crosbye, Walby, Brunskewgh, Carleton, Little Carleton & the wood

---

368 For the early history of Carlisle, see Summerson, *Medieval Carlisle*, pp. 15–30.
   Camden also records the plantation of Flemings (Denton's 'Dutchmen') in
   Carlisle by William Rufus, their removal into Wales and a later plantation of
   southern Englishmen (*Britannia*, p. 779) but the ultimate source of this tradition has not been traced.
369 M and J read 'Aldury'.
370 The reference to a pre-Conquest nunnery at Carlisle may derive from Bede's
   life of St Cuthbert, which tells of Ecgfrith's queen being 'in her sister's
   monastery' at Carlisle: *Two Lives of St Cuthbert*, ed. B. Colgrave (Cambridge,
   1985), p. 243. For the nunnery at Armathwaite (in Ainstable parish) and the
   spurious tradition that it had been founded by William Rufus in 1089, see:
   VCH Cumb., II, pp. 189–92.
371 For the foundation of the priory and bishopric of Carlisle, see Summerson,
   Medieval Carlisle, pp. 30–8; Sharpe, *Norman Rule*, pp. 57–62.

& the churches & rectories of St Cuthberts in Carlisle & Stainwiggs, which the king had given him and the same gift was confirmed both by the king and Bishopp Athelwold unto < them. >[372] [*In margin:* In the honour of St Cuthbert of Durham, who was lord of the same of auncient tyme and of 15teene miles about Carlisle.][373] The rectorye of St Cuthbert in Carlisle was founded by the former inhabitants in Carlisle before the Danes overthrew the citty. At the first foundacion of the church every citizen offered < a Cuthberts penny > a peice of money, which was a coyne in brass then currant which they buried under the foundacion of the church steeple there, as was found to be true at the late new reedifying of St Cuthbert's steeple anno domini ......, for when they tooke up the foundacion of th'old steeple they found well nere a London bushell of that money.[374]

After the said priors Athelwold and Walter, succeeded John (in the tyme of Bishopp Bernard) who gave Wate-croft in Flemby to the lord of Workington, Thomas filius Gospatricii; and after John Bartholomew, who in the tyme of Bishopp Hugh confirmed Orton in Westmorland to the prior of Conishead.[375] After him Radulph was prior who confirmed the impropriacion of the rectory of Burgh to [*p. 49*] the abbey of Holme Cultram in the tyme of Walter, bishopp of Carlisle.[376] After Radulph these were priors successively:[377] Robert Morvill; Adam Felton; Allanus; Galfridus; John de Horncastre; John de Penreath; William Dalston; Robert Edenhall; Thomas Hatton;[378] Thomas Barnby; Thomas Huthwaite; Thomas Gaddybar;[379] Symon

372 In M 'them' is omitted and the text runs on. For this charter (which was granted by Bishop Athelwold, rather than Walter himself), see H. Summerson, 'Athelwold the bishop', pp. 85–91 and *EEA 30: Carlisle*, no. 3. Walter is recorded as prior between 1133x1157 and *c.* 1175: D. Knowles, C. N. L. Brooke and V. C. M. London (eds), *Heads of Religious Houses: England and Wales*, I (2nd edn, Cambridge, 2001), p. 158.

373 In 685 Ecgfrith, king of Northumbria, granted to St Cuthbert 'Lugubalia, known as Luel, with 15 miles round about it': C. R. Hart, *The Early Charters of Northern England and the North Midlands* (Leicester, 1975), p. 133 (no. 146).

374 This may refer to a hoard of Roman coins found under the church, recorded by Stukeley in 1776: see D. C. A. Shotter, 'Roman coin hoards from Cumbria: addenda', *CW2*, 82 (1982), p. 198. The date of the rebuilding of St Cuthbert's church, referred to by Denton, is not known.

375 The confirmation can be dated to 1219x1223: *EEA 30: Carlisle*, no. 43.

376 The confirmation is dated 12 Apr. 1234: *EEA 30: Carlisle*, no. 88.

377 The following list of priors is incomplete: see *VCH Cumb.*, II, pp. 150–1; Smith and London, *Heads of Religious Houses*, II, pp. 359–60.

378 H: 'Hoton'.

379 H: 'Gudybour'.

Senos; Christopher Slee and Lanclott Salkeld, last prior and first deane after King Henry the eight had changed the priory into a deanry and cathedrall church[380] of a new foundacion at the suppression of abbeys, adding thereunto (for their better maintenance) the revenue of the dissolved priory of Wetherall, a cell of St Marye's abbey in York, dedicateing the church to the honour of the holly and indivisible Trinity, the Father, the Sone, and the Holy Ghost. After Salkeld next succeeded Sir Thomas Smith, after Sir John Woolley, knight, and now Christopher Parkins, doctor, enjoyeth the same.[381] The priory wanted not reliques of saints, for Waldieff the son of Gospatrick, earle of Dunbarr, brought from Jerusalem and Constantinople a bone of St Paule th'appostle and another of St John Baptist's, two stones of Christ's sepulchre, and the holy cross, which he gave to the priory together with a mansion nere St Cuthbert's church, where at that tyme stood an auncient building called Arthur's-chamber then taken to be a part of the mansion house of King Arthur the son of Uter Pendragon, of memorable note for his worthiness in the tyme of the beginning of the British kings.[382] And another auncient building called Lyons gaide often remembred in that history of Arthur written by a monck, the ruines whereof are yett to be seene, < as >[383] is thought, at Ravenglass distant from Carlisle according to that number of myles[384] in that historie reported, < placed > nere the sea and not without some reasonable conjecture probally thought therefore to be the same.[385]

< After the death of Richard, earl of Chester, who was drowned with the king's children, Ranulph Meschiens remov'd to Chester and was earl thereof. Presently K. H. 1st dyed and K. Stephen usurping the states gave this county of Cumberland to David K. of Scots to procure his end against H. 2, right heir to the late king. But the Scots

---

380 'church' repeated in M and J, but crossed though in M.
381 Christopher Perkins was dean 1595–1622. For the early deans of Carlisle see J. M. Horn, D. M. Smith and P. Mussett, *Fasti Ecclesiae Anglicanae 1541–1857*: XI (London, 2004), pp. 14–15.
382 H: 'in the time of the regiment of the Scottish kings.'
383 M: 'and'.
384 H: '50 miles', the figure being an interlineation.
385 M text runs on, omitting the next section from H. For the Arthurian associations of Carlisle, see A. Wheatley, 'King Arthur lives in merry Carleile', in McCarthy and Weston (eds), *Carlisle and Cumbria*, pp. 63–72. 'Lyons gaide' is a mis-transcription of 'Joyous Garde', Lancelot's castle in Malory's *Morte D'Arthur*. Fleming 1 MS [4], p. 68 gives the correct form: 'joyous guard'. The ruins at Ravenglass are Walls Castle, the bathhouse of the Roman fort there.

secretly favoured Henry, the son of Maude the empress, daughter
and sole heir to K. H. 1st, for his right sake and for that he had
made the said Henry Empress knight at Carliell, yet accepting the
gift of the county, whereunto he pretended his own right as before
granted to his ancestors by the Saxon kings. He made his eldest son
Henry filius David earl of Huntington and Carliell, which Henry
founded the abbey Holm-cultram in the time of K. Stephen, his
father David confirming his grant of the revenues wherewith he
endowed that house and so his son Malcolme, king of Scots after
David. After Henry son of David was dead and K. Stephen, K. Henry
fitz Empress took Carliell and the county from the Scots and granted
to the city the first liberties of their city (as I read of) which they
enjoyed after the Conquest.[386] But his charter was burned by casual
fire that happened > in the towne in the tyme of King [*Henry III*]
which defaced a great part of the same and all the records of greatest
antiquity of that place.[387]

At the repairing of the citty in William Rufus tyme it was devided
into streets as it is at this present without any great alteration. In
the great street now called Abbay Gate were placed those Irish men,
which dwelt there when it was waste in cottages *then called vicus
Hiberniensium*.[388] [*p. 50*] In the street now called < Castlegait from
the castle at the end thereof >[389] were the Frenchmen or Normans
first inhabitants placed and therefore then called vicus Francorum.
In the other streets vicus Richardi of the gate < & street > leading to
Richarby; vicus Bochardi of the port or street leading to Botchardby;
vicus Castri of the castle standing att the end thereof; and in other
most commendable places of the cittye leading to and nigh the
markett place and churches dwelt the chiefe and best citizens, natu-
rall Englishmen. In the surburbs of the citty beyond Caldew toward
Cawcotes of Caldew cottages and towards Dalston in Shadwingate
dwelt the remnant of those Flemings, translated aforesaid, whereupon that street was called vicus Flandrensis. In the lowest place
of the cittye were placed the fish shambles vicus piscatorum; in the
head whereof then stood the flesh shambles or butchers' raw, vicus

---

386 For the charter of Henry II *c.* 1158, see K. Smith, 'The dating of Carlisle's first
     charter', *CW2*, 54 (1955), pp. 272–3.
387 A major fire in 1251, the first of several to afflict the city, destroyed Carlisle's
     early charters: Summerson, *Medieval Carlisle*, p. 124.
388 The phrase marked here by asterisks is written in the margin.
389 M and J: 'C. street'.

Carnificum; in the middle the markett place; and on the south side the
< abbay or > priory.

[B3] Ulnedale & Gilcruce.[390] The mannor of Ulnedale lyeth above
Bolton, and is soe called of the Elne running through the same, which
river is diversly named as Elne, Alne < & Olne > and therefore the
Romans named Olena, and the valley there Uln-daile.[391]

This mannor or parcell of the barony of Allerdall Waldeif filius
Gospatricii comitis gave unto Adam filius Lyolf, brother of Phorne
filius Lyolff, baron of Greystock, together with the mannor of
Gilcruce, from which Adam they descended by a daughter to the
Bonkills,[392] who granted forth Gilcruce to a younger brother Robert
Bonkill, & the sonnes of the said Robert, Thomas Bonkill and Walter,
gave away their inheritance in Gilcruce to the abbey of Cawdre,
which Sir Ranulf Bonkill Kt, then lord paramount both of Ulnedale
and Gilcruce, confirmed the same[393] to the abbott.[394] Sir Ranulff had
issue Alexander, who had issue Adam, which Adam gave Auerth-
waite, parcell of his mannor of Ulnedale unto the priory of Carlisle. The said Adam had issue another Alexander Bonekill whose
daughter and heire first married to John Steward kinsman [*p. 51*]
to the king of Scotts, and afterwards to David Briegham, a Scotish
knight of great valour, < who > transferred the inheritance to the
familie of the Brieghames.[395] This David Briegham was a companion

---

390 Uldale (NY 25 37); Gilcrux (NY 11 38).
391 The name Uldale incorporates ON personal name Ulf, rather than the river
    name Ellen: *PNC*, II, p. 327. Camden (*Britannia*, p. 769) linked the Roman
    name Olenacum to Ellenborough rather than Uldale.
392 The grant of Uldale to Adam son of Lyulph is recorded in 'Chronicon
    Cumbrie': *St Bees*, p. 492. The Bunkles were a Berwickshire family.
393 'the same' deleted in both M and H.
394 Grants to the abbey of lands in Gilcrux by Robert Bonekill were confirmed
    by Henry III in 1231: Thorley, 'Estates of Calder abbey', p. 140. A charter of
    Walter son of Robert de Bonekil, granting a fourth part of the mill of Gilcrux
    to Calder abbey, survived in private hands in 2004 (inf. from John Thorley).
395 Sir Alexander Bunkle, who held Uldale in 1296 (*Cal Docs Scotland*, II, p. 171
    (no. 736)), was dead by 1300, when the manor was in the king's hand as his
    daughter, Margaret, was in Scotland (ibid., p. 290 (no. 1135); *Cal IPM*, III,
    no. 607). It was restored to her and her second husband, Sir David Brechin
    ('Breghyn') after the Scottish submission of 1304 and although Margaret soon
    died, it was still in Brechin's hands in late 1305 and perhaps for some years
    thereafter (*Cal. Docs Scotland*, II, pp. 464–5 (no. 1717); *Cal. Pat. Edw I*, IV, p. 407;
    Scots Peerage, ed. J. B. Paul (Edinburgh (1904–14), ii, 218–22). Once Margaret's
    son Alexander Stewart came of age, Uldale should have descended to him

of William Walleyes that was executed for treason (at London) comitted against Edw. the first by resisting that king's attempt for the superior lord<ship> of Scottland and the Ballyells' right to the crowne of Scotland, takeing part with Robert Bruce. Wallyce was a man of extraordinarie strength and David Briegham an exceeding good horseman, whereupon the Scotts thus ryhmed of them:

The man was ne're soe wight nor good
But wurthye Wallice durst him byde;
Nor never horse soe wylde nor wood
But David Briegham durst him ryde.[396]

David Briegham thereby forfeited his estate to Anthony Lord Lucy, then lord of Allerdale, so Ulldale escheated againe and became parcell of that auncient baronny, and the mannor extinguished of right. Yett was it continued as a mannor by the Lucies' posteritye and the Pierces, earls of Northumberland, the cattalogues of whose posteritye appeares in the tittle of Allerdale, untill Henry the < sixt > of that name earle of Northumberland gave his inheritance to Hen. the eight, which kinge granted forth that mannor of Ulnedale to Thomas Dalston and Elioner his second wife, and to the heires of their two bodyes. And now Christopher Dalston gentl. their heire as in that right enjoyeth the same.[397]

– but by 1318 it was in the king's hand, because of Stewart's 'rebellion' (*Cal. IPM*, VI, no. 159).

396 The last words of lines 1 and 3 have been altered in M to 'gead' and 'wead' and in H to 'guud' and 'wuud'. The source of this ditty has not been traced. Sir David Brechin (executed by Robert I in 1320) was a kinsman of John Comyn of Badenoch, which led him firmly into the anti-Bruce faction after Comyn's murder in 1306 (A. A. M. Duncan, 'Brechin, Sir David', *ODNB*). Alexander Grant has suggested to me that the stanza quoted by Denton might derive from a lost text about Brechin and his close companion, Sir Ingram de Umfraville (see John Barbour, *The Bruce*, ed. A. A. M. Duncan (Edinburgh, 1997), pp. 28–30), which would have been one of the pro-Comyn poems or ballads circulating in the early fourteenth century (see A. Grant, 'The death of John Comyn: what was going on?', *Scottish Historical Review*, 86 (2007), pp. 189–92, 199–207). It is striking that Brechin is associated with horsemanship in contemporary sources: 'Blind Hary' asked 'How bauld Breichin contrar his king coud ryd' (*Hary's Wallace*, ed. M. P. McDiarmid (Scottish Text Society, 4th ser., vol. 5, Edinburgh, 1969), bk XII, line 1199); he is also on horseback in Barbour's *Bruce* (ed. Duncan, pp. 328, 332). I am very grateful to Alexander Grant for references in this and the previous note, and for generously sharing his expertise in the pursuit of this stanza.

397 For the grant of the manors of Uldale, Brundholme, Caldbeck Upton and Kirkbride to Thomas Dalston in 1543 see *L & P Hen. VIII*, 18 (1), no. 981 (§

[*In margin of p. 50:*] Robt Bonkill, R. 1; Alexander, Jo.; Ranulph, H. 3; Alexander, Ed. 1; David Breigham, Ed. 2; Antho. Lucy.

[*p. 52*]

[B 4] Threpland,[398] contentionis terrae,[399] is now a village and the inheritance of John Salkeld, a younger brother of Lanclott < Salkeld > of the Whitehall. He holds it of Allerdale baronny and had it by purchase from Lanclott Skelton of Armanthwaite, Esq. It descended to him by ...... descent from the Skeltons from Thomas Skelton a younger brother who marryed the coheire of Henry Malton, knight, and Margarett his wife, in Edw. 3 tyme. Malton & his wife had it by fyne from William de Redness alias Mulcastre, anno 15 Ed. 2;[400] and the said William, Thomas and John Mulcastre brethren successively before Malton by guift of Michaell de Harcla in the tyme of Ed. 1st, father to Andrew, earle of Carlisle. < Before the Harcleys one Langus fil' Edredi, in the 19th year of H. 3 had it in the time of Walter Percy son to William Percy, who held it the eleventh of the same king. >[401]

[B 5] Blennerhassett & Uckmanby.[402] Blennerhassett and Uckmanby were parcell of Allerdaile, which Allan second lord thereof, the son of Waldeive, gave unto Radulph de Lindsey with the sister of the said Allan named Ochtred in frankmarriage. From them that inheritance came unto the Mulcastres.[403] In the tyme of King Henry 3 Robert de Mulcastre held the same; after him William his son, who had issue Walter, & he another William, whose son Robert transferred the Mulcastres' patrimony by a daughter to the Tillyolls, viz. Haiton, Turpenhow,[404] and by another daughter[405] to Roger de Quincy, earle

60). Dalston was settled on Thomas and Eleanor Dalston and their heirs in 1546: ibid., 21(1), no. 716 (§ 20).

398 Threapland (NY 15 39).

399 Denton's interpretation of the place-name is correct: it contains the dialect term 'threap' ('dispute'): *PNC*, II, p. 271.

400 FF Cumb. 16 Edw. II [1322–3] (*CW2*, 7 (1907), p. 233, no. 199). Henry de Malton was dead by 1326: *Cal. IPM*, VI, no. 678.

401 The first part of this sentence appears to refer to land in Blennerhasset, which Langusa daughter of Aldred had by fine from Walter de Percy in 1234–5: FF Cumb. 19 Hen. III [1234–5] (*CW2*, 7 (1907), p. 222, no. 47). The source for the reference to Percy's tenure in 11 Hen. III (1226–7) has not been traced.

402 Blennerhasset (NY 17 41); Upmanby (NY 190 423), in Allhallows parish.

403 M runs on here.

404 For the Mulcaster family, see *CFH*, p. 235. The daughter and heiress of Robert Mulcaster of Hayton married Peter de Tilliol (d. 1435): see above, section A42.

405 The punctuation is clearly wrong here, since the material in the remainder of the sentence refers back to the thirteenth century.

of Winchester and constable of Scottland, in the right of ...... his wife, one of the daughters and heires of Alane filius Roland filius Ughtred had the tuition of Sibell de Valonis and gave the king fifty marks 7° Hen. 3.[406]

[*In margin:*] 1. Rad. Lindsey, H. 2, dominus Blenr; 2. Nic. Stutvill, R. 1; 3. Wm Peircy, Jo., H. 3; 4. Walter Percy, < H. 3 >;[407] 5. Rob. Mulcaster; 6. Walter; 7. Wm; 8. Robtt.

[**B 6**] **Torpenhow.**[408] Torpenhow was att the conquest of England auncient demeasne of the barony of Allerdale, untill the said Alane Fitz Waldeive gave the same in frank marriage with < Gunyld >[409] his sister to Ughtred the son of Fergus, lord of Galloway, to be holden of him by <u>homage</u>, cornage and other services. In Hen. the 2 tyme, one Philipp de Valonis[410] in the right of his wife held the same of Reginold Lucy and Amabill his wife, then lord [*p. 53*] of the moietye of Allerdale < till > the king seized the tenure <u>because Reginold Duncane</u>. And in King John's tyme Robert Stutevill, brother to the lord Nicholas Stutevill, lord of Liddell < held it. >[411] Anno 31 Hen. 3 William filius Willielmi de Ulfbye gave three carracutes of land there to Robert Mulcastre,[412] and[413] held five parts of the same and Robert Brim[414] the other sixth part (which he adjoyned to his mannor of Bothill) of the lords of Lyddell, heire to Stutevile. The said five parts descended to the Mulcasters, and from them to the Tyliolls, whose coheires transferred the same with other lands to the < families >[415]

---

406 Roger de Quincy (*c*.1195–1265) married (1) Helen, daughter of Alan, lord of Galloway and constable of Scotland. On his father-in-law's death in 1234, he received the constableship of Scotland: see R. D. Oram, 'Alan, lord of Galloway', 'Quincy, Roger de', *ODNB*. De Quincy was fined for the wardship of land of Sibilla de Valoniis in Torpenhow in 1222–3: *Cal. Docs Scotland*, I, nos. 840, 847–8.

407 M: 'H. 5'.

408 Torpenhow (NY 20 39).

409 As above (section A30), M again renders her name 'Gymild'.

410 H: 'Valomes'.

411 Testa de Nevill explains that, because Reginald de Lucy refused the homage of Robert's predecessor, Philip de Valoines, Henry II had taken his homage: *Book of Fees*, p.198.

412 FF Cumb. 31 Hen. III [1246–7] (*CW2*, 7 (1907), p. 224, no. 83).

413 H: 'who'.

414 H: 'Richard Brune'.

415 M: 'family'.

of the Morresbies and the Covills.[416] It is called Tor-pen-how, every
sillable of which word in severall languages of the people which
successively did inhabitte the place doeth signifye after a manner
one thing. The Brittons first called a little riseing hill ther[417] Pen.
The Saxons next succeeding, not well understanding the significa-
tion of Pen, called it Tor-Pen (the pinackle Pen). The last, as wee
doe yet, called it Tor-pen-how, the how or hill Torpen.[418] Others
have thought it soe named upon this occassion: the Saxons called a
village Dorp, and finding the hill there to be named of the Brittons
(there forbeares)[419] Pen, a head or hill topp, they named Dor-pen or
the towne hill. Others will have it soe named of one Torpe, whom
they suppose to have beene lord thereof, of which name they finde
of record one Robert Torpe, sometyme lord of Edenhall,[420] but with
better probabillity they may conjecture Edenhall to have beene first
a country village and therefore the sayd Robert to be rightly called
Robert de Dorp,[421] and that dorpe or village to be called afterwards
Edenhall, or the hall upon Eden, after his auncestors [had][422] seated
themselves there and built a hall or capitall messuage and mannor
house. I read of one Robert de Torpenhow but I know not whether
he was father to Alice Stutevile or issue maile to Ughtred Valonies
or Stutevile.

[B7] Bolton in Allerdall to beneath Derwent.[423] Bolton or Bothillton was auncient demeasne of Allerdaile till the said Alane Fitz
Waldieve gave the same with Bastingthwaite and the Isle of Eastholme to his bastard brother Gospatrick the son of Waldieve,[424] one

416 For these families, see Wilson, 'Some extinct Cumberland families III: the Tilliols', pp. 98–9.
417 H: 'a rising or little topped hill there'.
418 Denton's interpretation of the name, which has entered popular historical folklore, is only partly correct. The first two elements are both Brittonic, the compound *torr-pen* meaning 'peak head'. The third element is thought more likely to be OE *hoh* ('ridge or hill spur') than ON *haugr* ('hill'): *PNC*, II, p. 326.
419 Altered to 'forrunners' in M; 'forebearers' in H.
420 Robert Tourp or Turp (d. 1314), held two-thirds of Edenhall: *Cal. IPM*, V, no. 446.
421 The entry for Torpenhow ends here in H: it is followed by a series of dashes, presumably indicating that text has been omitted. The missing text is, however, found in Mawson MS [8], the sister manuscript to H.
422 Supplied from J; M reads 'and'.
423 The extensive parish of Boltons. Bolton Hall and the parish church are at Boltongate (NY 229 408).
424 As recorded in 'Chronicon Cumbrie': *St Bees*, p. 493.

of whose posteritye tooke their surname of Bastingthwaite. I read
of diverse knights of that name, one Sir Robert de Bastingthwaite
in Hen. ..... tyme [*p. 54*] and Adam his son, and one Alexander in
Edw. 1 tyme. The said Gospatrick seated himselfe at Bolton, from
whom it descended unto the Lassiells by Christiane uxor Duncani
in 2 Rich. 1[425] < and Thomas his son > in Hen. 3 tyme < and >
Thomas de Lasciells < his son >,[426] lord of Bolton, married Christian filia Willelmi de Ireby, confirmed to the abbott and monckes
of Holme Cultram the hermitage of St Hyld, called now Hyldekirk,
and granted them common in Bolton.[427] His widdow Christian
Irebye filia Willelmi,[428] wife of Robert Bruce, dyed 33 Ed. 1 < and >
seized of Heslespring in Westward, Gamelsby and Unthank beyond
Eden, and of Markett Irebye, which Ireby she held of John Boyvill of
Thorseby.[429] In Ed. 2 tyme Roger Mowbray, lord of Bolton, forfeited
his estate therein by takeing part with Robert Bruce.[430] Afterwards it
came to his sonne Robert Mowbray in Edw. 3 tyme, and to Alexander
Mowbray, and after to the Nevills. In the 12 of Rich. 2 John Nevill of
Raby dyed seized of Bolton and the Mowbrays' lands in Gamelsbye
and Unthanke.[431] In the 22th of that king's raigne Radulphus Nevyll
held Bolton & Bassinthwaite of Maude Lucye.[432] Thenceforth the
Nevills, lords Latimer, held the same, untill it fell to Henry now earle
of Northumberland, by the death of his mother the countess, one of
the daughters and coheires of ...... last Lord Latymer, of that name
of the Nevylls.[433]

[*In margin:*] Wm Latimer had Gamelsby, Glassonbye and Unthank in
the parish of Adingham [*followed by the following descent:*] 1. Waldevus,
Hen. 1; 2. Alanus, H. 2 & Stephen; 3. Gospatr' bastard filius Waldevi,
H. 2; Christianae uxor Duncani Lascell, R., Jo.; Thom' Lascell, H. 3.

---

425 H: 'in K. Richard the first's time'. Cf. Pipe Roll, 2 John (1200): *VCH Cumb.*, I,
     p. 386. In margin: 'Duncan Lacells test to a deed of Ranulf Bonekill.'
426 'his son' is interlined in H.
427 See *Holm Cultram*, p. 78, no. 225, dated to *c*. 1227.
428 Gilpin, p. 145: 'MS. was originally Daughter but it is rased & Widow interlind
     by another hand' and 'MS. she is called Lascels & Ireby by another hand'.
429 Inquisition, 1305: *Cal. IPM*, IV, no. 280.
430 In 1318 the manor was in the king's hand by reason of the enmity of Sir Roger
     de Mowbray: *Cal. IPM*, VI, no. 159.
431 Inquisition, 1388: *Cal. IPM*, XVI, no. 735.
432 Inquisition, 1398: *Cal. IPM*, XVII, no. 1247 (p. 471).
433 Henry Percy, 8th earl of Northumberland (d. 1585) married Katherine
     (d. 1596), daughter and heir of John Neville, Lord Latimer: *Complete Peerage*,
     VII, p. 485; IX, p. 732.

15; Thom' Las', Hen. 3. 53; Galfred' Mowbray, Ed. 1; Joh' Mowbray, E. 1. 33; Robt Mowbray; Alex. Mowbray; Robt Mowbray, 39 Ed. 3; Jo. Nevill, 12 R. 2 et Eliz. Mowbr' uxor'; Radulphi Nevill 22 R. 2; Geo. dominus Latimer, 10 E. 4.[434]

Robt Bruce et Christian uxor, filia Roberti filii Adae de Bassingthwaite q' voc. Remig' de Pocklington q' voc. Jeoffrey Mowbrey ad warrant' priori Hospital' sancti Johannis in Jerusalem carracut terrae in Skelmerbeck < in Bastingthwait > 16 Ed. primi.[435]

[*p. 55*]

[B 8] Dovenby.[436] Dovenbye or Dolphinbye in Allerdaill was first soe called of one Dolphin the son of Alleward who first seated himselfe there and called the name of his mansion house Dolphinbye.[437] Of that place, his posterityе were called Dovenbyes corruptly, but rightly Dolphinbies. In Henry the < 2nd's > tyme, one Richard de Dovenbie possessed the same, his son Benedict de Bridekirke confirmed to the abbott of Cawdre lands in Gilcroose. The Lord Waldave, first lord of Allerdaill, gave unto the said Dolphin the son of Alwarde, < with Maude his sister, >[438] Applethwaite beside Keswick, Little Crosbye, Lanrigg[439] and Brigham, with the patronage of Brigham.[440] Aleward his father seated himselfe at Alewardbye, nameing the place after his owne name.[441]

[*In margin:*] uxores Lampleugh, Kirkbride, Pennington, Highmore, Harrington, Curwen, Preston, Salkeld, Breithwaite.

After the issue male of Dolphin extinguished, in the tyme of Hen. 3, Dovenbie fell by marryage to the familye of the Rawlles or Rowlles. In the 51th yeare of Hen. 3 one Roger de Rall was possessed of Dovenbie.[442] After him one Allan de Rall held the mannor of Dovenbie in 33

434 Gilpin, p. 146 notes of this descent: 'MS. but in another hand this pedigree is inserted in Marg[in]'.
435 16 Edw. I = 1287–8. Gilpin, p. 146 (beside this paragraph): 'MS. but another ancient hand'.
436 Dovenby (NY 09 33).
437 The personal name incorporated into the place-name is more likely to be Irish *Dufan* than Dolfin: *PNC*, II, p. 284.
438 In M the phrase is corrupted to 'which marr'd his sister'.
439 'Langrigg' (the form in J) is meant.
440 As recorded in 'Chronicon Cumbrie': *St Bees*, p. 493.
441 Allerby (NY 08 39) does contain the personal name Ailward (OE Æðelward): *PNC*, II, p. 306.
442 51 Hen. III = 1266–7. The source has not been traced.

Ed. 1 of Thomas Lucy.[443] In the 23 yeare of Edw. 3, Richard Kirkbride was lord of Dovenbie and dyed then seized thereof, leaveing his son Richard a ward.[444] He dyed in the 22 of Rich. 2 or the 1 of Hen. 4.[445] By his daughter or sister Dovenbye was transferred into the familye of the Lampleughes, and was[446] married to a younger brother of Sir Thomas Lampleughs of Lampleugh, in whose issue male the right thereof remaineth yett to this day.[447]

[*p. 56*]

[B 9] Bothill.[448] Bothill was demeasne of Allerdaile untill Waldeive lord of Allerdall gave the towneshipp to Gamell the son of < Brune >[449] in Hen. 1 tyme, whose posteritye long enjoyed the same in the issue male. His father's chiefe mansion was at Brunskewghe beneath the river Eden neare unto the wastes; whereupon Radulph filius Gamell was called Radulfus de feritate, Ralph of the wastes, and soe his son Robert de feritate. They were lords of Beamont, Glasson, Drom-brughe and Bowness, which they held of the lords of Burghe. In Hen. 3 and Edw. the 1st tyme, Richard < Brune > was lord of Bothill, of the vi[th] part of Torpenhow, and the premisses.[450] And after Robert < Brune >, in Edw. 3 tyme. Afterwards Bothill and the < Bruns' > lands fell to three coheires marryed to Nicholas Harrington, a brother or kinsman of the lord of Harrington; William Culwen of Workington; and one to Thomas Bowett. To < Nicholas >[451] Harrington in his part succeeded James who dyed 5[to] Hen. 5o,[452] and after James, Sir Richard Harrington, knight, 7 E. 4,[453] and now in the possession of Thomas Denton of Warnell by Ellen his wife.[454] To William Curwen's part the

---

443 Inquisition, 1305: *Cal. IPM*, IV, no. 322, which renders his name Alan de Roule.

444 Inquisition, 1350: *Cal. IPM*, IX, no. 225.

445 The correct date is 22 Rich. II. See inquisition,1399: *Cal. IPM*, XVII, no. 1174.

446 M: 'and was' crossed out and replaced by 'shee being'. J and H read 'and was'.

447 For the Lamplugh family of Dovenby, see S. Taylor, 'The Lamplugh family in Cumberland, part II', *CW2*, 39 (1939), pp. 71–108.

448 Bothel (NY18 38).

449 Here and below M renders the name 'Brim'.

450 Richard le Brun was dead by 1313: *Cal. IPM*, V, no. 393.

451 M and J read 'Thom.' but Nicholas is presumably meant.

452 At his death in 1417 James Harrington's estate included the manors of Bothel, Bowness and Beaumont and the vill of Brunstock: *Cal. IPM*, XX, no. 689.

453 See inquisition, 1467–8: *Calendarium inquisitionum post mortem sive escaetarum*, IV, p. 341.

454 Harrington sold his share to Thomas Lord Dacre, who granted it and other

heires of Workington, his posterity, untill Sir Henry Curwen knight, father of Nicholas, sold the same to Anthony Barwise of Hyldkirk Esq. Bowet's part of Bothill is now enjoyed by Thomas Ellis, whose auncestor < William Ellis > purchased the same of Nicholas Bowett by fine levyed 8 Ed. 4.[455]

The towne stands on the side of a hill, where in old tyme the watch was keept day and night for seawake, which service was performed by the < country >[456] beneath Derwent at that place, and above Derwent in Copeland att Bothill in Millam and att Bothelton in Egremont barrony. It is called servicium de Bodis in old evidence, whereupon the hill was named the Bode or Bothe-hill, and a village at the foote of it Bothillton – bodorum collis. The country people call a lanthorne a bowett, which was the name and was [*p. 57*] then in use for a light on the shore to direct saylors on the night; properly signi-fieing a token, and not a light or lanthorne, as they call a message warranted by a token a bode-word at this day; and the watchmen called bodesmen, because they had a bod or watch word given them for the enemies fraud on the night.[457]

[*In margin:*] Tho. Bowett Margarett ux' 5 H. 6 Wm Bowett [m'] Amie[458] ux' Joha' filia H. 7 Nich. Bowet [m'] vendit Ellis. [*The following forms a separate marginal entry in M and J*] Harington part Nich. [m'] James. Rich. [m'] Nich. [m'] q' vendit Tho. Dna Dacre 22 H. 7 Jo. et Tho. Denton de Warnell Tho. Denton Hen. fil' Geo fratris Thomae.[459]

---

lands to John Denton of Warnell in 1506, in exchange for the manor of Denton in Gilsland: Denton, *Perambulation*, p. 161.

455 FF Cumb. 8 Edw. IV [1468–9] (*CW2*, 7 (1907), p. 249, no. 366).

456 M: 'county' but both J and H have 'country'.

457 In margin: 'Bode, a token'. The derivation of the place-name Bothel is OE *boðl* ('building with a special purpose'), usually taken to indicate a high status site: *PNC*, II, p. 271; Phythian-Adams, *Land of Cumbrians*, 88–9. It is conceivable that Denton's attempt to explain the name preserves a garbled memory of early dues being rendered at Bothel. He confuses 'seawake', a coastal guarding duty found in Copeland and Allerdale, with the service of 'bode' (providing messengers) and uses the latter to explain the place-name. Despite the confusion, could it be that he is recalling a distant memory of an association between places containing the element *boðl* and early 'public' services performed by settlements in Allerdale and Copeland?

458 H: 'Mary'.

459 The interpretation of the symbol rendered '[m']', which occurs five times in this marginal entry, is uncertain. In M and J it is almost identical to the looped 'm' found as the standard abbreviation for *misericordia* ('amercement') in the margins of manor court rolls, yet, from the context here, the meaning cannot

[B 10] Ishall.[460] When Ishall was demeasne of Allerdall it conteined Rughthwaite, Blencrake, < Warthole >,[461] Redmayne, halfe of Plumland and Sunderland, with their appurtenances.[462] Allan the son of Waldeive gave Ruthwaite and the third part of the wastes of Isall unto Gamell < le Brune >,[463] lord of Bothil, < ad >[464] tertiam partem unius villae.[465] And he gave the principall mannor of Ishall cum pertinentiis, Blencrake with the services of Newton, to Radulphe Engayne.[466] Raduph had issue William Engayne, and he a daughter named Ada mother to Sir Hugh Morvill. Of her it was written by a monck that in th'old age of her husband she grew enamoured of one Lyolphe, a young gentleman that served her husband, whom by noe meanes she could perswade to abuse himselfe towards his master, but dutifully he avoyded every occasion that might further her desire. But being commanded one day by his master to carry upp a dish of meat to her when she kept her chamber, after he was entered, she caused a gentlewoman to make fast the doore and forthwith shamed not to move him to lye with her, as oftentymes before she had done. But he continued resolutely faithfull to his master, and would not consent for any thing she could doe or say. Whereupon feareing < that > he would discover that her lewd incontinencye and turneing her inordinate lust into wrath,[467] she presently made her gentlewoman to make a great outcry. When her husband heard them he ran[468] into the chamber and his servants [*p. 58*] and in a great rage asked the cause of such disquietnesse. She accused the young gentleman that he would have ravished her, and thereupon he commanded him presently to be bound and to be cast into a lead full of scalding water. Sir Hugh Morvill his sonne by that wife, afterwards killed Thomas Beckett, th'archbishopp of Canterbury, where-

be the same. In the single occurrence in H it is rendered as four minims, the last carried below the line, as in a lower case Roman numeral ('iiij').
460 Isel (NY 15 33).
461 M: 'Wathole'.
462 The places listed are Ruthwaite (NY 23 36); Blindcrake (NY 14 34); Wardhall (cf. Wardhall Common: NY 14 37); Redmain (NY 13 33); Plumbland (NY 15 39); and Sunderland (NY 17 35).
463 M: 'de Brim'.
464 M and J: 'at'.
465 See 'Chronicon Cumbrie', which, however, does not mention the third part of the wastes of Isel: *St Bees*, p. 493.
466 Ibid.
467 H: 'revenge'.
468 H: 'came'

fore the monckes of that tyme < gladly > tooke hold of whatsoever might disgrace him or his parents to posterityе.[469]

After Radulph Engayne, William his son, Sir Hugh Morvill's father in the right of the said Ada Engaine his wife, it fell by her death to himselfe and, after his death, with his daughters, Sir Richard Lucye, lord of Egremont, and Sir Richard Waryn or Werrne enjoyed the same with the baronny of Burgh; and after them to Thomas filius Thomae de Multon, as appeareth in the title of Burgh. Thomas de Multon in the tyme of Hen. 3 entayled Ishall and Blencrake with the appurtenances to his two younger sonns Edward & Hubbart, and their heires generall successively. Soe lost the lords of Ishall the services of Newton, first because that tenour remained to the grauntor Thomas Multon and his heires as it had to him descended.

By that entayle Hubbert Multon enjoyed Ishall and William his son after him,[470] whose daughter Margarett brought th'inheritance into the familye of the Lighes in Ed. 2 tyme, whose issue male have enjoyed it untill old Thomas Lighe, the last of that name, gave it to his wife Maud Redmayne, whom he married a widdow after the death of his first wife; a lustye younge gentlewoman, who granted it presently after his death to Wilfrid Lawson her present husband.[471]

[p. 59]
[B11] Newton.[472] Newton in Allerdaile is now the inheritance of Edward Musgrave second son to William and his wife ..... Martindale, one of the coheires of ..... Martindall, last of that name lord

---

469 This is a variant of the story recorded in the lives of Thomas Becket to blacken the name of Hugh Morvill. In most versions Hugh Morvill's mother (some say his wife) called out that Lyulph had drawn his sword when her advances were rebuffed: *Materials for the History of Thomas Becket*, ed. J. C. Robertson (Rolls Series 67A, 1875), I, p. 128.

470 William de Multon had inherited Isel and come of age before 1311: *Cal. IPM*, V, no. 328. His inheritance was not straightforward, since his father had remarried after divorcing William's mother, Ada la Brune, on grounds of affinity: *Northern Petitions*, ed. C. M. Fraser (Surtees Society Vol. 194; Gateshead, 1982), no. 61.

471 In margin of M, the arms of Leigh of Isel. Thomas Leigh d. 1573; his widow Maud (née Redman) (d. 1624) married Sir Wilfrid Lawson (1545–1632): *CFH*, pp. 199, 203.

472 Westnewton (NY 13 44). In margin of M a sketch of the arms of Martindale of Westnewton, annotated with tinctures: Argent two bars Gules over all a bend Or.

of Newton.[473] To him it descended from one Roger Martindall his auncestor, who marryed the daughter and heire of Thomas de Newton lord thereof in Edw. 3 tyme, which Thomas and his auncestors the Newtons lineally decending from father to sonn enjoyed the same in the tyme of King Stephen untill the death of Thomas filius Thomae, filii Richardi, filii Adami, filii Richardi, fratris Adami, filii Ketell de Newton, filius[474] Odardi de Wigton, to which Odard Alan 2 lord paramount of Allerdall gave Newton, and afterward granted the services thereof to Radulphe Engayne with Ishall.[475]

[*In margin of M:*] The coppy whereout this transcript was taken is rent in the remainder of this title of Newton, as alsoe in the severall titles following; yet blanks are left in case a faire[476] coppie may be comed by.

< The said Ketell filius [*Adam, son of Odard de Wigton, gave*] to Alane of Hensingham his third son a piece of [*ground by the sea, where*] he first [*erected*] his capitall messuage and named it Al[*lanby*] .... now that township so called to this day .... the inheritance of William the son of [*Flembie*] married another heir of Martindall. >[477]

[*p. 60*]

[B12] Wigton Baronny. Wigton was auncient demeasne of Allerdaile untill Waldeive fitz Gospatrick comitis gave that baronny unto Odardis de Logis.[478] It conteined Wigton, Waverton, Blencogo, Dundraw and < Kirkbride >[479] with their appurtenances, which five towneshipps are severall mannors within themselves knowne by meeres and boundes and lye within the baronny of Wigton. Odardus built Wigton church and endowed the same. He lived untill King John's tyme. K. H. 1 confirmed Waldeive's grant of the baronny to him; therefore it appeareth probally that he lived above a hundred

473 Edward Musgrave was son of William Musgrave (d. 1596) and his wife Isabel, daughter and heir of James Martindale: *CFH*, p. 238.

474 'filius' is followed by a blank in M.

475 As recorded in 'Chronicon Cumbrie': *St Bees*, p. 493. The text of H runs on here. M finishes the paragraph with '&c', presumably to indicate material omitted from the defective copy.

476 J: 'fairer'.

477 The text of this paragraph, referring to Allonby (NY 08 43), has been partially reconstructed from what appear to be versions of it in *Accompt*, p. 59 and Denton, *Perambulation*, p. 187.

478 See 'Chronicon Cumbrie': *St Bees*, p. 492.

479 M and J: 'Bridekirk', but Kirkbride is meant.

yeares. The Earle Randolph de Meschienes gave Stainton to him, and King Hen. 1 gave him Blackall & Melmerby. He had issue Adam, and Adam had issue Odard the second, whose son & heire Adam the second dyed without issue; therefore the inheritance came to his brother Walter who had issue Odard the third, who dyed without issue, and Odard the 4th likewise, wherefore their brother John de Wigton filius Walter entered & had issue < a >[480] sole daughter & heires, Margarett, who in anno domini ...... granted the church of Wigton to th'abbott & covent of Holme Cultram, which they presently did impropriate to their house in the yeare of grace 1334.[481] In K. Ed. 3 time < Margret was married to Sir John Denham, kt and >[482] she was impleaded for her birthright, and her mother Idyonise Lovetot, the wife of Sir John de Wigton, < was > for a tyme hindred of her dowry. Yet her adversary did not prevaile.[483] Wigton barony shortly after her death came to Thomas Lucy[484] < the [*last*] of that name lord of Allardall and thereby in right that seignory was extinguished & became again parcell of the ancient barony of Allardall, though it is yet taken and reputed as a mannor of it selfe. From the Lord Lucy it thencforth as other lands descended to the Lucyes & earles of Northumberland as appears in the title of Allardall, and the rest [*of*] Wigton's lands to others as appeareth in the[*ir titles*] .... purchased by Richard Cromely of Pickinglithe .... 28 4 H. 6 confirmed by K. H. 8th 17 anno.>[485]

[*In margin:*] Odard; Adam filius eius; Odard filius eius; Adam filius eius; Walter frater Adae; Odard filius eius; Odard frater; John frater

---

480 M: 'his'.

481 In 1332 John Gernoun and Margaret his wife granted Wigton church to Holm Cultram abbey in consideration of the losses incurred through the depradations of the Scots: FF Cumb. 6 Edw. III [1332–3] (*CW2*, 7 (1907), p. 236, no. 225); *Cal. Pat. Edw III*, II, p. 266.

482 The insertion from H occurs as a note in the margin of M, which renders the name 'Denam'.

483 For this dispute and the complex affairs of the much-married Margaret de Wigton (*c.* 1293–1349), see T. H. B. Graham, 'Margaret de Wigton', *CW2*, 29 (1929), pp. 81–90, and J. R. Magrath, 'Sir Robert Parvyng', *CW2*, 19 (1919), pp. 30–91.

484 The account of Wigton in M ends here with '&c. &c', again indicating the omission of additional material from the defective copy. The text of J ends here.

485 Text reconstructed from *Accompt*, p. 63 and Denton, *Perambulation*, p. 202. The latter identifies Blencogo as the estate purchased by Richard Cholmeley in 24 Hen. VII [1508–9], for which see *Cal. Pat. Hen. VII*, II, p. 595.

eius; Margarett filia, uxor John Denom; John Gernon; John Weston anno domini 1332.

[*p. 61*]

[B 13] **Kirkbryd.**[486] The mannor of Kirkbryde conteines the townes of Kirkbride and Oulton (a hamlett of the same) with their appurtenances. It was first granted forth from the baronny of Wigton by Adam filius Odard, second baron of Wigton, in K. John's tyme to Adam filius Adae his second son, a knight, brother to Odard the second. His posteritye tooke their surname of their mansion house at Kirkbride and therefore are called Kirkbrides. The church there founded before the Conquest and dedicated to the honour of a religious Irish woman of great sanctimony called Brydoch and corruptly St Bride, which gave first name to the towne.[487] The said Adam filius Adae was witness to a deed of gift of his cousen Henry filius Adae de Waverton, made to the moncks of Holm Cultram of lands in Waverton;[488] had issue Richard de Kirkbride and Richard had issue Robert whose issue male enjoyed the moiety of Kirkbride untill it fell to the coheires of George Kirkbride the last of that house, who transferred his inheritance to the Dalstons, Clebburnes & Weddalls who marryed his daughters according to the pedigree in the margent.[489] Th'other moiety went forth by a daughter of .... whose posterity sold that part in successe of tyme to the lord paramount of Wigton, in whose handes it continued till the earle of Northumberland gave his patrimony to K. Hen. 8, which king sold it to Thomas Dalston, grandfather to John Dalston, now entyre lord of the same.[490]

[*In margin:*] Adam filius Adae; Richard filius Adae; Rich' filius Rich'; Rob' filius Richardi; Rich' frater Roberti 23 Ed. 1; Walter; Richard 5

---

486 Kirkbride (NY 23 56). In the margin of M a sketch of arms, presumably those of Kirkbride: [Argent] a cross [Vert]: see *CFH*, p. 191.

487 Denton interprets the place-name correctly: see *PNC*, I, p. 144.

488 This charter has not been identified in *Holm Cultram*.

489 The pedigree in the margin, printed at the end of this paragraph, does not include the daughters and co-heiresses of George Kirkbride (d. 1511), who were: Elizabeth (b. *c.* 1478), wife of John Dalston; Isabel (b. 1482), whose second husband was Gilbert Weddale; and Emmotte (b. 1490), wife of Robert Cleburn: *CFH*, p. 191.

490 Thomas Dalston was granted Kirkbride and other manors in 1543: *L & P Hen. VIII*, 18 (1), no. 981 (§ 60). At the end of this paragraph M again adds '&c', presumably to indicate missing material. In H the account of Kirkbride is followed by fragmentary material referring to places in Millom seigniory, clearly misplaced.

Ed. 3; Walter 10 Ed. 3; Rich' 23 Ed. 3; Rich' 22 Ric. 2; Rich' Kirkbride;
Ric'.[491]

[*p. 62*]

[B 14] Caldbeck[492] was long after the Conquest a waste forrest
ground parcel of Allerdale. It is a dale betweene Warnhill-fell and the
mountaines < Carock >[493] & Grisdale fells.[494] It was first soe called
Caldbeck of a rill or beck that falleth downe eastward through the
same into Caldew, and therefore Caldewbeck, contractly Caldbeck;
or of the coldnesse of the place which is for the most part in winter
covered with snow, and therefore called the < Coldbeck, which they
pronounce > Caldbeck.[495] It conteyneth that dale now inhabitted,
and a great parte of the mountaines of Mosedale and Grisedale[496]
untill the white water dash at the head of Elne[497] or Aln that falleth
into < Ulnedale. >[498] The two dales there on the east side of the
mountaines are soe called Mossdale of a great moss ground there;
Grisedale of a store house < there, >[499] which the barons of Gray-
stock and the Dacres held of Caldbeck; they keept sheepe, cattle and
swyne, and suffered the porklins to run wylde in the woodes that
grew in the skirtes and borders of the mountaines.[500]

Out of Westmorland and th'east <u>of</u> part of Cumberland there lay
(as yett doth) an high way or beaten streete through Caldbeck into
the west country of Cumberland, which was dangerous then to

491 For the inquisitions after the deaths of members of the Kirkbride family, see
     Cal. IPM, VII, no. 317 (Richard, 5 Edw. III [1331]); VIII, no. 53 (Walter, 10 Edw.
     III [1336]); IX, no. 225 (Richard, 23 Edw. III [1350]); XVII, no. 1174 (Richard,
     22 Rich. II [1398–9]).
492 Caldbeck (NY 32 39). Additional seventeenth-century copies of the account
     of Caldbeck survive in CRO, D/Lec, box 129 and Oxford, Bodleian Library,
     MS Gough, Scotland 4. The text of the latter is very close to that of M.
493 M: 'Carrick'.
494 i.e. Warnell Fell (NY 338 412), Carrock Fell (NY 34 33) and the fells in
     Mungrisdale township, Caldbeck's neighbour on the south.
495 Denton's second suggestion is correct: Caldbeck is simply 'cold stream': *PNC*,
     II, pp. 275–6; *Dict. LDPN*, p. 63.
496 Here and in the following sentence, the transcript in D/Lec, box 129 has
     'Swin(e)side' in place of 'Grisedale', presumably referring to Swineside (NY
     342 323).
497 M: 'Elme'. Whitewater Dash is a waterfall on Dash Beck at NY 273 313.
498 M: 'Ulvedale'.
499 M: 'the'.
500 Denton's interpretation of the names Mosedale (NY 35 32) and 'Grisedale'
     (now Mungrisdale, NY 36 30) are correct: *PNC*, I, p. 226; II, pp. 304–5.

passengers, who were often robb'd in that < thevish >[501] place by theives that haunted the woods & mountaines there, whereupon Radolphe[502] Engayne, the chiefe forrester of Englewood, ... granted the prior of Carlisle lycence to have[503] a hospitall for the reliefe of poore travellers that might happen to be troubled by those theives or by the stormes & snow in winter[504] < and gave further liberty to the prior to inclose a part of the same where the church stands at this time, which inclosure became part of the glebe of the church.[505] The prior procured not his consent for his right in the soyl but without his consent it could not be inclosed, for that great large deere lodged continually in the woods and mountains there, and it was then used as a park or forrest; but the right of the soyl was the barons heirs of Allerdall, who was ..... Doncane the aunt son of Allane, second baron of Allerdall, by Octred the sister of Waldeive fitz Gospatricii, yet then another Gospatrick filius Ormi & of Gamile the said Waldeive's sister clamed a moyety of Allerdall coparcener. >

[*p. 63*] After this hospitall was built they founded the church there in the honour of St Mungo and the place became inhabitted fully in that part of the same called Caldbeck Upperton; and after under the fell sides, which latter buildings they call Caldbeck Underfell. First that part towards Greystock, as Heskatt and Haltcleugh, was brought to tillage as best fitting for corne, which is the lower end of the dale, and therefore the hamlett at the church standing higher in the dale was called Caldbeck upp in the towne, and soe contractly Caldbeck Upperton.[506] The priors became patrones of the rectory there by the grants and confirmacions of William de Vescy and Burgha his wife, and of Dame Alice Romley, ladye of Allerdall. They then dissolved the hospitall and endowed the church with the lands thereof, about

---

501 'theivish' deleted in M.
502 H: 'Hugh' with 'Randolf' interlined.
503 H: 'procure' with 'build there' interlined.
504 M: adds '&c, &c' to indicate the material omitted from the defective copy.
505 Ranulph Engaine (d. before 1158) was hereditary chief forester as lord of the barony of Burgh. The late Peter Gaskins suggested to me that 'Hugh' in H may reflect confusion with a later forester, his great-grandson, Hugh de Morvill. The *hospitalem domum de Caldebech* and the church there were given to Carlisle priory by Gospatric son of Orm before 1170: *VCH Cumb.*, II, p. 204; *Monasticon*, VI, p. 144.
506 The suffixes of the two divisions of the parish, Caldbeck Underfell and Caldbeck Upton, describe their positions: 'below the hill' and 'the higher settlement': *PNC*, II, p. 276.

King John's tyme. In Henr. 3 tyme[507] one John Francigena (Fraun-
coyes or French), a kinsman of Gilbert Francoyes, lord of Rocliffe,
was parson & gatt a great < inclosure >[508] on Warnell banck in the
forrest of Englewood, which he joyned to the glebe, yet the monckes
of Holme soe quarrell'd him that he was glad to part stakes and gave
them that moiety of the same now called Frierhall, and the other
moietye called the Parson's park remaines yett.[509] < att .... priors
successor Bartholomew granted the [*advowson of this church to*][510]
Walter Malclerk and to his successors .... the seigniory descended
.... Allerdall from Waldeive .... coparceners daughters and heirs
.... then Caldbeck fell to Dame .... which part came to the other
two .... Caldbeck was allotted to the .... was first in the right
of his .... between his daughter Mabell .... Alice who enjoyed
the .... gave the Lucyes' lands to the earles .... in Rich. the
second's time .... of all his possessions to > [*p. 64*] King Hen. 8th
< which king > sold Caldbeck Upperton to Thomas Dalston in fee
simple and[511] the earle before his grant to the king had first given in
fee tayle;[512] and Caldbeck Underfell to Thomas Lord Wharton and
to his heires male, who being warden at that tyme of those West-
marches so entreated the said Thomas Dalston that he was glad to
sell him Upperton alsoe.[513] Now Philipp Lord Wharton his grand-
childe enjoyeth the same. After Queene Mary restored the earle of

507 The copy in CRO, D/Lec, box 129 has in margin 'Anno Dom 21', presumably
     indicating the year 1221 (5 or 6 Hen. III).
508 M and Bodleian Library MS Gough Scotland 4 read 'embleme', presumably
     a misreading of 'enclosure'.
509 M adds '&c &c.' presumably referring to the defective material which follows
     in H. Gilpin, p. 152: 'Here the MS. is defaced'. The transcriber of the Queen's
     College MS [12] also noted (p. 154): 'so torne out I cannot make any perfect
     sense here'. Friar Hall (NY 324 399) and Parson's Park (NY 335 401) lay on
     the north side of the Cald Beck in Sebergham parish.
510 Text reconstructed from Denton, *Perambulation*, p. 176, where the rest of the
     account of the descent of the manor appears to be a paraphrase, rather than
     a close copy, of the defective text here.
511 Corrected to 'which' in margin of M.
512 Thomas Dalston was granted the manors of Uldale, Brundholme, Caldbeck
     Upton and Kirkbride in 1543: *L & P Hen. VIII*, 18 (1), no. 981 (§ 60).
513 Dalston received licence to alienate Caldbeck Upton to Thomas Lord Wharton
     (*c.* 1495–1568) in 1546: *L & P Hen. VIII*, 21 (1), no. 970 (§ 62).

Northumberland [she][514] granted the reversion of this Caldbeck to him & his heires mailes.[515]

Both the Caldbecks were one entire mannor to Dame Alice Romley. By her death it was devided by the two sister children of the house of Albemarle and the Lucyes. After the line of Albemarle ended all fell to the Lucies, who continued that late devision of the mannor < ...... > by two severall graveshipps < or >[516] collectors in Caldbeck Underfell and Upperton; and accompted the profitts of them to the lord as of two severall mannors for the raiseing services.[517] The wastes were not knowne to be devided.[518]

[*End of Part One*]

---

514 Supplied from Hutton John MS (CRO, D/Lons/L.12/4/5/1), p. 38.

515 Thomas, earl of Northumberland, was granted the reversion of Caldbeck in 1557: *Cal. Pat. Philip & Mary*, IV, pp. 187–8.

516 M: 'as'.

517 The copy in CRO, D/Lec, box 129 reads 'rents & services', which is probably meant. H reads 'for ..... services.'

518 In M there follows a paragraph in Thomas Machell's hand recording that Richard Machell, of the Crackenthorpe family, had lived in Caldbeck in the time of Henry VIII and Edward VI and discussing his descendants. In the margin of M, beside this paragraph, is a note in William Nicolson's hand stating 'This is an interpolation by Mr T. M.' Since the paragraph is clearly not part of Denton's text, it has been omitted.

Second part of Mr J Denton's book.²

[C1] Crofton.³ Crofton is the next towne and mannor to Thursbye
< in the parish of Thursby > and lyes betweene Thursbye and Parton
towards the east and west, and betweene the rivers of Wampole and
the Pow on the south and north. It is called Croftowne of the word
croft, as the towne standing upon the crofts.⁴ The first lord that I reade
of the same was a knight, Sir Gilbert filius Gilberti de Dundraw. He
gave a parcell of the same to the hospitall of St Nicholas of Carlisle
and boundred it out called Gillmartinridden.⁵ He lived in King
John's tyme. He bound that land to grind att his milne at Crofton.
Next after him the lords de Crofton had to their surname Crofton, as
John de Crofton, Robert de Crofton, John de Crofton and Clement de
Crofton. They had lands in Carlisle and Birkscewgh which corruptly
they call Braskowgh and Briscoe. One Robert de Briscoe marryed the
heire of Crofton, whose posteritye in the issue male have enjoyed
the same, and at this day John Brisco an infant, filius Willelmi, filii
Johannis, filii Roberti (which Robert was slaine at Sollom-moss) is
lord thereof.⁶ They were called de Birkscewgh because their first
auncestor dwelt at Birkskewgh or Birtchwood, a place by Newbiggin
in a lordshipp belonging to the priory of Carliell which land they
enjoyed then.⁷ And when Gualo, cardinall of St Martin in K. John's

---

1 Part 2 is paginated separately, starting afresh at p. 1. The figure in round
brackets is the later, consolidated pagination of Machell MSS Vol. VI, in which
the transcripts of Denton's history are bound.
2 At the head of the page in M, in the hand of William Nicolson. On the previous
folio of M, also in Nicolson's hand, are pedigrees showing the descent of the
manors of Cardew and Great Dalston, headed 'Before the 2nd part of Mr
Denton's MS in a copy lent to me (W. Carliol) by Mr Bird of Brougham, Jun. 3
1708, there are these pedigrees.' The pedigree for Cardew is of some interest,
as it is headed by Thore and Thorfin, strongly suggesting that the compiler
was aware of the reference to Thorfynn mac Thore as a landholder in Cardew
and Cumdivock in the eleventh-century Gospatric's writ (see *PNC*, III, p.
xxvii). I am grateful to David Parsons for drawing my attention to this. It is
striking that Denton's account of Cardew (below, D 9) gives no indication that
he was aware of Gospatric's writ.
3 Crofton (NY 30 49).
4 Denton's interpretation is correct: see *PNC*, I, pp. 154–5.
5 H: 'Gillmartin'. W. G. Collingwood reported a reference to 'Gill martyne
ridding prope Crofton' *temp.* John (cited in *PNC*, I, p. 157) but the source has
not been traced.
6 For the Brisco family, see below, note 19.
7 H: 'enjoy yet.' Denton is referring to Brisco (NY 42 51), which derives from OE

tyme, and after him Randolph in King Hen. 3 time made < distribu-
tion >[8] of the lands belonging to the church of Carliell betweene the
bishopp and the prior (which till then were holden pro indeviso till
the said cardinall, as legate from the pope, devided them), the said
first named John de Crofton held the same land in Briskoe as a freeholder.[9] They give to their armes three grey houndes sable currant
in a field de or, which as I think the harrold devised alluding to the
word vriskogh[10] which in the Brittish tongue implyeth < agility >[11]
or leeping, from which word the Saxons tooke their word to frisk
or leape.[12] But their right surname is de Birkskewgh. These words
Scewgh, Schowgh, Skaw, Shaw, I have seene in auncient evidence so
differently written yet alwayes importing the name, a wood ground
standing on a hill[13] as Birkskewgh, Whinow-Skaw; the down[14] land
called in old evidence Midleskewgh and Midleskowghe;[15] three
peeces of woodland in Dalston called the Skaw, the first Skaw[16] and
Rayson-Skaw, and in old evidence Scawgh or Schowgh. John Briscoe,
grandfather to the ......, added to his coate for a creast a greyhound
sable beareing.[17]

[*p. 2 (84)*] John de Crofton gave lands to the priory of Carliell, his
< arms > was a pellican and her young ones in a nest under her.
Robert his sonne gave them land alsoe; he sealled with a lillyie pott
of those flowers.

< [*In margin of H:*] Robert Briskoe, dom' de Briskoe; Alan filius
Roberti; Jordayn filius Allani; Robert Brisko filius Jordayne; John

---

bi(e)rce + sceaga ('birch copse'): PNC, I, p. 148.
8 M: 'disturbance'.
9 For the division of properties between the see and the priory of Carlisle, see
   EEA 30: Carlisle, no. 41 and explanatory notes, p. 32–3.
10 H: 'Briskogh'.
11 M: 'agillitir'.
12 Denton is presumably alluding to Welsh brysg / Gaelic brisg ('lively'), both of
   which are, however, derived from the English 'brisk'.
13 H: 'a wood growing or standing on a hill'. These names derive from the
   cognate elements OE sceaga or ON skógr, both meaning a wood or copse: PNC,
   III, pp. 489, 491.
14 H: 'skue'.
15 H: 'Schowgh'. Middlesceugh (NY 40 41), in Inglewood Forest, is probably
   meant.
16 H: 'the litle Skaw'.
17 H: 'added to his coat for a crest 2 grayhounds'. The Briscos' crest was a greyhound courant sable holding a rabbit or hare proper between his forepaws:
   CFH, p. 38.

Brisko filius Roberti anno 6to Ed. 2^{di} as appears by a release made to him by his mother of her dower;[18] Isold Brisko who married Margret sole daughter & heir of Sir Jo. Crofton, kt, anno Richardi secundi; Christofer filius Isold, lord of Crofton, Brisko & Dundraw; Robert filius Christofer; Robert filius Roberti; John filius Roberti; R. filius Johannis; Robert filius Rich', who was slain at Solemn Moss; Jo' filius Roberti; William filius John; Jo' filius Willelmi, an infant anno 1582. >[19]

[C2] **Aickton** villa quercum[20] is a mannor, towne and parish within the barrony of Burghe super <u>Sabulones</u>, the principall seat of Johan de Morvill, the second daughter and one of the two coheires of Sir Hugh Morvill, lord of Burghe. A little hamlett there now called < Downhall >[21] (and ever soe named after the Scotts burnt it < or because placed on the of [*sic*] a downe >) was the capitall messuage of Aikton where the said Johan Morvill and her husband Sir Richard[22] Gernonns dwelt, and after them another Richard Gernonn and Hellewise his wife, he the kinsman of thelder Richard and she the daughter to John Morvill, to whom Johan gave six carracatts of land for their maintenance in franckmarriage. Johan dyed in the 31 y. of K. Hen. 3, and Helewise her daughter 34 H. 3.[23] By her death the land fell to Ada her sister and heire, late wife to Randolph Boyvill de Levyngton, and then wife to William Furnivall; the same Ada dyed 55 H. 3.[24] And after Ada, her daughter and heire Hawiss the late wife of Eustace Balioll did succeed in the inheritance of Ada and of Radulph Levington her husband, which Hawise dyed 55 H. 3 without issue.[25] Therefore Radulph Boyville of Levington land

---

18 This document of 1312–13 has not been located.

19 The pedigree in H continues 'Since this account: Wm. fil' Jo'; Jo' fil' Wm; Wm f' Johannis'. Genealogies of the Brisco family are given in *Visitation of the County of Cumberland … 1615*, ed. J. Fetherston (London, 1872), pp. 11–12; CRO, Machell MSS, VI, p. 631; and J. Nicolson and R. Burn, *The History and Antiquities of the Counties of Westmorland and Cumberland* (London, 1777), II, pp. 202–4. Fleming 1 MS [4], p. 68 contains a transcript of the Brisco pedigree copied from the St Bees School MS [26]. Gilpin MS (p. 239) contains a drawing of 'Sigillum Adae de Crofton' with a note by Gilpin: 'in Mr Denton's MS'.

20 Aikton (NY 27 53). Denton's interpretation is correct: see *PNC*, I, pp. 118–19.

21 M: 'Townhall'. Down Hall (NY 283 525) is meant.

22 H: 'Hugh'.

23 *recte* 54 Hen. III (1269–70): see *Cal. IPM*, I, nos. 106 (Joan de Morvill, 1247), 738 (Helewisa wife of Richard de Wernune, 1270).

24 Inquisition, 1271: *Cal. IPM*, I, no. 752.

25 Inquisition, 1272: *Cal. IPM*, I, no. 811.

fell to his six sisters and coheires, and her < sisters > 4th part (viz:) the moiety of her grandmother's moiety of the Morvills lands in Burghe and Kirkoswald to Thomas de Multon de Gilsland. And the mannor of Aikton and the other 4th part of Burgh baronny to Roger filius Walter Colvill and Margarett his wife, in the right of the said Margarett by desent (as some think) from Hawise; but it seemes otherwise, for the land is found to be holden of the lords of Burghe afterwards, and not of the king immediately.[26] After Roger succeeded Edward Colvill his sonne and heire (the 14 Ed. 1), lord of Aikton.[27] His mother Margarett dyed 9 E. 3, and then Robert Colvill son or kinsman to Roger was found heire.[28] In the 23 of Ed. < 3 >[29] Thomas Daniell dyed lord of the same and th'other lands in Burghe then in the right of Issabell his wife, the heire of Colvill, and left his daughter Margarett a child of three yeares age his heire,[30] who in the 4th y. of K. Ed. 3[31] entayled the land to theirs males of John Ratcliff her husband and hers. The remainder to Richard their son for life; after to the heires males of [*p. 3 (85)*] Robert, Thomas, Richard and John, sonnes of the said Richard successively; after to the heires males of Henr' filius Kather' de Cliftley; after to the heires mailes of John the sonn of William Radcliffe of Longfeild; after to the heires males of Robert filius Willelmi filii Ricardi Radcliffe; after to the right heires of Margarett Daniell, the grandmother, for ever.[32] She dyed 44 Ed. 3.[33] Afterwards those lands and mannor were sold in the tyme of King H. the 6th to the Lord Thomas Dacre, father of Humphred, by Sir John Savage, kt, in whose blood they continue till this day and soe are become demeasne of the lord paramount of Burgh and united to the auncient segniory from whence they were devided

---

26 The inquisition taken on the death of Roger de Colevill in 1288 does not mention any part of the barony of Burgh. He held the manor of Aikton by free marriage with his wife Margaret, 'who ought to hold it of the king in chief by cornage and render 13s 3d yearly': *Cal. IPM*, II, no. 688.

27 14 Edw. I = 1285–6. Roger's son is named Edmund in the 1288 inquisition: ibid.

28 Inquisition, 1335: *Cal. IPM*, VII, no. 653.

29 M, erroneously, gives the date as 23 Edward I.

30 Inquisition, 1349: *Cal. IPM*, IX, no. 193. Thomas Daniell held Rockcliffe, but not Aikton, jointly with Isobel his wife. Cf. FF Cumb. 22 Edw. III [1348–9] (*CW2*, 7 (1907), p. 239, no. 263), by which Robert de Cohull of Bitham, knight, and Cecily his wife conveyed the manor of Aikton and land in Burgh by Sands to Thomas Danyers, knight.

31 *Sic; recte* 40 Edw. III (1366–7).

32 FF Cumb. 40 Edw. III [1366–7] (*CW2*, 7 (1907), p. 240, no. 278).

33 44 Edw. III = 1370–1. Margaret Daniel (b. 1348) came of age in 1362: *Cal. IPM*, XI, no. 386. No inquisition *post mortem* has been located.

by the partition of Sir Hugh Morvill's daughters, Ada first wife of
Richard Lucye and after of Thomas Multon, and Johan Morvill wife
of Richard Gernonn aforementioned, in the tyme of King John. < It is
now in the queen's hands by the attainder of Dacre, lord of Burghe. >

[C3] **Parton**,[34] a manner and towneshipp soe called, adjoyneth to the
west side of Crofton and is devided from the same by a rill called
Cattbeck. It lyes betweene the river of Wampole on the south and
the Powbeck on the north, extended from Cattbeck unto the Karrs-
mouth, where the rill called Powbeck falls into Wampole. The first
lords after the Conquest tooke their surname of the place and towne
and were called Parton. Th'eldest lyne of ..... of by a daughter transferred th'inheritance to one Richard Mansell whose son and heire
John Mansell sold the same to Robert Mulcaster, who gave the same
to Robert de Grinsdale in H. 3 tyme.[35] Robert Grinsdale had issue
Gilbert Grinsdale who had issue Allane and Robert; Allane by his
wife Margery had issue Thomas and Henry who dyed without issue
of their bodyes. Therefore their lands att Carliell fell to Sir William
de Arthurett kt, and Marriott their sister, his wife, after the death
of Henry Grinsdall, her brother, as heire generall. But Parton fell to
Margarett the wife of Gilbert Pepper in Ed. 3 tyme, another heire of
the Grinsdales, who dyeing without issue, for that she was of half
blood, her part fell to Robert Grinsdall. Marriott made John Denton
of Cardew her heire, and Margarett gave her part to Robert Roose
her second husband, whose nephew and heire Richard Roose [*p. 4
(86)*] sold the same to John Carliell, parson of Kirkland. [*In margin of
p. 3:* Robert Roose fr[atr]es Tho' Roose de Kendall milit'; Rich' Roose
filius Thomae]. His brother's son,[36] Robert filius Roberti Carliell, sold
to William Denton the sonne and heire of John Denton aforesayd the
moietye of Parton, whose posteritye in the issue male enjoy the same
at this day.[37] The mannor and towne < containeth >[38] the hamletts of
Parton, Micklethwaite, Whinhew and Whinshill; and Dromblening

---

34 Parton (NY 27 50).

35 The dating of this sequence of events appears to be incorrect, since John Maun-
    seyl, son and heir of Richard Maunseyl, did not release his right to lands in
    Parton to Robert de Mulcaster until 1308: CRO, D/Lons/L5/1/55, D.2(a).

36 H ends the previous sentence here.

37 The sale by Robert son of Robert Carlell of Carlisle can be dated to 1429, when
    he and his mother Margaret, widow of Robert Carlell, released their interest
    in half the manor of Parton to William de Denton of Carlisle: CRO, D/Lons/
    L5/1/55, D52, D55.

38 M: 'conteining'.

was parcell of the same mannor untill the lord paramount purchased
the same of Thomas < Briscoe, >[39] heir generall to John Dalston,
sometyme freeholder of lands in Parton. All Parton is in the parish
of Thursbye, saveing that Dromleyning[40] which is in the parish of
Aikton, <u>and now doeth service to the mannor of Aikton</u>. It is called
corruptly Dromleyning; the right name thereof is the Myer-dromble-
heyning, < i.e. > the frith or freed-spring of the bittures.[41] Wee call a
bitture a myer-dromble because she haunteth myres, fennes, boggs
and < carrs >,[42] and for that she hath a thundering voyce which we
call rombling, and a wood new cutt for springing, a frith, a spring,
a heyning, of the word heyned, which signifies freed or spared or
forborne.[43]

[C4] **Gamelsby**[44] is the next towne to Parton, and standes upon the
north side of the river of Wampole, betweene it and the feilds of
Aikton. It conteines the two hamletts of Gamelsbye and Bigglands,
which is soe called <u>Bigglands</u> of that kind of graine called beer
or barley[45] which <u>plentifully</u> growes their, <u>which kinde of graine
Cumberland calls bigg and thereupon the hamlett is named Bigg-
lands</u>. Those two hamletts were aunciently a mannor. The cheife
capitall messuage stood att Gamelsbye, which was soe called of one
Gamell that first builded there.[46] It was aunciently parcell of Burgh
and granted forth to William Brewer by the baronns of Burgh, to be
holden as a part of the same mannor, as the baron held the rest of
the king. It is called in auncient evidence Gamelsby iuxta Aicton,
therefore not de Aicton nor within the bounders [*p. 5 (87)*] of the
same. Before Gamell built there it was a woodie waste haunted
with deere. The next lord thereof that I read of was one Adam de
< Crookdayke >[47] who had it by fine of William Brewer.[48] After it

---

39 M: 'Birko'.
40 Drumleaning (NY 271 518).
41 i.e. bitterns.
42 M: 'karch'.
43 Denton's ingenious interpretation is almost certainly incorrect: Drumleaning
    is a Gaelic place-name, *druim-Linán* ('Linán's ridge'): *PNC*, I, p. 119.
44 Gamelsby (NY 258 524).
45 H: 'beer-barley'. Biglands (NY 256 532) lies north of Gamelsby. Denton's inter-
    pretation is probably correct: *PNC*, I, p. 120.
46 Like Gamblesby (below, section D11), Gamelsby contains the Scandinavian
    personal name Gamall: *PNC*, I, p. 119.
47 M: 'Crookdale'
48 FF Cumb. 23 Edw. I [1294–5] (*CW2*, 7 (1907), p. 230, no. 158), where Brewer's
    name is rendered 'Breouse'.

descended by two daughters to the familyes of the Raughtons and of those Bevills which were lords of West Linton, and therefore called de Levington or Linton. Raughton's part descended to a daughter named Katherine, the wife of John Aspilon, a Buckinghamshire man, who sold the same to the Warcopps, who sold the same to the Crackenthropps or Southaikes, who exchanged the same with the Dentons of Cardew for their land in Skelton.[49] One of the posteritye of the Dentons sold the same of late to the severall inhabitants and tennants of that part, who now enjoyeth the same. And the other moiety, the Levingtons' part, descended long in the heir maile, till by a daughter the same was transferred to one Alexander Highmore of Harbybrow, whose heire sold the same to the Lord Dacres. And it is now in the queene's hand by the attander of the Lord Dacres.[50]

[C5] **Wathinpoole**[51] or Wampoole is next unto Bigglands & Gamelsbye, and is soe called of the river Wampoole because it standeth upon the bancks of the same. The eldest that I read of that were lords of the same was one Robert Brunne the son of Radulph, which was called Robert de Wathinpole. He married Margarett the daughter and heire of Richard de Trute,[52] lord of Newbye beneath Carliell. She confirmed Newby to the abbey of Holm Cultram, being

---

49 The exchange took place in 1522, when Robert Warcop and Elizabeth his wife exchanged property, including 2 messuages in Gamelsby and 3 tenements in Biglands, for one-sixth of the manor of Skelton with William Denton of Cardew: CRO, D/Van, Skelton deeds, 18 June 1522. A detailed descent of the manor of Gamelsby, drawn up by John Denton from escheats in the Tower of London, survives in CRO, D/Lons/L5/1/55, D.2. The manor was divided after the death of John Crookdake in 1322–3, the moiety described above passing to John Tolson (d. 1347–8), son of Robert, son of Roger Tolson and Julian his wife, aunt of John Crookdake. It descended through John Tolson's daughter, Eleanor, wife of John Raughton (d. 1369–70) to Katherine, wife of John Apsilon and was sold in 1437–8 by Katherine Apsilon, wife of Thomas Manington to Robert Warcop.

50 H: '… attainder of the heirs of the said Dacres'. Denton's more detailed account of the descent of this moiety states that it passed from John Crookdake (d. 1322–3) to Christian wife of Michael Apulby, daughter of Crookdake's aunt and co-heir Christian, wife of Robert Castlecarrock. It descended in the female line through Christian, wife of William Ritson, and their daughter Mariot, wife of Thomas Allonby, to their daughter who was the wife of John Levington of Westlinton. After her death it passed to Elizabeth wife of Alexander Highmore, who held it at his death in 1478–9: CRO, D/Lons/L5/1/55, D.2.

51 Wampool (NY 241 546).

52 H: 'Richard fil' Trute'.

covert baron,[53] therefore Harrey de Wampoole, Robert de Dunbraton, William de Feritate and Radulph his brother were her pledges for that assureance.[54] The familye of that place tooke their surname and were called Wathinpooles. Afterwards the Warwicks of Warwick were lords thereof, whose heire Richard Warwick lately sold the same to the inhabitants, who <u>now</u> are lords of the freehold. It is held of the baronny of Burgh. It was aunciently a demeasne but now devided into foure tenements. [*In margin:* Blennerhassett i; Dacre i; Warwick ii.] Warwick's moiety descended from Thomas de Whitrigg, knight; Blennerhassett part from William Arthurett, k[night], heir to Adam de Crofton,[55] <u>viz. terr' q' Wm Wallas de Laithes tent'; m' et vii acr' q' Johanni ten'; v acr' q' Thom' Patronelson; di m' et vii acr' Jo Agotson tent. Itum m' et xvi acr q' Wm Fitz Ada; m' et vii acr' q' Robert de Wampole tent; in[56] et 5 acr q idem Robert tent et alia di' m' et vii acr' q' Jo. Agatson ter' fuit assign Adae Staffal heraed'.</u>

[*p. 6 (88)*]

[C6] **Leathes**[57] is a hamlett next unto Wampoole, and was soe called first of a graing or farm which the lord of Whitrigg had there. Of that place the familie of the Laithes tooke their surname, which aunciently well nigh the Conquest have enjoyed the same in the issue male untill Adam Leathes now owner of the demeasnes thereof sold the < tenements >[58] and the residue of that hamlett to th'inhabitants.[59] It was aunciently parcell of the demeasne of Whitrigg, and given by Robert de Dunbretton to his kinsman, whose posterityes as aforesaid were called de le Laithes. Wee call a barne for corne a leath, where-upon the place was soe called, being a very good corne soile and aunciently keept in tillage.[60] It is of the parish of Aicton.

53 A legal term, describing the status of a married woman: 'under the authority and protection of her husband': *OED*.
54 See *Holm Cultram*, p. 11 (no. 32).
55 The entry in H ends here, a dashed line suggesting that material following has been omitted.
56 *Sic* but 'm' (for 'messuagium') is presumably intended.
57 Laythes (NY 244 556).
58 M: 'tennants' but 'tenements' is clearly meant.
59 Adam Leathes (d. 1621) was founder of the Dalehead family. He bought the estate, near Keswick, in 1577 and appears to have removed there from Laythes soon afterwards: B. L. Thompson, 'The Leathes family of Dalehead', *CW2*, 60 (1960), pp. 112–13.
60 Denton's explanation is correct: the name is ON *hlaða*, 'a barn': *PNC*, I, p. 119.

[*In margin:*] Robt filius Roberti de Dunbreton dedit Lathes Henr' fratri suo anno Henr. 3, 1.[61] < Robt filius Henrici de le Leaths; Willm: Ed. 3; Richard: Ed. 3, Ric. 2; Robert: H. 6; Robert; Ed. 4; Robert: H. 7; Edward: H. 8; Robert; H. 8; Lawr' & Jo' fra. 4 Eliz; Adam: 12 Eliz; Thomas: 42 Eliz; Christofer: 20 Jac; Thomas: 3 Caro. >[62]

[C7] **Whitrigg**[63] or the Whiteridge, a great long white rigg upon the bancks of Wathinpoole, was soe called of the waste ground there fashioned like a corne rigg.[64] It was first inhabitted by the Bruns, which were aunciently a great familie. Whiterigg was the inheritance of Robert de Dunbretton, soe called because he dwelt att Dunbretton, but his surname was Brun; his posterlye were called Whiteriggs of the place. Another hamlett belonging to the same is called Whiterigg-Leyes which was the pasture ground and leye of Whiterigg when it was demeasne.

Towards the sea coast at the foote of Wampoole, stood an old village called Caer-Durnok, a British name which signifies the towne of the thornes,[65] of a wood there then all of thornes, which was long after called the Eyen Thornes, or old thornes; and now are all wasted away. In the place where they did grow stands now a village called yet Ainthorne.[66] There is also a hamlett called Lang-crofts, parcell of Whiterigg, soe called of the long ridges of land which lye betweene the towne and Wampoole.[67] There is another village called Finland, Fingland and Fenneland, which is almost envirorned with a moss or fenny ground.[68] All these were the Brun lands and did belong unto and were parcell of their mannors of Bowness and Drombughe.

< These Brunes in a short time became devided into 5 families; there first seat was at Brunskeugh called also de feritate of there being so neer the waists; att Drumbough, Whitrigg, Leathes & Wampool. >[69]

61 H: 'Robt de Dunbreton alias Brune dedit Leathes Hen. fra suo anno Hen. 3.'
62 For the later generations of the Leathes family, see Thompson, 'Leathes family of Dalehead', pp. 109–19.
63 Whitrigg (NY 22 57).
64 Denton's interpretation of the name is correct: *PNC*, I, p. 126.
65 Cardurnock (NY 17 58). The modern interpretation of the name is British *caer* + *dornoch* ('fort at the pebbly place'): *PNC*, I, pp. 123–4.
66 Anthorn (NY 19 58) is ON *ein* + *þorn* ('solitary thorn tree'): *PNC*, I, pp. 123.
67 Longcroft (NY 21 58).
68 Fingland (NY 25 57). Early forms of the place-name do not favour derivation from 'fen'. ON *þing* ('assembly') or Irish *fionn-ghleann* ('white glen') have been suggested: *PNC*, I, p. 125.
69 This paragraph is inserted in H in a different hand.

[*p. 7 (89)*]

[C8] **Bowness**[70] is a common name to the mannor, towne and parish of Bowness. One of the first barons of Burghe after the Conquest gave the same to Gamell de Brunne. It conteines on the north side where the sea flowes upp into the river of Eden, the towne of Bowness it selfe, Glasson, < Drumbugh >[71] and Easton, where the bounder of the same crosseth over southward on the east side of Fingland and Whiterigg untill Wathempoole, and conteyneth all the fore remembred townes of Whiterigg < part in Aikton parish >,[72] Whiterigg Lees, Langcrofts, Fingland, Ainthorne and Cardronock, all which make a great poinct of land into the sea, thrusting in betweene the waters of Wampoole and Eden; a goodly mannor whilest it was intire, but now devided into severall parts. Bowness was aunciently called Bulgeum-blatum of the Romanes, who, as I think, framed this word Bulgeum of a word now in use with us, Bulge, which signifieth a breaking in, as the sea, there swelling, breakes in.[73] But whereof they took this word Blatum I cannott perceive unless of that place in Scottland a little from Tordoff called Blawtwood, which soundeth[74] the sea swelling in at Blawth. But this name Bowness as some have thought was given to the place Noose, which the Scotts and this countey[75] call Neese. They commonly call a point of land into the sea a neese, and for that it makes a crooked point < in > the sea att Bowness like a bow, it is called Bowness, which signifieth a crooked poynt. Others have written it Bowlness as a word made of bowling which is swelling, and the said word ness a point; for that often-tymes the tyde comeing with a wind the sea breakes in att that point with great furie.[76]

---

70 Bowness-on-Solway (NY 22 62).

71 M: 'Drunnbugh'. Drumburgh is meant.

72 This phrase, which appears both in the body of the text and in the margin of H, is only in the margin of M.

73 Denton is following Camden's identification of Bowness on Solway with 'Blatum-bulgium'. Camden, however, suggested that the second element derived from a British word, *Bulch*, 'that signifieth a separation': *Britannia*, p. 775.

74 H: 'boundeth'. Thomas Denton's borrowing from John Denton's account (Denton, *Perambulation*, p. 210) reads 'sundereth', which may be the sense intended.

75 H: 'they Scots and this country people'

76 The elements in the place-name Bowness are OE *boga* or ON *bogi* ('a bow') and OE *naess* or ON *nes* ('headland'), meaning a 'rounded or bow-shaped headland': *PNC*, I, p. 123.

Howsoever it was called, it was a most auncient thing < and great
buildings > as appeareth by the auncient foundacions and paved
streets which are daily found in the common fields by the inhabitants. It is seated att the west end of that memorable Romane work
called the Picts-wall. The church is placed at Bowness, but the capitall messuage is seated at Drumbugh where the said Gamell Brun
and his posteritye dwelt. It is called Drumbugh of that fennish myre
or bogg, then full of shrubbs and haunted with bitternes which the
people call myre drummes [*p. 8 (90)*] or myre drumnle, soe as that
word Drumbogh signifieth the bittures' fenn.[77] The next hamlett to
it is Easton for that it is the eastermoste towne of that mannor. The
other hamlett, Glasson, was soe named by the Irish inhabitants being
a greene at the river side. Glass is in Irish green, and Oan a river.[78]
That place gave surname to a gentleman named Glasson, som of
whose[79] race builded att Glassonbye beside Kirkoswold, nameing
the place after his name Glassonbie. The last of that name William
de Glasson, who held <u>Glasson of Robert Brunne de le Feritate, lord
of</u> Bowness, forfeited the same, being outlawed for the death of one
Patrick Tayler the 6 yeare of Edw. 1.[80]

After the foresaid Gamell de[81] Brunne, divers of the Brunes were lords
of Bownes successively, as Robert, Radulph, < Robert >, Richard.
One of the said Robertts and Radulph his father had a mansion
house without Eden nye a bush of wood, called therefore Brunes
skeugh or Brun'swood where the towne of Brunskewgh now standeth.[82] And for that the same is seated towards the wylde wastes, they

---

77 Drumburgh (NY 26 59) is probably from the Old Welsh *drum* ('a ridge') with
an uncertain second element (perhaps *bwch*, 'buck') which has been confused
with OE *burh* ('fortified place'): *PNC*, I, p. 124.

78 Glasson (NY 25 60). In this instance, Denton's suggested interpretation of the
place-name is broadly accepted by modern scholars: *PNC*, I, p. 125.

79 H: 'one of whose'. In M 'and whose' has been altered to read 'som of whose'.

80 6 Edw. I = 1277–8. See *Calendar of Inquisitions Miscellaneous*, I, no. 1104. The
manor had been in the king's hand for 'a year and a day' in June 1278. It
was ordered that it should be delivered to Robert de la Ferete the following
September: *Cal. Close Edward I*, I, p. 477.

81 H: 'le'.

82 A reference to Brunstock (NY 41 59), near Carlisle. The origin of the name
is unclear, but the second element is not *skógr* ('wood') but ON *skeið* ('race
course' or, more probably in this instance, 'boundary'). The first element is
probably *bruni* ('burning'), rather than the personal name *Bruni*: G. Fellows-
Jensen, *Scandinavian Settlement Names in the North West* (Copenhagen, 1985),
p. 111; cf. *PNC*, I, p. 109.

were called de le Feritate, but their surnames were Bruns. Their lands were devided amongst three copercioners, the daughters and heires of Richard Brunes, the last of that name. One of them named Hellen was marryed to the house of Workington; another to the Harringtons of Harrington; and another to Bowett < ..... >, whose posteritye sold the same to Elles, who yet enjoyeth that third part in Bothell, but hath sold his part in Bowness parish to Robert Graham of the Fold.[83]

[*p. 9 (91)*] The next hamlett to Easton in the parish of Bowness is Bowsteedhill, soe named of a bow < of >[84] kine there keept for their dairie by the lords of Burgh;[85] and next unto Bowsteed hill is a hamlett named Langbarugh, soe named of the auncient word bargh which signifieth a riseing ground;[86] both which were auncient demeasne to Burgh, and their pasture ground, and now for better strength of the borders letten foorth to tennants. [*In margin:* And without Lambargh now a hamlett called Dykesfeild, which gave name to the Dykes, a familye of gentlemen.] Next to the same stands Burgh it selfe,[87] where the barons of Burgh had a capitall messuage, the ruines whereof are seene yett at the east end of the towne. And betweene Burgh and the sands was a mannor house [*In margin:* called yet the Sands-feild][88] where one Henry de Sands a gentleman resided[89] and held there of the barons of Burgh a carrucate and a halfe of land in demesne, of which place he, his auncestors and posteritie took their surname, and were called in old evidences de Sabulonibus, whose issue male is now lord of [*Rottington*];[90] but that their mannor house

---

83 According to *CFH* (p. 44), the heiresses of le Brun were the sisters of Robert le Brun: Elena (d. *c.* 1395), whose second husband was Sir William Curwen (d. 1403) of Workington; Margaret, wife of Sir William Lengleys; and Elizabeth, wife of Thomas Bowet. In 1633 Robert Graham's grandson, George Graham of the Fold, released his rights in Bowness and Cardurnock to Thomas, earl of Arundel: H. Warne (ed.), *The Duke of Norfolk's Deeds at Arundel Castle – catalogue 1: Dacre estates in northern counties* (Chichester, 2006), p. 79.
84 M: 'or', presumably in error.
85 The modern interpretation derives Boustead Hill (NY 29 59) from OE *burhstede* ('fortified place'): *PNC*, I, p. 127.
86 Longburgh (NY 308 588). Denton's interpretation is correct: the second element is OE *beorg* or ON *berg*, 'a hill': *PNC*, I, p. 128.
87 Burgh-by-Sands (NY 32 59).
88 Old and New Sandsfield (NY 33 61) stand on the Eden estuary at the mouth of Powburgh Beck.
89 'resided' is interlined.
90 M: 'Rottingham'; H: 'Kottington'. Rottington (NX 96 13), near St Bees, is meant.

and the lands belonging to the same lyes now waste and are the
pasture grounds belonging to the inhabitants of Burgh. Next unto
Burgh towards Carliell is a little hamlett called Woormorbye or
Woormanbye, soe named of the first inhabitants there.[91] On a faire
hill next unto it stands the towne of Beaumont, < so > named of the
faire hill from whence lyeth every way a goodlie prospect, which
gave occasion of the name.[92] It was aunciently a mannor belonging
to the Brunnes, lords of Bowness, who were patrons of the church;
but of latter tymes the barons of Burgh have bought it of the coheires
and granted the towne foorth in customary tennants.[93]

Next unto Beamont standes the parish & towne of Kirkanders[94] [*In
margin:* It tooke name of the church dedicated to St Andrew], which
the auncient lords of Burgh, as I think, with the < service > of the
mannor of Orton did aunciently grant unto the baronns of Levington
and severed the same from the baronny of Burgh; soe they lye not
within the same and are not part thereof.

Upon the next office found by inquisition after the makeing of the
statute of Magna Carta in Henry the third's tyme the barron's lands
of Levington, wheresoever they did lye were found to be one baronny
by inquisition, as other men's [*p. 10 (92)*] lands were then < that >
were holden in capite of the king, as Lessingby which is distant some
six miles yet is found to be parcell of Burgh; and Skelton soe farr
remote from Kirklevington yett soe found to be parcell of the same
barrony of Levington.[95] The lords of Burgh have annexed < Kirk-
Andrews >[96] towne againe unto the segniory of Burgh; but Orton is
holden still of Levington yett lyes in Burgh.[97]

---

91 Wormanby (NY 336 588). The name is a compound of ON *by* ('settlement') and
a personal name, perhaps Middle English *Wilmer* or *Winmer*: PNC, I, p. 128.
92 Beaumont (NY 34 59). Denton is correct: the name is the Norman-French *beau
mont* ('beautiful hill'): PNC, I, p. 121.
93 Text in M runs on but a line has been drawn between the entries for Beaumont
and Kirkandrews.
94 Kirkandrews-on-Eden (NY 35 58), taking its name, as Denton states, from the
dedication of the church: PNC, I, pp. 141–2.
95 Skelton and Kirkandrews were *disjecta membra* of Kirklinton barony: see
T. H. B. Graham, 'The Levingtons of Kirklinton', CW2, 12 (1912), p. 61; PRO,
C132/10/15 (inquisition after death of Richard de Levington, 1250).
96 M: 'Kirkland', clearly in error.
97 Text runs on in M.

Next unto Kirkanders lyes Grinsdall,[98] a parish, towne & mannor within Burgh baronny & holden of the same. It gives surname unto a familye of gentlemen called Grinsdall. The most auncient of that name that I read of is one Udard de Grinsdall, and after him Asktill filius Roberti de Greensdall; they lived in the tymes of Henry the first, Stephen and Henry the second. The eldest lyne failed about King John's tyme when th'inheritance fell to two daughters, whereof one was marryed to the lord of Newton in Allerdale; one Thomas de Newton held it by that right, the moiety of Greensdall of Thomas Multon, lord of Burgh, in Henry the third's tyme. And the other moiety was then soe holden by one William de la Sore, whose auncestor had married th'other coparcener.[99] A second brother of Asktill named Robert was a citizen of Carlisle and became an inheritor of lands there and in Perton,[100] which descended according to the pedegree in the mergent,[101] untill the coparceners and their heires sold the same to the Dentons of Cardew in Henry the fowerth's tyme, whose issue male enjoyeth the same at this day. Newton's moiety of Grinsdall fell by marriage to Martindall, and to one of the Dacreses named Richard Dacres, in the right of his wife as coheire of Martindall. His issue William Dacre & himselfe for following Leonard Dacre in the last[102] rebellion lost the same & now it is in the queen's hand by attainder. Th'other is Michaell Studholme's lands, filius Ricardi filii Johannis filii Johannis filii Ricardi filii Nicholai[103] filii Johannis filii Richardi filii Willelmi, who bought the same of the lord of Kirkanders[104] filius et heres Johannis de Parton et Kirkanders, anno domini < E. 3. 10 >.[105]

[*In margin:*] Udard; Robert; Asktill; Robt fr'Asktill; Gilbertt; Robert; < Gilbert; >Alane; Henry; Marriott & Margarett.

It is called Greensdall or Grinsdall for that the townefeilds was aunciently a low greene bottome < valley >[106] or dale by the river

---

98   Grinsdale (NY 36 58).
99   The two moieties of Grinsdale were held by Thomas de Newton and William de Sore in 1271: *Cal. IPM*, I, no. 758.
100 H: 'Parton'.
101 Printed at the end of this paragraph.
102 H: 'late'.
103 H: 'fil' Michaelis'.
104 H: '… of John de Kirkandrews'.
105 10 Edw. III = 1336–7.
106 M: '[.....]Allyes'.

side of Eden.[107] That race of gentlemen are worne out unless the Greensdalls be of their posteritye.

[*p. 11 (93)*]

[**C9**] **Orton.**[108] Above Greensdall and Kirkanders more towards the south stands Orton or Overton, which name is common to the parish, mannor and towne, being named of the scituation and higher standing of that place in respect of Kirkanders and the lower townes towards Eden and the border of < the > countey.[109] It is parcell of the < barony >[110] of Levington and holden of the same and gave surname to a familye of gentlemen of mark called Orton.[111] They gave for armes vert a lyon rampant argent crowned and armed gules. The first of that name I read of was Symon, who had issue Allan de Orton to whom King Henry the third granted free warren in Orton.[112] After him succeeded John his son (they were all knights), and after him Gyles whose daughter and heire Johane was wife to Sir Clement de Skelton, to whom she had fower daughters and heires; one named Agnes married to the Lighes of Issall; another named .... to Bellases; another named [*Alice*] marryed to Ridley; the fowerth to Blennerhassett. They devided the mannor into three partes which Lighe, Ridley and Blennerhassett enjoyed and charged the land with a rent of viii[li] to Bellasses, whose heires sold the same to one Coldall, a merchant in Carliell, which Robert Brisco filius Leonardi, a younger brother's sone of the Briscoes of Crofton, yett enjoyeth, in the right of Eleoner his wife, filia Ricardi Coldall[113] filii Johannis filii Johannis.[114] And the mannor is now th'inheritance of John Briscoe of Crofton an infant, filius Willelmi, filii Johannis, which John the grandfather purchased

---

107 An alternative explanation derives Grinsdale from the ON personal name *Grennir*: *PNC*, I, p. 141.

108 Great Orton (NY 32 54).

109 Modern scholarship derives this Orton from ON personal name *Orri* rather than OE *uferra* ('higher'), which is the root of most other instances of the name: *PNC*, I, p. 144.

110 M: 'mannor'.

111 For the Orton family, see T. H. B. Graham, 'Great Orton', *CW2*, 32 (1932), pp. 38–44.

112 See *Cal. Charter R*, II, p. 76.

113 M: 'Coldan', presumably a transcription error.

114 The four daughters were Alice, who married Nicholas Ridley as her first husband; Joan, whose first husband was Ralph Blennerhasset; Agnes, who married Sir William Leigh (d. 1429); and an unnamed daughter who married ..... Bellasis. The descent of the manor is traced in C. M. L. Bouch, 'The manor and advowson of Great Orton from 1369', *CW2*, 40 (1940), pp. 46–55.

the Lighs' part from Wilfrid Lawson and Maud his wife, late wife of
Thomas Lighe, to whom he gave his lands; and of Thomas Blennerhassett of Carliell another third part; and another third part Nicholas
Ridley sold to the tennants there, whereof one sold his purchase to
Denton of Cardew, another keept his part, and the third < the > right
of patronage of the rectory. The residue sold < their >[115] parts to the
said William Briscoe, the infant's father.[116]

[*In margin:*] Symon de Orton; Allan; John; Gyles; Johan < uxor > de
Clementis Skelton.

< **[C10] Wiggonby.**[117] Next unto Orton stands Wigornby, which was
anciently the Ortons' lands, and (as I think) parcell of Orton. Yet I
have seen offices that have found it a manner of itselfe. It descended
with the Ortons' lands as Orton did to the coheirs. Lighe sold his
part to George Porter of Bolton; Blennerhasset yet holds his part; and
Ridley sold his part to the inhabitants. >[118]

[*p. 12 (94)*]

[C11] Bampton mag' et parva.[119] Bampton villat' Bembae vel
Bembe[120] is a townshipp within Burgh baronny. It was the principall seate of Hildred de Carliell, a knight in the tyme of King Hen.
the second.[121] The towneshipp conteynes Great-Bampton, Little-
Bampton, Ughtredby and Studholme. The rectory lyes in Great
Bampton. In the particion of Hildred's estate after his death his
grandchildren Richard and Robert the sons of Odardae filius Hildred
parted this mannor. [*In margin:* Adam de Usher mediet' Comquint
et Edmond de C aliud demid' 19 Ed. 3.[122] Adam filius Roberti filii
Odard filii Hillred dedit Hildred dedit [*sic*] ecclesiae dm' St Nicholai

---

115 M: 'the'.

116 John Brisco purchased the Lawsons' share in 1574 and Blennerhasset's in
     1580. Nicholas Ridley sold his share to 48 tenants in 1577. Some tenancies
     were re-purchased by Brisco in 1583; the remainder by William Brisco in
     1587: Bouch, 'Manor and advowson of Great Orton', p. 50.

117 Wiggonby (NY 29 53).

118 The entry for Wiggonby is missing from most Series A manuscripts.

119 Kirkbampton (NY 30 56) and Little Bampton (NY 27 55).

120 Denton appears to interpret the first element of the place-name as a personal
     name, whereas modern scholarship regards it as OE *bēam* ('tree'): *PNC*, I, pp.
     142–3.

121 Hildred of Carlisle was a key royal official in Carlisle under Henry I. He
     accounted for the farm of Carlisle in the earliest surviving Pipe Roll (of 1130)
     but was dead by 1133: Sharpe, *Norman Rule*, pp. 7–21, 64–5.

122 19 Edw. III = 1345–6. The source has not been traced.

Carliell.[123]] And Eudo de Carliell tennant of the same gave in the xi[th] of K. H. 3 fower carracatts in Uchtredby and Little Bampton to Walter de Bampton by fyne,[124] which by inquisicion taken 23 Ed. 1 was valued to xx[li] land, and to be holden of the mannor of Burgh.[125] Another part Dame Elizabeth Mountacute, countess of Sarum, held 36 Ed. 3 as of th'inheritance of Wm Mountacute, earle of Sarum;[126] and the same yeare Sir Bryan Stapleton of Bedell in Yorkshire also, as by purchase I think, whose posteritye in < H > the ..... tyme sold it to Thomas Dacre of Leonardcost, and Christopher hath now sold it into many parts to the inhabitants.[127]

Walter de Bampton, David de Marshall, Robert de Wampoll et Margarett uxor eius, filia Ricardi filii Ricardi filii Troite carracate in Cumbersdale, duo carr' in Cumbquint' 4th carr' in Uchtredbye et Bampton parva 11 Hen. 3 < per > finem levatum inter eos et Eudonem filium Adam filii Roberti filii Odard filii Hildred de Carliell.[128]

Walter filius Bernard pro heredae Ricardi filii Troite (15 Regis Jo.)[129] Robertus de Wampole pro terris Ricardi filii Ricardi filii Troite 10 Hen. 3.[130] Willelmus le Mariskall pro terr' Walter filius Bernard 10 Hen 3. Wm de Arthurett de jure Mariotae uxoris relictae Thomae Morpait medietatem de Cummersdale feofato in feodo tam cum Thomae predicto et 4 partem alterius medietatis iure hereditatis eiusdem uxoris per decessum Adae de Crofton alias de Usher sive de Marshall avunculi eius; alteram quartam partem de perquisisione ab Adamo de Stafole facta per Willelmum de Arthur[et]; et Thomas de Whitrigg tenet alias quartam partem in quabus duabus partibus ultimo dictis Newby continetur.

---

123 Adam son of Robert gave half the tithe sheaves of Little Bampton to St Nicholas' hospital Carlisle, 1204x1214: *VCH Cumb.*, II, p. 200.
124 FF Cumb. 11 Hen. III [1226–7] (*CW2*, 7 (1907), p. 220, no. 29).
125 23 Edw. I = 1294–5. This inquisition has not been traced.
126 *recte* 28 Edw. III [1354]: *Cal. IPM*, X, no. 173.
127 In margin: 'Brian Stapleton'. For Sir Thomas Dacre (d. 1565), illegitimate son of Thomas, 2nd Lord Dacre and recipient of Lanercost after the Dissolution, see H. Summerson and S. Harrison, *Lanercost Priory, Cumbria* (Kendal, 2000), pp. 44–8. The Dacres' property in Kirkbampton appears to have been at Oughterby: ibid., p. 48.
128 FF Cumb. 11 Hen. III [1226–7] (*CW2*, 7 (1907), p. 220, no. 29). This and the remaining paragraphs concerning Kirkbampton are slightly indented in M.
129 Walter son of Bernard had the wardship of the heirs of Richard son of Truite in 1213: Pipe Roll, 15 John: *VCH Cumb.*, I, p. 417.
130 10 Hen. III = 1225–6. The text in H, which is an insertion, written down the margin beside the entry for Dundraw, ends here.

Adam de Crofton et Robert de Whitrigg jun' Cumbquintin; Egli-
onby tenet nunc partem Adae Crofton et Skelton partem Roberti
Whitrigg.[131]

[*p. 13 (95)*]

[C12] **Dundragh**, collis quercum, an Irish name.[132] It is a hamlett
of the baronny of Wigton in the forest of Allerdall. Ranulph Bohun
de Meschienes, lord of Cumberland, gave < Allerdall >[133] to Waldieff fitz Gospatrick, comes Dunbar. Waldeif gave Wigton to Odard
de Logis. Odard gave Dundragh to Gilbertt his son, which place
gave surname to the said Gilbertt and his posterityye. After Gilbert
succeeded Gilbert his sonne and after him I read of one Symon de
Dundragh who lived in the 17th yeare of King Hen. the third,[134]
but whether he held the mannor or not, I know not yett; for the
4[re] daughters and heires of the second Gilbert of Dundragh did
inherit his lands in Dundraigh, Crofton, Thackthwaite & Distington,
viz. Cicilie the wife of Jordan Clapell who gave her part by fyne to
William Cundall,[135] in whose right succeeded Ralph Cundall. Matild
the wife of William Multon[136] gave her part of Distington to Thomas
filius Lambert de Multon lord of Egremont, and her part of Thackthwaite to Thomas Lucy, the son of Alice and of Alane Multon. Isold
the wife of Adam de Tinmouth, who sold her part of Thackthwaite
to Thomas Lucy, & of Distington to Thomas filius Lambert Multon.
And Adae the wife of Stephen de Crofton whose part descended by
the Croftons till the tyme of K. Hen. 4, thenceforth to the Briscoes,
which yet enjoyeth the same in Dundraigh and Crofton; and she
gave her part in Distington to Thomas Moresbye and Margarett his
wife and to the heires of Thomas; and her part of Thackthwaite to
Margarett the sister of Thomas Lucye and wife to Thomas Stanley.[137]

---

131 The indented paragraphs, underlined to show that they are missing from H,
  occur neither in Gilpin's nor in Thomas Denton's re-ordered transcripts (MSS
  [11], [13b]), perhaps suggesting that they are additions to the original text.
132 Dundraw (NY 21 49). Modern scholarship interprets the name as a compound
  of Welsh *drum* or Gaelic *druim* ('ridge') and ON *drag* ('steep slope'): *PNC*, I,
  pp. 139–40.
133 M: 'all'.
134 17 Hen. III = 1232–3. The source has not been traced.
135 FF Cumb. 40 Hen. III [1255–6] (*CW2*, 7 (1907), p. 226, no. 101).
136 H: 'Millon'.
137 See above, Distington (A27); Loweswater (A25) for Thackthwaite.

[C13] Baronia de Gilsland.[138] The great barony of Gilsland was given by the Earle Randulph Mescheins to one Hubertus de Vallibus, soe called of the word vallis or vaulx, which signfies dales, where-upon that countey was first called Gilsland, being full every where of those little < gills >.[139] That French word Vaulx, pronounced Vaus, became thenceforth a surname unto the said Hubbert and his poster-itye there, and to divers other families that tooke their begining from [*p.14 (96)*][140] younger brothers of his house, as Vaulx of Tyremane, of Ainstipligh, of Catterlen, of Caldbeck.

Hubertus was a kinsman or follower of the sayd Earle Randolph in the latter end of the Conqueror's tyme, when the peace of the countey begun to be established, and served under the earle's brother William Meschiens there in Gilsland. After he was possessed of the baronny peaceably he gave divers parcells thereof by the name of mannors as Denton in Gilsland to one Wescopp, Farlam to one Wesfalan, [*Corby*][141] to one Odard and divers other mannors and lands there some to the auncient inhabitants and others to his friends and kinsmen. Such as he soe preferred he bound them by allyance and marryages to his house and by all other good meanes he could devise. Yett his new reconciled enemies continued but a short tyme his friends, for in King Stephen's tyme (when the Scotts under their King David and Earle Henrey Fitz David possessed the countey of Cumberland) they stood with the auncient heir one Gillesbeuth or Gill filius Bueth, against Hubbert's tittle to Gilsland. But afterwards (when Henry FitzEmpress obtained the crowne of England and tooke Cumberland againe from the Scots) one Robert de Vallibus, son of the sayd Hubbert, entered to the barony of Gilsland and enjoyed the same peacablly. He kil'd the said Gill at a meeting which they call a trist, for which act he became greatly repentant, and therefore for expiacion he founded the priory of Lannercost in Gilsland.[142] This Robert Vaulx was a valerous gentleman and well learned in the lawes of this land, < for > he was justice itenerant into Cumberland in the 24 yeare of K. Hen. 2, with Ranulph Glanvill and Robert Piknett

---

138 The earlier sections of this second account of Gilsland repeat material in the first entry: see above, A43.
139 M: 'hills', clearly in error.
140 M: the page is wrongly numbered '97'.
141 M: 'Kirkby'; H: 'Kork'. Corby is meant: see T. H. B. Graham, 'The manor of Corby', *CW2*, 14 (1914), pp. 238–40.
142 For Gillesbueth and the tradition concerning the founding of Lanercost, see above, section A43.

his associates.[143] King Hen. 2 did little in Cumberland without the advice and councell of the said Robert de Vallibus.

The said King Hen. 2 gave againe the said baronny to Hubbert de Vallibus in haec verba [sic]: Totam terram quam Gillbertt filius Bueth tenuit et de incremento < Korkby >[144] quam < Wescubright >[145] filius Willelmi Stephen tenuit et Catterlen cum molendino q' Willitred filius Halden tenuit.[146] Afterward, about the 10 Hen. 2, Hubbert dyed, and the king remitted to this Robert xviii[li] cornage rent due out of those lands.[147] He was fyned for suffering money to be currant < in his liberties > which the king had forbid by proclamacion, and for escape of certaine prisoners.[148] Robert dyed without issue male.[149]

After succeeded Ranulph de Vallibus in the segniory of Gilsland in Rich. the first his tyme; and after Ranulph the baronny descended to his son and heir Robert de Vallibus otherwise called Robert filius Radulphi. This was the same Robert Vaux that was found tennant to the land by inquisicion [p. 15 (97)] taken in King John's tyme, remaining yet of record.[150] He confirmed to the priory of Wetherall certaine lands in < Korkby >,[151] Denton, < Newby > and Burdaswold, as lord paramount.[152] After this Robert Vaulx, his son Hubbert was barron of Gilsland, whose daughter and heire Matild or Maud

---

143 See above, A43, note 332.
144 M: 'Kirkby'. Corby ('Korkebi' in original) is meant.
145 M: 'Westnbright'.
146 The charter, of 1158, is reproduced in *VCH Cumb.*, I, opp. p. 306.
147 Pipe Roll, 11 Hen. II (1165): *VCH Cumb.*, I, p. 341. Robert de Vallibus was pardoned for £18 13s. 3d.
148 Pipe Roll, 31 Hen. II (1185): *VCH Cumb.*, I, p. 358.
149 This paragraph is written in the margin in M; in H it is placed here. In Gilpin MS, pp. 365–6 (printed in *Accompt*, p. 131) the following text links the final sentence of this paragraph with the beginning of the succeeding one: '… Robert dyed without issue male and Hugh his kinsman & next heyr succeeded him, to whom K. Hen. 2 for the better strengthening of his title confirmed the Barony of Gilsland, as appears by the old inquisicion aforesaid taken in K. John's tyme, to whom succeeded Ranulph de Vallibus …'. In the margin beside this text Gilpin noted: 'This is legible in the originall MS. but is crossed out by another tho an antient Ink, which makes Ranulph immediately to succeed Robert fil' Hub. but this seems inconsistant with the Inquisicion where Hugo not Hubert is named and therfor I have restored the MS'.
150 i.e. 'Testa de Nevill' of 1212: *Book of Fees*, p. 197.
151 M: 'Kirkby'. Again, Corby is meant.
152 *Wetheral*, no. 193. In H material from the previous paragraph is repeated in the margin here.

Vaulx, lady of Gilsland, the wife of Thomas filii Thomae de Multon
< lord of Burgh > and Adae Morvill filiae Hughonis Morvill < et
coheredis >, by whom she had issue the third Thomas Multon,
called Thomas de Multon de Gilsland, that dyed the < 23 > yeare
of K. Ed. 1.[153] By this Maud the Vaulx's lands in Cumberland were
transferred to the Multons, who enjoyed the same in the issue male
fower descents lyneally from father to son, named all successively
Thomas with some addicion. The first Thomas Multon marryed Ada
Morvill, late wife to Richard Lucy, <u>by whom she had issue Thomas
the second, called Thomas filius Thomae; and by a former wife he
had issue Lambert Multon and Alane Multon, whom he marryed to
the two daughters and coheires of Richard Lucye</u>, named Amabill
and Alice. Lambert by his wife Amabill became lord of Egremont,
and Alane by his wife Alice was lord of the moiety of Allerdall, and
the xx[th] part of Egremont.[154]

The second Thomas Multon <u>named</u> filius Thomae marryed Matild
Vaulx and by her had issue Thomas Multon de Gilsland, his heire of
Burgh and Gillsland, and two younger sonnes Edward[155] & Hubbart
to whom he gave Issall, which Hubbart bare for his armes the same
coat which the Lighes of Issall his heires by blood now give, viz. five
peeces barwise, azure & argent.

[p. 16 (98)]
[C14] Skelton.[156] Skale-towne (villa ad Skallingas), now called
corruptly Skelton, is a village in the forrest of Englewood in that
place where of auncient tyme the country people that had their
sheepe, swine and milk-beasts agghested in the forrest, had certaine
sheeles and little cottages to rest in, whiles they gathered the summer
profitts of such goods.[157] And about the tyme of Henry the first the
Boyvills, then lords of Levington, first planted an habitation there
for themselfes and afterwards sett some tennants, in whose possession it continued with their heire mailes untill the death of Randolph

---

153 Inquisition, 1295: *Cal. IPM*, III, no. 285. M gives the date, incorrectly, as 24
   Ed. I.
154 For the Multon family, see *Complete Peerage*, IX, pp. 405–8; T. H. B. Graham,
   'The de Multons of Gilsland', *CW2*, 28 (1928), pp. 157–66; C. L. Kingsford, rev.
   R. V. Turner, 'Moulton, Sir Thomas de', *ODNB*.
155 M: 'Edd'; H: 'Edw'.
156 Skelton (NY 43 35).
157 Modern scholarship sees Skelton as deriving from a Scandinavianised variant
   of OE *scylf* ('shelf or ledge') rather than ON *skali* ('hut, shieling'): *PNC*, I, pp.
   239–40.

de Levington. And his daughter and heire Hawiss the wife of Sir Eustace Balioll, knight, dying without issue of her body, the Boyvills' lands in Levington, Kirkanders and Skelton, were devided amongst the six sisters of Radulph < Levington, >[158] aunts and next heires to the said Hawise for the segniory thereof.[159] Howbeit their father Richard < de Levington > and his auncestors had given forth before that descent divers parts of the same in frankmarriage to them and others to whom it descended.

The purpart of < Euphemia >[160] wife of ..... Kirkbride there continued in her blood six descents & then Walter Kirkbride sold it to Robert Parving.[161] Sir Adam Parving, sister sonn to the said Robert, sold it to John Denton of Cardew and his posteritye enjoyed it fower descents untill they sold it to the South-aikes,[162] who held it three or fowre descents and now John < Southaik >[163] hath sold it to the land tennants and customary possessors.[164]

---

158 M: 'de Lo'.

159 On the death of Helewisa de Levynton in 1272 her aunts and co-heirs were named as Euphemia de Kirkebrid, Isabel de Twynham, Agnes de Corri, Margery de Hampton, Juliana de Carrig and Eva de Sutheayt: *Cal. IPM*, I, no. 811. See above, Kirklinton barony (A39).

160 M: 'Euphinia'.

161 FF Cumb. 9 Edw. III [1335–6] (*CW2*, 7 (1907), p. 236, no. 232). Cf. inquisition *post mortem* of Robert Parving, 17 Edw. III (1343): *Cal. IPM*, VIII, no. 458. For Robert Parving (d. 1343), see J. R. Magrath, 'Sir Robert Parvyng, knight of the shire for Cumberland and Westmorland and chancellor of England', *CW2*, 19 (1919), pp. 30–91; C. L. Kingsford and W. Ormrod, 'Parning, Sir Robert', *ODNB*.

162 The sale took place in 1522, when William Denton of Cardew exchanged one-sixth of the manor of Skelton for property in Gamelsby, Biglands, Thornby and Caldbeck with Robert Warcop and Elizabeth his wife, who then exchanged the sixth part of Skelton for other property with William Southaik of Hardrigg: CRO, D/Van, Skelton deeds: 18 June 1522, 24 July 1522. For the Southaik family, see *CFH*, p. 315.

163 M: 'S.'

164 At the time of his death in 1601, John Southaik held one-third of the manor of Skelton, presumably representing this sixth part and the third portion (see below). The sale to tenants appears to have taken place after his death: his widow Alice, son Francis and his wife Juliana obtained letters patent in Aug. 1602 to grant eight messuages and lands in Skelton to tenants: CRO, D/Van, Skelton deeds: copy inquisition 12 Jan. 1601/2; copy letters patent, 1 Aug. 1602.

The second part fell to Margery uxor Roberti de Hampton, whose nephew & grandchild William Lochard[165] filius Symon L, sold the same to John Seaton whose son Christopher forfeited his right to K. Ed. 1 and the said king gave it to Robert Clifford,[166] in whose blood it remained till George, now earle of Cumberland, sold it to the inhabitants.

[*p. 17 (99)*] The third porcion was allotted to Issabell the wife of Patrick Southaik, filius Gilberti filii Gospatricii de Workington, from which Patrick it descended to John < Southaik >[167] who sold it the customary tennants there.[168]

The 4th part one Walter Corry held in the right of Eva his wife, but their son and heire, takeing part with Robert Bruce and the Scotts against the king, forfeited his estate, which the king granted to one William Marmion.

The < 5th >[169] coheire Julian uxor Patricii Trump had issue another Patrick Trump who sold that part to Robert < Tillioll >,[170] knight.

The 6th porcion fell to Agnes the wife of Walter Twinham knight, who had issue Adam father to Walter the younger, and he sold it to Walter Kirkbride.[171]

[C15] Langrigg.[172] Langrigg is a hamlett of Bromfeild. 51 Hen. 3[173] Agnes ux' nuper Adae de feritate petit versus Adam de Feritate iii partem duarum bovat' ibidem. 9 Ed. 1[174] Agnes uxor Gilberti de Langrigg petit versus Jo. Crookdale 25 acrr' terr' 15 acr' prat' et 2s 5d reddit ibidem. Eadem versus Cecilia Tradagill iiii acr ibidem. Eadem versus Thom' de Langrigg 30 acr' terr' et xiiii prati ibidem. Agnes uxor Ranulphi de Osmunderley et Alice ux' Thomae de Laithes fil'

---

165 H: 'Lachard'.
166 For these grants to Robert de Clifford in 1306–7, see *Cal. Charter R*, III, pp. 77, 84. On Clifford's death in 1314 the property was described as one-third of Skelton, excluding the dower of Ermina de Seton, mother of Christopher de Seton: *Cal. IPM*, V, no. 533 (p. 300).
167 M: 'S.'
168 See above, note 164.
169 M: 'first'.
170 M: 'Tallioll'.
171 Below this entry in M: '20 Ed 1 placita'.
172 Langrigg (NY 16 45).
173 51 Hen. III = 1266–7.
174 9 Edw. I = 1280–1.

et hered' Thomae de Langrigg. [*interlined:* Regist' Cart' de Holme Cultram].[175]

30 Hen. 3.[176] Fines levat inter Hugh Langrigg et Matild ux' eius q' et Rich Bouch de ii partibus & bovatar' in Bromfield et de iii partes manerii de nova Sowerby habend' Hugho et Matildae et heredibus.[177]

39 Ed. 3. Johannes de Bromfeild et Thom' fil' Lother tenent terr in Langrigg et reddunt in cornage vis viiid et per vigilia maris viid velent [*sic*] per anum vli.[178]

22 Ric. 2. Thom' Lother et Rich' Egglesfield ten' 3 part' de Langrigg pro cornag' xxd et vigil' maries iid.[179]

39 Ed. 3. Jo. Brumfield tenet libere et reddit 3d et ad cornage xs iid et pro vigil maries vd et valeunt per annum vli.[180]

42 Ed. 3. Joh' Br[*ounfeld*] et Thom' Lother in Langrigg ut super. Et Jo. Br[*ounfeld*] per cert terr in Bromfield xd cornage iiis xd et vigil' maries vd Ad Anand Munciux ii mess' et et iiii bovat' ad cornage vid.[181]

[*p. 18 (100)*] 46 Ed. 3. Thom' fil' Issabell de Langrigg felo ten' mess et iiii acr in Langrigg et postea Jo. de Langrigg fil' dict' Thomae et Matild uxor eius tenner.[182]

16 H. 6th. Christofer Sowerbye ten iiii mess' et mollend' ventriticum in Langrigg ii cot' in Meldrig et Dundraw.[183]

[*p. 18 (100) contd.*]
[D1] Wetherell Cell.[184] The cell of Wetherall was first founded att the instance of Stephen first abbott of St Marie's att Yorke, the first

---

175 This interlineation may refer to Holm Cultram's grants of Bromfield Marsh, which was bounded by Langrigg Beck: *Holm Cultram*, pp. 79–82 (nos. 234–47).

176 This and the following dates are written in the margin against each entry.

177 FF Cumb. 30 Hen. III [1245–6] (*CW2*, 7 (1907), p. 223, no. 69), where the land conveyed is described as 'land in Brunefeld and a moiety of one-third of the manor of New Sowerby.'

178 Inquisition after death of Thomas de Lucy, 1365: *Cal. IPM*, XII, no. 17 (p. 20).

179 Inquisition after death of Maud, wife of Henry Percy, earl of Northumberland, 1398: *Cal. IPM*, XVII, no. 1247 (p. 471).

180 Inquisition after death of Thomas de Lucy, 1365: *Cal. IPM*, XII, no. 17 (p. 19).

181 Inquisition after death of Anthony de Lucy, 1368: *Cal. IPM*, XII, no. 233 (pp. 212–13). The holding of Amand de Mounceux is said elsewhere (*Cal. IPM*, XII, no. 17) to have been in Waverton.

182 Inquisitions, 1372, 1374: *Cal. IPM*, XIII, nos. 179, 303; *Calendar of Inquisitions Miscellaneous*, III, nos. 85, 937. Thomas son of Isabella died in 1356; his felony was the killing of William Tabard at Bromfield in 1348 or 1349.

183 Inquisition, 1438–9: *Calendarium inquisitionum post mortem sive escaetarum*, IV, p. 188.

184 The Benedictine priory at Wetheral (NY 468 542), a daughter house of St Mary's abbey, York.

yeare of William Rufus, anno domini 1086 by the Earle Randall
Meschiens who gave his mannor of Wedder-hall to the sayd Stephen
with other lands thereunto belonging in pure almes to the abbey of
York.[185] Stephen dedicated the same to God and St Mary and to St
Constantine and gave all such things as the sayd abbey held in Westmorland and Cumberland to the sayd cell or priory of Wedder-hall,
as the fishing in Eden and the milne there, the two churches of St
Laurence and St Michaell in Applebye, < all > of the gift of the Earle
Randall Meschiens, with the church of Wedder-hall & the chappell
of Warthwick and the chamber of St Constantine and two oxgangs of
land in Korkbye; of the gift of Adam the son of Swene a great baron,
the hermitage of St Andrew, on the east side of Eden; of the gift of
Ughtred the son of Lyolf, the third part of Croglin lands in Eston
and Cumbquinton, the tithe of Sowerby demaines and Scotby milne.
Of the gift of Enisant filius Walter a carracate of land in Colby. The
church of Morland and three carrucatts of land there which < Ketell
filius Eldred >[186] gave them. The church of Bromfeild, the mannor
of Salkeld and the tithe of that demaine which Waldeif the son of
Gospatrick gave with his body there to be buryed.[187]

[*p. 19 (101)*]

[D2] Blackhall[188] or Blackhill, commonly Blackhill, is the name of
the towne and mannor of Blackhill, soe called of old before it was
inhabitted, being a black heathie ground then of the auncient forrest
of Englewood,[189] and given by Henry the first to Odardus de Logis,
baron of Wigton and cittizen of Carliell, after the Flemings were
thence translated. Odardus first builded there and planted habitacions, holding part in demasne and the residue in services, some
free which he granted foorth to be holden freely; others in bondage
and villenage, some both persons and land, others land only, lett to
freemen, the persons that age called < drings >[190] and the land soe

---

185 For the history of Wetheral Priory, see *VCH Cumb.*, II, pp. 184–9. The founda-
     tion of the priory can be dated to 1101x1112: ibid., p. 184; Sharpe, *Norman
     Rule*, pp. 47 (n. 119), 54 (n. 141).
186 M: 'Kekell fil' Elred'.
187 The details of these grants appear to have been taken from the confirmation
     charter of Henry II: *Wetheral*, no. 14.
188 The name is preserved in Blackwell Hall (NY 397 528) and Blackhall Wood
     (NY 386 512), to the south of Carlisle.
189 Early forms of the name suggest that the second element is OE *h(e)all* ('hall'),
     rather than 'hill': *PNC*, I, p. 148.
190 M: 'Deing'.

holden the tenour in law is called Drengagium.[191] Blackell thus made
a mannor by Odardus and his posteritye, it descended by his issue
maile according to the pedigree of Wigton untill the tyme of Edward
the third, when Margarett de Wigton, sole daughter and heire to Sir
John de Wigton knight (last issue male of the eldest sonn of that
house) to defend her birthright was glad to give away this mannor of
Blackhill, Melmorby and Stainton, to Robert Parving, then the king's
serjeant at law, for her strength at the common law;[192] the rectory of
Wigton to the Abbey Holme for the civill law, and Wigton it selfe
to the Lord Anthony Lucy for his helpe in the country, because her
mother Idonysa Lovtot was bitterly taxed of incontinency at the
instance of Sir Richard Kirkbride next heire maile apparent to the
land. But Margarett de Wigton reserved an estate in all things but the
rectory to the heires of her body and dyed without issue.[193] Therefore
Bleck-ell fell to Sir Robert Parving who marryed Katherine the sister
of the sayd Sir Richard Kirkbride to Adam Parving (als. Peacock)
the sonne of John Peacock who married Johane one of the daughters and coheires of the sayd Sir Robertt Parvings. After Adam it
descended in the blood of the Parvings some few descents, untill
Margarett [p. 20 (102)] the wife of Thomas Boyt[194] and William Boyt
his son descended of the said Johane.[195] And Matild Walker filia
Alice Attewood and Thomas Whitelockman son and heire of Margarett Pape daughter and heire[196] to Emma wife of John Skailby, the
other daughter and coheire of the said Sir Robert Parvings,[197] sold

---

191 Drengage was an archaic form of tenure recorded widely across northern
    England. Drengs were normally free men but early records show that they
    nevertheless owed labour services. Jolliffe suggested that drengage was a
    ministerial tenure, the dreng originally being a steward holding land freely
    and supervising the services owed by a demesne township: J. E. A. Jolliffe,
    'Northumbrian institutions', *English Historical Review*, CLXI (1926), pp. 15–19.
192 FF Cumb. 7 & 8 Edw. III [1334] (*CW2*, 7 (1907), p. 236, nos. 226–7).
193 See above, section B12, note 483.
194 H: 'Boyl'.
195 H: 'John'.
196 H: 'daughters & heirs'.
197 The heirs of Robert Parvyng junior were named in 1405 as Margaret, wife of
    Thomas Bowet; Maud, formerly wife of John Walker of Cockermouth and
    daughter of Alice de Wode; and Thomas Qwytlokman, son of Margaret Pape,
    the last two being descendants of Emma de Skateby, sister of Robert Parvyng
    junior: *Cal. IPM*, XVIII, no. 1176.

the same to William Stapleton and Matild[198] his wife of whom the Lord Dacre did purchase it.[199]

[D3] Chorkby.[200] The mannor of Chorkby in Gilsland hath from the Conquest of England beene a gentleman's seate. It was given by Hubbert baron of Gilsland to one Odard to whom alsoe the Earle Randolph gave the mannor of Warthwik on the west side of the river Eden. Odard had issue Osbert and William, who succeeded in the inheritance, and granted to the house of Wedderhall the chamber of St Constantine, and < diverse > liberties in Chorkby and lands in Warthwik.[201] Osbert dyed without issue, wherefore the mannor fell to his brother William, who had issue John and Robert by his wife Osanna. John was eldest yett he seated himselfe at Warwik and lett his brother Robert possess Chorkby. William filius Odard had issue another son named Allan who was lord of Langthwaite, his brother Robert gave him lands in Warthwik, and another son called Raulf.

After Robert filius Willelmi filii Odard, I find one Adam de Chorkbye, a knight, and Allan[202] filius Roger and Osanna his wife lords thereof. < K. John in the 10th year of his reign gave Chorkby to one Henry Brebar. >[203] < In > the 23th yeare of King Ed. the first one Walter de Routhbury was lord thereof,[204] and in Ed. 2 tyme Andrew Harcla, earle of Carliel, forfeited the same to the king.[205] And in Edw. 3 tyme Richard Salkeld &c.[206]

---

198 H: 'Maryote'.
199 FF Cumb. 8 Hen. VI [1429–30] (*CW2*, 7 (1907), p. 247, no. 348).
200 Great Corby (NY 47 54).
201 See *Wetheral*, no. 38. Osbert and William had also granted fishing rights: ibid., nos. 35–6.
202 H: 'Hen.'
203 10 John = 1208–9. This sentence is placed between brackets in H. Gilpin (p. 374): 'In the MS. after Wm fil' Roger & Oswina his wife 'tis legible in the originall that [K. John in the 10 yere of his raigne gave Chorkby to one Henry Brebor] but it is expunged with fresher Ink' (square brackets as in Gilpin MS).
204 i.e. at the death of Thomas de Multon of Gilsland in 1295: *Cal. IPM*, III, no. 285, p. 185.
205 The reading of this phrase, which is not in H, is uncertain. The reading given here assumes that M reads: 'to ye k'.
206 In Gilpin MS, p. 374 an incomplete pedigree follows: 'Odard de Chorkby; Osbert filius Odard; Wm frater Osbert; Robert fitz William; *****; Adam de Chorkby; *****; Wm filius Roger & Oswina uxor; *****; Henry Brebor; *****'. Gilpin notes that this 'is expunged with fresher Ink … and with a later (but yet an auncient) hand this following pedigree [*i.e. that in the margin of M, printed below*] is subscribed in the room therof'.

[*In margin:*] Willelmus; Stephanus; Wescubright; Hubbert de Vall';
Odardus; Osbert filius Odard; Willelmus frater Osbert; Roberttus
filius Wm; Roger Lascells; Wm filius Roger et Osanna uxor; Robert
filius Wm; Alan de Lascells et Issabell uxor; Adam Lascell; Robert
filius Adam; Issabell filia, uxor Walter Routhberry; Andrew Harcla;
Rich. Salkeld.

[*p. 21 (103)*]

[D4] **Combquinton.**[207] The mannor of Combquinton was att the
Conquest the lands of Hildred a knight, to whom the Earle Randolph
gave the same and King William Rufus and Henry Beuclark a great
seignory and large possessions on the east side of the river Eden. He
dwelt at Carliell and was therefore called Hildredus de Carliell,[208]
he left that surname to that auncient familie the Carliells which were
knights successively untill Edw. 1st's tyme, when their cheife seated
himselfe in Scottland, at Kynmoont, when K. Ed. 1 invaded Scottland, at which tyme he sold most of his lands here in England. His
name was William Carliell; of him the barons Carliell in Scottland
are lyneally descended, whose heire maile of the eldest issue ended
of late in my tyme and his liveing is fallen to a daughter. But there
are yett a great number of that surname and race both in England
and Scottland.[209]

Hildred had issue a sonne named Odard who dyed in his tyme,
therefore Combquinton descended to his nephewes and grandchildren Richard Carliell & Robertt, betweene whom he devided his
lands. And this mannor, to make the particion equall, was parted
into two moietyes, which till this present tyme is not yett united, for
the Skeltons enjoy one part, the Agillanbyes another part, and the
deane and chapter of Carlisle a peece, which the cell of Wedderall
purchased in Ed. 3 tyme of Robert Parving who bought it of Edw.
Combquinton.[210]

< [*At foot of page in three columns:*] Richard had issue Robert; Robert
filius Richard; Eudo; Willelmus; Eudo; William sold to Mansel;

---

207 Cumwhinton (NY 45 52).

208 For Hildred of Carlisle, see Sharpe, *Norman Rule*, pp. 7–22.

209 For the Carlyles of Kinmont, whose male line ended with the death of
Michael, 4th Lord Carlyle in 1575, see *The Scots Peerage*, ed. J. Balfour Paul, 9
vols (Edinburgh, 1904–1914), II, pp. 369–94.

210 There is no reference to this purchase in *Wetheral* but the priory had received
grants of land in Cumwhinton in the twelfth and thirteenth centuries: *Wetheral*, nos. 14, 71, 76–83.

Richard Mansell; John Mansell; Adam le Usher et Elizabeth uxor; William Arthuret; Aglionby.[211]

[*At head of following page:*] Robert filius Odard; Adam; John; Eudo; William; Edmund de Comquinton sold it to Robert Parvinge the wood; John; Thomas Whiterig; Robert Whiterig; .... Skelton. >[212]

[*p. 22 (104)*]

[**D 5**] **Agilanby.**[213] The mannor of Agillunby (corruptly called Agli-onby), was first soe called of one Agillun that came into England with the Conqueror & into Cumberland under Randolph Meschiens. He gave name to the place of his dwelling there and named his seat or capitall mansion Agillunby, Agillun's building.[214] His alliance to the house of Warthwik or attendance under the abbott of York and priory of Wetherall preferred him to that place of his dwelling and first seat; which successively they have holden from the Conquest, and their heires maile so do at this day, without any great differ-ence or alteration of their first estate by riseing or fall. In success of tyme they withdrew themselves into Carliell and lett their mannor in tennancies, which is now become a towneshipp and is holden of Warthwik.[215] The first auncestor was called Walter Agillun, he had issue Everard and Lawrence and Werrye. Werrie had issue Elias and he Allan, father of William, who had issue Adam. John his son had issue another Adam, from whom th'inheritance descended to Thomas and these his posterytye successively, vizt: William, Thomas, John, Thomas, < Edward >,[216] John, Edward[217] and Edward now an infant.[218]

---

211 Gilpin, p. 298, at the head of a variant of this pedigree (printed in *Accompt*, p. 107): 'These following pedigrees of Hildred Carliel is in the MS. but crossed out with the same Ink with which it is writ, ideo quere'.
212 Gilpin, p. 299: 'And the pedigree of Robt fil' Odard fil' Hildred stands thus in the MS. but is likewise rased with antient Ink'.
213 Aglionby (NY 44 56).
214 Denton's interpretation of the name is correct. Aglionby contains the Norman-French personal name *Agyllun* and can probably be identified with Walter Agullon, who witnessed a charter of Hildred of Carlisle *c.* 1130: *PNC*, I, p. 158; Summerson, *Aglionbys*, pp. 17–19.
215 H: name erased.
216 M: 'Everard'.
217 M: 'John, Edward' repeated.
218 For the Aglionby family, see Summerson, *Aglionbys*.

[*In margin:*] Walter; Everard filius Walter; Lawr' frater Everard; Werricus frater Eterr';[219] Elias filius Werric'; Alanus filius Elias; Willelmus filius Allan; Adam filius Willelmi; Johannes filius Adae; Adam filius Johannis; Thomas filius Adam; Willelmus filius Thomae; Thomas filius Willelmi; Johannes filius Thomae; Thomas filius Johannis; Edwardus filius < Thomae >;[220] Johannes filius Edwardi; Edwardus filius Johannis; Edwardus filius Edwardi.

[D6] Newby.[221] Newby on the Moore, < nighe > or in the boundes of Cumbersdall, was the lands of Hildred Carliell and descended, as afore in Combquinton, untill it came to Richard filius Ricardi filii Trute, who gave the same to Reginald de Carlielli, and he gave it to th'abbey of Holme Cultram, to whom the heire of Richard filius Ricardi filii Trute (< viz. >[222] Margarett the wife of Robert de Wampole) released it, and the abbott exchanged it with the prior of Carliell.[223] Now the deane and chapter hold it of the king.

[*In margin:*] Hilde; Trute; Robertus filius Trute; Ricardus filius Trute; Ricardus filius Ricardi; Margaret[224] = Ro. Wathempole; Helwis = Jo' Crofton; John Crofton; Helena [=] Adam Crofton.

[*p. 23 (105)*]
[D7] Warthwik.[225] The mannor of Warthwik was first th'inheritance of Odard first lord of Chorkbye, who left the same to his second son William filius Odardi, and to Osbert his heire he gave Chorbye. Osbert dyed without issue, therefore William became lord of all. He had issue John & Robert and diverse other children whom he preferred. John his eldest son held Warthwik and lett his brother Robert have Chorkby. He is named in old evidence John filius Willelmi filii Odardi.

---

219 M: *sic*, for 'Everard'. H reads simply 'Werricius frater'.
220 M gives Edward son of John, presumably in error.
221 Now represented by Newby West (NY 368 538) and Newby Cross (NY 365 531) in Cummersdale.
222 M: 'by'.
223 For these charters, see *Holm Cultram*, pp. 10–11, nos. 30–36. The exchange with Carlisle Priory has not been traced: *Holm Cultram* no. 36 refers only to a dispute over tithes of Newby between Holm Cultram Abbey and Carlisle Priory.
224 H: 'Combquint'.
225 Warwick-on-Eden (NY 46 56).

[*In margin:*] Odard de Loge de Wigton; Willelmus filius Odardi; Johannes filius Willelmi; Willelmus filius Johannis; Robertus filius Willelmi; Willemus filius Roberti.[226]

[*Between entries for Warwick and Botcherby, a genealogy of the Aglionby family and their marriages in reverse order:*]

< Invertitur ordo >

2º Jac	Edw Aglionby [=] filia Hen Brougham[227]
20 Eliz	Thomae Edw [=] filia Cuth Musgrave de Crookdake[228]
10 Eliz	Johannes [=] filia .... Salkeld de Corby[229]
20 H. 8	Edw [=] filia[230]
3 H. 7	Thom [=] Johana filia .... Skelton[231]
14 Ed. 4	Jo' [=] Johana filia Alani Blennerhassett[232]
3 H. 5	Thom' [=] Katherin < filia .... Skelton >[233]
14 Ric. 2	Wm [=] Mariae < filia Alani >[234]
< 43 > Ed. 3	John[235]
22 Ed. < 3 >[236]	Adam [=] Julian Whitfeild[237]
	John[238]

---

226 Gilpin, p. 295: 'This pedigree is writ with another hand & through inadvertancy mistakes this Odard for Odard of Wigton'.

227 Edward Aglionby (d. 1648) married Jane Brougham *c.* 1608. This and the following glosses are based on Summerson, *Aglionbys*, pp. 23–55, 88–90.

228 Edward Aglionby (d. 1599) married Elizabeth Musgrave *c.* 1584. 'Thomae' presumably refers to his elder brother who was dead by 1584.

229 John Aglionby (d. 1584) married Katherine Salkeld, 1539.

230 In the tabulation in M the positioning of the spouses does not exactly match: 'filia' is repeated twice between this and the next marriage. Edward Aglionby (d. 1553) married Anne Middleton before 1521.

231 Summerson does not record the surname of Joan, wife of Thomas Aglionby (d. before 1530).

232 John Aglionby (d. 1477) married twice. Summerson does not record the name of his first wife; his second was Janet Ratcliffe, whom he married in 1464.

233 Thomas Aglionby (d. 1474) had married Katherine Skelton by 1411.

234 William Aglionby (dead by 1411) married Marion or Mary, daughter of Alan Blennerhasset *c.* 1373.

235 M: '22 Ed. 3'; H: '22 43 Ed. 3'. This John does not appear in Summerson's account of the family. The confusion over the date may suggest a copying error.

236 M: '22 Ed. 7' but Ed. III is meant.

237 Adam Aglionby (d. 1368) married Gillian Whitfield *c.* 1338.

238 John Aglionby died *c.* 1356. H adds: 'Adam [=] Julian Whitfeild' with the comment 'again but seems to be mistaken.'

[D 8] **Botchardbye**,[239] villa Bochardi was th'inheritance of one Bochard a Fleming, one of those that first peopled Carlisle.[240] He had a grainge there for provision of his house in Carliell, and when the Flemings < went >[241] to Anglesey in Wales he left that patrimony to Guy the forester, with his daughter Isold. To this Guy the hunter K. H. 1 confirmed Botchardby to hold the same by cornage paying yearly vi*s*. ii*d*. to the cornage silver to the king.[242] It is gildable & vicomitile and gives ayde with < Combquinton >[243] to the shiriffe yearely 4*s*.4*d*. turne silver. It lyneally descended in the issue maile unto William the son < of > Otho or Oden filius Radulphi filii Guidonis venatoris de Botcharby. This William lived in the tyme of King John and held then the mannor of him.[244] Then William de Bochardby and Adam de Bochardby, descended of the younger brethren, held part of the same. In the 12 yeare of Hen. 3[245] Radulph the son of the said William Botchardby entred to the segniory. His sisters Alice, Pavy, and Agnes were his heires. Alice and Agnes gave their parts to < Jokolin de Blonde >[246] of Carliell, and Pavy her part to Adam Leger her son, and to William filius Ivon.[247] The five daughters of Jokolin did inherit: Summinott,[248] Johan, Matild, Julian, and Marriott.[249]

[*In margin:*] Guydo venator; Radulph filius Guydonis; Odo filius Radulphi; Willelmus filius Odonis; Radulph; Walter; Adam; Robt Parving; Adam Parving; Robt Parving; Wm Stapleton; Wm Stapleton; Margaret Stapleton; .... Musgrave; Tho. Birkbeck.

---

239 Botcherby (NY 42 55).
240 Denton's explanation of the name is probably correct: *Bochard* is the French form of the Germanic personal name *Burchard*: *PNC*, I, p. 42.
241 M: 'were'.
242 As recorded in 'Testa de Nevill' of 1212: *Book of Fees*, p. 199.
243 M: 'commission'.
244 See *Book of Fees*, p. 199.
245 12 Hen. III = 1227–8.
246 M: 'Jokalin de Blande'.
247 The coheirs of Ralph de Botcharby disposed of their shares as follows: Alice's son, Thomas Snaubol, and Agnes herself gave their parts to Jakolin le Blund; Pavia's descendant Adam Leger gave his part to William son of Ivo of Carlisle: *Cal. IPM*, II, no. 105.
248 The reading of this name is unclear: in H it is rendered 'Sunimot'. In *Cal. IPM*, II, no. 104 she is called 'Sunnota'.
249 The inquisition after the death of James le Blund, alias Jakelin Albus of Carlisle, in 1275 names his heirs as his daughters Joan, Maud, Juliana and Marjory, and Elizabeth and Joan, daughters of his daughter Sunnota: *Cal. IPM*, II, no. 104.

[*p. 24 (106)*]

[**D 9**] **Cardew.**[250] The mannor and towne of Cardew in the barony of Dalston were aunciently called Car-thew, id est palus sive mariscus < deorum >[251] and tooke first name of that great fenny ground att the head of the river Wathenpole now called Cardewmire and of the auncient inhabitants Car-thew which is by interpretacion God's-fenn or God's-bogg,[252] and soe called by them for that it adjoyned unto Thursbye, where the Danes had a house or temple of sacrifice, or a publique place where those pagans offered upp the blood of their captives to a god whom in that sort they honored, as Everrardus sometyme abbott of Holme Cultram hath registered to posteritye, who lived in the dayes of King Henry the second.[253]

Cardew was aunciently a forrest ground (as all the rest of the baronny of Dalston was before it was inhabited) and parcell of that great forrest of Englewood & became first inhabitted in William Rufus tyme or Hen. 1 tyme. The first auncestor that I read of was one William who tooke surname of the place and was called William de Carthew. I read of that name and of one Stephen and one Thomas de Carthew.[254] The last inheritor sold his patrimony to one Berrington a chaplein, which Berrington gave the same to the bishopp of Carliell in trust to the use of John Burden.[255] John Burden had issue a sonne called alsoe John, to whom his father gave the land, to him and the heires of his bodye, and for default of such issue to John Denton and < Johan >[256] his wife and the heires of their bodyes, whose issue

---

250 Cardew (NY 34 49) was John Denton's seat.

251 M: 'idro', which is clearly an error.

252 Modern place-name scholars have suggested that Cardew may represent the Brittonic *caer-ddu* ('black fort'): *PNC*, I, pp. 131–2.

253 For Everard, first abbot of Holm Cultram, 1150–1192, see *VCH Cumb.*, II, pp. 168–9. A tradition that Everard wrote Lives of several saints was recorded in the seventeenth century, but none of his writings are now known: R. Bartlett, 'Cults of Irish, Scottish and Welsh saints in twelfth-century England', in B. Smith (ed.), *Britain and Ireland 900–1300: insular responses to medieval European change* (Cambridge, 1999), p. 260n.

254 In margin beside above section: 'Hugho: Jo'; Adam: H. 3; Henr: H. 3; Wm: 2 Ed 1'.

255 Denton appears to conflate two grants: *c.* 1322 [25 Mar. 1322 x 3 Mar. 1323] John de Bermington ['Bermeton'], rector of Denton, granted lands in Cardew to John Halton, bishop of Carlisle. In 1327, John son of William de Panetra granted lands in Cardew which he had had by grant of Bishop Halton to John de Bordon: CRO, D/Lons/L5/1/55, D.3, D.8.

256 M: 'Iran'.

maile, lyneally descended from father to son, enjoyeth the same at this day in that right.[257] The said John Denton was lord also of Ainstipleagh and of the forrest of Garnerie and Kirkpatrick Aigingrey in Scotland, which he had of the gift of Edward Balioll, king of Scottland. His letters pattents thereof were sealed in the Isle of East holme.[258] The said John Denton was then steward of all Annerdale, under the Lord Humphry de Boune,[259] earle of Heriford & Essex, high constable [*p. 25 (107)*] of England, to whom the sayd Edward Ballioll or < John > Baliell his father gave the whole seignory of Annerdale which was aunciently the Bruces' landes. The said John Denton deserved soe well in those warrs betweene the Balliols and the Bruces, competitors to the crowne of Scottland, that < the > Balioll then king preferred him to that forrest, late the bishopp of Glascoe's lands, and to Kirkpatrick late the lands of Sir James Frissolld, adherent to the Bruces' faccion.[260] And the earle of Hereford preferred him to the stewardshipp of Annerdall, the principall office in that seignory, for that he first entred to the same and held it to the earle his master's use in despite of the Bruces' faccion.[261] And when Balioll was banished Scottland he keept still the principall

257 The charter (of *c.* 1340) by which John de Burdon, rector of Rothbury, Northumberland, granted the manor of Cardew to his son John, with remainder to John de Denton and Johanna his wife and their heirs, survives in CRO, D/Lons/L5/1/55, D.11.
258 The text of this grant, which refers to the forest of 'Garnery' but does not mention Kirkpatrick Irongray, is printed in F. W. Ragg, 'Five Strathclyde and Galloway charters', *CW2*, 17 (1917), pp. 226–7. See also, below, note 260. The 'Isle of East holme' is Hestan Island (NX 83 50), which lies off the coast of Galloway.
259 H: 'de Boam'. Recte Humphrey de Bohun.
260 See above, note 258. The grant of Kirkpatrick Irongray has not been traced; it is not noted in 'The *Acta* of King Edward Balliol', in A. Beam, *The Balliol Dynasty, 1210–1364* (Edinburgh, 2008), pp. 329–44. 'Sir James Frissold' was either James Fraser of Frendraught (third son of Sir Andrew Fraser of Touch-Fraser), who was killed at Halidon in 1333, or his son, also called James. The latter presumably regained Irongray after 1356, because in 1463 it belonged to his great-great-granddaughter and eventual heiress, Janet Dunbar of Frendraught. See *Scots Peerage*, III, pp. 61–4; VI, pp. 304–6; VII, pp. 425–6; *Registrum Magni Sigilli Regum Scotorum*, II, ed. J. Balfour Paul (Edinburgh, 1882), nos. 760, 2911.
261 John Denton was given custody of Lochmaben castle and the lordship of Annandale in 1361, during the minority of the heir of Humphrey de Bohun, earl of Northampton: *Rotuli Scotiae in turri Londiniensi et in domo capitulari Westmonasteriensi asservati* (Edinburgh, 1814), I, p. 861b. I am grateful to Alexander Grant for the references in this and the preceding note.

< house >[262] till it was fired under him, beaten and undermyned readye to fall, whereupon his heires gives now in remembrance thereof < for a chrest a castle flaming with a lyon rampant issuant with a sword in the dexter paw brandis'd. >[263]

[D 10] **Ireby**,[264] saith Cambden, was called Arbeia in the Romanes' tyme, where the band of souldiers called Barcarii Tigriensis were then placed.[265] At the Conquest it was a gentleman's seate and a village, called then Ireby, and now < it > is become two mannors, viz. High-Ireby, in evidence named Alta-Ireby, because it stands higher < then the hill's side, and Low Ireby, > in auncient writeings named Ireby-base, and Markett-Irebye aloe, of a liberty to hold a faire and markett there granted by the K. .... to ...... lord thereof, and ever since soe continued.[266] The High-Ireby is more auncient, howbeit th'other, seated in the better place and being the lands of greater men successively, hath alwayes beene of more account and some deall obscured th'other.

High-Ireby was first parcell of the demeasne of Allerdall in Waldeive's tyme, and his son and heire Alane granted it to Gospatrick filius Orme, lord of Seaton and Workington. The same Gospatrick gave it to his younger son Orme filius Gospatrick who was thereupon called Orme de Ireby, & from him all the Irebies are descended [*p. 26 (108)*] and take their surname. Robert de Courtney & Dame Alice his wife, one of the 3 coheires of William Fitz Duncane, lord of Allerdall, gave this Orme de Ireby Emelton in Rich. the first's tyme, and he held lands in Waverton.[267] He had issue Adam his heire, and William a preist that gave lands in Gilcruce to th'abbey Holme.[268] Adam had Thomas his heire, William, lord of Gamelsbye and Glassonby, and Alane, father of Isaac that gave his dwelling house in Ireby (called Isaacbye, < now > Priorhall), to the priory of Carlisle.[269] Thomas had

---

262 M: 'use'.
263 In M the description of the arms ('a sable castle flameing and a lion rampant with a sword in his paw') is an addition in the hand of William Nicolson.
264 Ireby (NY 23 38) and High Ireby (NY 23 37), in Allerdale.
265 *Britannia*, p. 769C. The identification of the name Ireby with *Arbeia* is fanciful: Ireby is ON *Irabýr* ('settlement of the Irishmen/man'): *PNC*, II, pp. 299–300.
266 The market at Ireby originated in the grant of a market charter to William de Ireby by Henry III in 1236: *Cal. Charter R 1226–1257*, p. 225.
267 FF Cumb. 7 Rich. I [1195–6] (*CW2*, 7 (1907), p. 218, no. 2), calendared in *Cal. Docs Scotland*, I, no. 233.
268 See *Holm Cultram*, pp. 40–1, nos. 104–106a.
269 In the memorandum on the descent of the lordship of Allerdale, drawn up *c.*

issue John, and he Thomas, the father of William Ireby, the last lord of that name of Ireby-alta that I read of.

[*In margin of p. 25:*] Waldeiv; Alane; Gospatr' filius Orme; Orme filius Gospatr': Jo'; Adam; Thom'; Wm: Jo', H. 3; John issa H. 3; Thom: Ed. 1; Wm: Ed. 2.

Irebye-base, or Markett-Irebye, is now Musgrave's lands of Crook-dake, and was the Tiliolls from the death of Robert Tilioll, that dyed 39 Ed. 3.[270] Robert had it of Thomas Midleton filius Petri filii Adae, to whom Christian the daughter of William de Irebye the wife of Robert Bruse, & late widdow to Thomas filius Duncane Lascell of Bolton gave it by fyne 33 Ed. 1.[271] She held it of William < Boyvill >[272] of Thursbye, kt, whose father Guydo < Boyvill >[273] marryed the heir generall de sanguine of the Thursbyes; whose auncestor one Herbert de Thursbye had first made it an assert in the forrest and rented it to the king and William de Irebye her father was but a younger brother, but was advanced by K. John to farr better estate then his eldest brother, and made him knight and preferred him to the marryage of Odard's daughter and heire, lord of Glassonby and Gamelsbye, then the king's ward.

[*p. 27 (109)*]

[D 11] Glassonby and Gamelsby ultra Eden.[274] Glason-bye beyond Eden was first named Glass-oon by the Irish inhabitants, viz: the greene towards, or nigh, the river, being then a pasture ground and not inhabited; and afterwards by the Saxons Glassonbie, id est, habi-tatio <u>sive</u> villa ad Glasson, as the other village is named Gamelsbye, i.e., habitatio Gamelli, the first founder there of any building.[275] And Gamelsbye was a towne before the Irish possessed the place. Both

---

1275, the 'service of the ancestors of Isaac of Ireby in *Ysacby*' is listed along with the churches of Crosby and Ireby (which later belonged to Carlisle priory) among grants said to have been made by Alan son of Waldeve, lord of Allerdale in the mid twelfth century: *St Bees*, pp. 531–2.

270 Robert Tilliol died at Ireby on 6 April 1367 (i.e. 41 Edw. III). He held the moated manor house there from Anthony de Lucy: *Cal. IPM*, XII, no. 170. See also, J. Wilson, 'Some extinct Cumberland families III: the Tilliols', *The Ancestor*, 4 (1903), p. 97.

271 FF Cumb. 31 Ed. I [1302–3] (*CW2*, 7 (1907), p. 231, no. 166). Christian is described as the widow of Robert de Brus.

272 M: 'Baylioll'.

273 M: 'B.'

274 Glassonby (NY 57 38) and Gamblesby (NY 61 39).

275 Both place-names contain personal names which can be identified with their

were one seignory bounded in then on the north by the rill or little beck called ....[276] that falleth from the east mountaines by ....[277] and soe descendeth westward through Kirkoswold < park >[278] into Eden which doeth bound it on the west, from whence the lordshipp is extended of great breadth into the mountaines untill < it > bounds with Aldred's-towne-moore,[279] a great waste on the east.

Gamelsby and Glassonby were given by Henry the first (William Conqueror's son), king of England, unto one Hildred and his heires to be holden by cornage of the crowne in capite reddend' per annum ii^s de cornagio,[280] from whom it descended to a daughter named Christian being ward to King John who gave the wardshipp to William de Ireby. She was the daughter of Odard filius Odardi filii Odeline, son to the sayd Hildred.[281]

William de Irebye had by Christian his wife two daughters and heires, Christian and Eva. Eva had a rent charge out of the land and was married to Robert d'Estvil[282] and after to Allan de Charters. She relased to her sister Christian the wife of Thomas Lasscells of Bolton,[283] who had issue Arminia[284] Lasscells marryed to Thomas Seaton whose son Christopher Seaton forfeited the same and other lands to the king Ed. 1 by takeing part with Robert Bruce and the Scotts.

The king gave his lands in Gamelsbye and Unthank to William Latimer, father to William,[285] who had issue William Latimer father

early twelfth-century owners, Glassan son of Brictric and Gamel son of Bern: *PNC*, I, pp. 192, 194; Sharpe, *Norman Rule*, pp. 10, 12.

276 Thomas Denton's transcript (Appendix I, no. [13a]) supplies the name of the stream as 'Daleraughan'. The name survives in Daleraven Bridge (NY 566 396), where Glassonby Beck joins the Eden.

277 The same transcript supplies the name 'Unthank' (NY 610 405).

278 M: 'part'.

279 i.e. Alston Moor.

280 The writ charter granting Gamblesby and Glassonby to Hildred of Carlisle, 1129x1130, is printed and discussed in Sharpe, *Norman Rule*, pp. 7, 10–14.

281 In 1212 William de Ireby's wife was described as the daughter of Odard de Hodalm: *Book of Fees*, p. 199.

282 H: 'd'Evill'.

283 FF Cumb. 29 Hen. III [1244–5] (*CW2*, 7 (1907), p. 223, no. 66), where Eva is described as widow of Robert Avenel.

284 H: 'Arumna'.

285 See *Cal. IPM*, VII, nos. 50 (William Latimer, 1327); 689 (William Latimer, 1335).

to Elizabeth the wife of John Nevill, father to [*p. 28 (110)*] Raulf
Nevill, earle of Westmorland, who gave his lands in Cumberland
and diverse others to George his .... son Lord Latimer, from which
George they descended as their limitacion directed to the Lords
Latimer named in the mergent untill the last lord ...... dyed, and then
the fowre coheires of his daughters entred. The heir maile is Edmund
now Lord Latimer.[286]

[*In margin of p. 109:*] Hildred; Odeline; Odard; Odard; Christian uxor Willelmi Ireby; Christian uxor Thomae Lasscell; Armina
uxor Johannis Seaton; Chr Seaton. Wm Latimer; Wm Latimer; Wm
Latimer; Eliz Latimer uxor Johannis Nevill; Radulphus comes Westmorland; Geo. Nevill dominus Latimer.

[**D 12**] **Carghow** alias Carighow (collis ad petram)[287] is now a village
on the northeast side of the river Eden betweene Rocliff and Stainton.
It was first a mannor and demeasne, in the inheritance or possession
of John de < Lacy >,[288] constable of Chester, who held the same of the
King immediately by cornage. This John < Lacy > granted the same
and Cringledike, a territory there to the same belonging, to William
de Vescy and his heires, lord of Alnewick in Northumberland and
of Malton in Yorkshire, to be holden of the donor and his heires
for a meiw'd-hawk yearely for all services. William Vescy gave it
< to > Ewan Carlisle, knight, for lands in Yorkshire reserving to him
& his heires the same services. And afterward, in the second yeare of
Edward the first, Robert de Ross, lord of Werk in Tindall, dyed seized
thereof, and held the same of < Sapience >[289] the wife of William de
Carlile younger, reddendo per annum a hawk or a mark of money
yearely; and discharging the said [Sapience][290] of forreigne services
due to the king, viz., xxiii[d] de cornagio ad scaccariam Carlieli.[291]
From this Robert Ross it descended by many descents in the issue

286 For the Latimer family, see *Complete Peerage*, VII, pp. 461–76, 479–87. Edmund
    Nevill (*ante* 1555 – *c.* 1640), heir to the earldom of Westmorland, styled
    himself 'Lord Latimer': ibid., pp. 486–7.
287 Cargo (NY 36 59). Denton's interpretation of the name is broadly correct: it is
    probably a compound of Brittonic *carrecc* ('rock') and ON *haugr* ('hill'): PNC,
    I, p. 95.
288 M: 'Lucy'.
289 M: 'Sapirne'.
290 M: 'Sapirne'; H: 'Stephen'.
291 Inquisition, 1274: *Cal. IPM*, II, no. 70. The cornage due was 32*d.*, not 23*d.*

maile untill the < 32 > yeare of Ed. 3;[292] and shortly after Elizabeth Ross the heire generall transfered the inheritance to the familie of the Parrs of Kendall with other lands, in which house it descended by many descents untill William Parr late marquess of Northampton, who dyeing without issue, the widdow Dame Ellen exchanged it with Queene Elizabeth and tooke other lands for her joynture;[293] soe it rests now in the crowne and in the possession of the inhabitants as customary tennants.

[*p. 29 (111)*]

[D 13] Culgaith.[294] Culgaith and other lands in Cumberland beyond Eden were given or confirmed by K. H. the first unto Adam filius Sweni filii Ailrichi, to be holden per cornage, reddendo de cornagio Cxii^s < viii^d > regi. Adam his two daughters named Amabill and Matild were marryed to Alexander Crenquer and Adam de Montbegon. Amabill was wife after to William de Nevill by whom she had issue Thomas de Burgo, or a daughter to him marryed; and Thomas had issue another Thomas de Burgo who gave the moncks of Brecton in Yorkshire or to them confirmed his right to those lands which William Nevill his grandfather and Amabill uxor eiusdem Willelmi gave them and which Adam filius Sweene gave them before.[295] The said Thomas de Burgo younger gave to Symon filius Walter and to Sara his wife diverse of the lands by fyne in the 7th yeare of King John;[296] in whose tyme Roger de Montebegon, <u>Symon filius Walteri & Alexander de Nevill held the lands in Cumberland that were Adam fil' Sweni his inheritance.</u>[297] <u>The said Roger de Montebegon</u>

---

292 The last male heir was John son of Thomas de Roos of Kendal, who died in 1357, leaving his daughter Elizabeth (aged 2 years) as his heir: *Cal. IPM*, X, no. 427. In M the date is given wrongly as 2 Ed III.

293 Cargo was assigned as dower to Helen, marchioness of Northampton, in 1572. She had exchanged it with Elizabeth I by 1574: see *Cal. Pat. Elizabeth I*, V, no. 2725; VI, no. 1511.

294 Culgaith (NY 61 29).

295 For these charters, which refer not to Culgaith but to property in the vicinity of Monk Bretton, near Barnsley, see *Abstracts of the Chartularies of the Priory of Monkbretton*, ed. J. W. Walker (Yorkshire Archaeological Society Record Series Vol. LXVI, 1924), pp. 13–15. The chapel of St Andrew near Culgaith had been granted to Monkbretton by Adam son of Swain, as confirmed in 1154: J. E. Burton, *The Monastic Order in Yorkshire 1069–1215* (Cambridge, 1999), p. 63.

296 FF Cumb. 7 John [1205–6] (*CW2*, 7 (1907), p. 220, no. 27). The recipient was Walter son of Sarah brother of Thomas; Skirwith was granted with the consent of Sarah, whose *maritagium* it was.

297 See *Book of Fees*, p. 199.

was son to Adam de M. and to Matild his wife aforesaid. They had issue also Clementia a daughter marryed to .... de Longviller who (as I think) was heire to Roger her brother.

[*In margin:*] Aylrichus; Sweenus; Adam filius Sweni; Alex' Crenquer et uxor eius filia Adae; Adam de Montebegon et Matild filia < 2º > Adae uxor eius qui postea fuit uxor John Monseil.[298]

In the 16th yeare of K. H. 3 one William filius Johannis by fyne gave the moietye of Culgaith to one Gilbertt or Gilfrid de Nevill and to Mabell uxor < Gil. >[299]

In the 6th yeare of the next King Ed. 1 Michaell de Harcla, father to the earle of Carlisle Andrew Harcla,[300] held the moietye of Culgaith, & Walter Mulcastre and Gilbertt filius Roberti Hawksley th'other halfe.[301]

[*p. 30 (112)*] Andrew Harcla his part was forfeited by treason in Edw. the second's tyme. The residue became the land of Sir Christopher Morrisby. In the 28th yeare of Ed. 3 he dyed thereof seized,[302] from whence it descended to .... the Lady Knivett, the heire generall to the Pickerings and Morresbyes,[303] who sold the < park >[304] to Henry Crackinthorpp of Newbiggin Esq., and the lands to fower feoffees who assigned to the tennants.[305]

[D 14] Blenkarne.[306] Blenkarne was parcell of the barony of Adam filius Sween and William de Nevill's lands at the first, but afterwards it was granted forth in frank marriage and became freehold, holden

298 H: 'Wansale'.
299 FF Cumb. 16 Hen. III [1231–2] (*CW2*, 7 (1907), p. 221, no. 41), where the recipient is named Geoffrey Nevill.
300 H: 'Michael de Hartcla's father earl of Carliell & Andrew Hartcla'.
301 6 Edw. I = 1277–8. The source has not been traced.
302 Inquisition, 1348: *Cal. IPM*, IX, no. 105. Denton cites the regnal year incorrectly; it should be 22 Edw. III.
303 'Lady Knivett' was Anne (1517–1582), daughter of Sir Christopher Pickering of Scaleby Castle, whose second husband was Sir Henry Knyvett. Sir Christopher Pickering (1485–1516) had inherited the Moresby family estates from his mother, Anne, daughter and heir of Sir Christopher Moresby (d. 1499): *CFH*, pp. 192, 232, 262.
304 M: 'same'.
305 The manor of Culgaith was conveyed by Francis Vaughan of Sutton-upon-Darwen, Yorkshire, to Thomas Lambert, Thomas Robinson, George Sewell and Hugh Stevenson of Culgaith in 1585: CRO, SPC 7/1.
306 Blencarn (NY 63 31).

of the heires of Adam and William Nevill; and some part in franck almaigne granted to the priory of Carliell.[307]

In the tyme of King John and before, the Thursbyes of Thursby < & the Terribye of Terrybe & the nunns of Armythwait > held a moietye, and the Whitbies th'other moietye.

In the 11th yeare of King Henry the third[308] Evon de Vipont and Sibell Thursbye (filia Adae) his wife gave 6 bovats in Blenkarne to Barnard Thursbye, and her lands in Ainstable and Waverton; all which William Boyvill had in possession in his owne right as heire to the Thursbyes[309] in the 6th yeare of King Edw. the first[310] he granted part thereof to the priory of Carliell which the deane and chapter there yett hold. The residue descended to Edmund Boyvill his second son, who sold it to John Harcla. His brother Andrew Harcla, earle of Carliell, did forfeit it to the king, who granted it to William English father to William brother to Julian uxor Radulfi < R[estwold] >,[311] mother to William Restwold father to Richard Rest-wold whose heires sold it to < .... > Lough.[312]

[p. 31 (113)]

[D15] Skirwith.[313] Skirwith was parcell alsoe of the said baronny. In the tyme of King John one Jordan Spiggernell had freehold there and others rent.[314] The first I read of there held the towneshipp as meane lord thereof was Robert filius Walteri whom I take to be one of the Lancasters; he held it in Ed. 1 tyme, and in the latter part of the raigne of King Hen. 3. After, one John Lancaster de Helgill[315] was owner and dyed seized thereof in the 8th of Ed. 3's raigne and < held the same of >[316] Thomas de Burghe,[317] then one of the heires of the great baronny < or segnory > of Adam filius Sweene afore-

307 M: in margin 'Hen. 1'.
308 11 Hen. III = 1226–7.
309 Punctuation between this and following phrase not clear: M has '&' inter-lined at this point.
310 6 Edw. I = 1277–8.
311 M: '2'. 'Restwold' is presumably meant.
312 For the Restwold family, see T. H. B. Graham, 'The development of Ingle-wood and an account of the Skeltons of Armathwaite and the Restwolds of High Head', CW2, 12 (1912), pp. 19–28.
313 Skirwith (NY 61 32).
314 H: '& others. But the first …'.
315 H: 'Holgill'.
316 M: 'sold the same to'.
317 Inquisition, 1334: Cal. IPM, VII, no. 604.

said. From John Lancaster it descended to his cossen[318] Richard
filius Richardi Place, whose heire gave it by fyne to one William
de Lancaster, whose heire generall marryed to John Crakenthorpp,
father to William Crakenthorpp, father to John, whose three daughters and heires were marryed to Hutton of the Forrest, Sandford of
Askham, & to Midleton. Now afterwards the Midletons were lords
thereof; and now ...... Hutton son of Thomas of the Forrest and of
...... Midleton his wife, daughter and one of the coheires of Midleton
enjoyeth the same in her right, a part of the rest by purchase of the
coparceners.[319]

[*p. 32 (114)*]

[D 16] **Melmorby.**[320] Melmorbye, habitatio < ad planicem magn' >[321]
is the name of the townes parish and capitall messuage there, now
the dwelling house and seat of ...... Threlkeld of Melmorby, Esq.
It lyes betweene Gamelsbye and Ulnesby and was parcell of the
baronny of Adam filius Sween. In the raigne of K. Henry the third
Odardus, then lord of Wigton, dyed seized thereof,[322] after whose
death his son Walter de Wigton, John filius Walter and Margarett,
sole daughter and heire of the said John and Dionisia Lovetott his
wife, were successively lords thereof.[323] Margarett was marryed to
two husbands, John Denom, knight, and Sir John Weston, knight,
by whom she had none issue. She gave Melmorby to Sir Robert
Parving, kt, the king's serjeant at law, and Blak-hall alsoe.[324] After
Sir Robert his sister's son Adam filius John Peacock, who named

---

318 H: 'issue & heir'.
319 H: 'in her right a part & the rest by purchase …'. The owner of Skirwith when
     Denton was writing was Lancelot Hutton (b. 1582) of Hutton in the Forrest,
     who sold Skirwith in 1604. He was son of Thomas Hutton (1549–1601) of
     Hutton in the Forest and Barbara, daughter and coheir of Thomas Middleton
     (d. 1580): *CFH*, pp. 176, 226.
320 Melmerby (NY 61 37).
321 M: 'planitioy mag'. Denton's suggested etymology ('large level area')
     presumably assumes that 'Melmor-' represents *melr* (ON: 'sandbank') + *mor*
     (Gaelic: 'great'). The accepted modern interpretation is that the first element
     is the Gaelic personal name Melmor: *PNC*, I, p. 224. Denton hints at the latter
     interpretation below, under Ousby (D17).
322 Inquisition (undated): *Cal. IPM*, I, no. 843.
323 Walter died before 1286, when his son Sir John de Wigton was his heir, aged
     22: *Cal. IPM*, II, no. 603. For Margaret de Wigton, see above, section B12,
     note 483.
324 See FF Cumb. 8 Edw. III [1334–5] (*CW2*, 7 (1907), p. 236, nos. 227–8).

himselfe Adam Parving. He dyed 4th Ric. Regis secundi[325] and then
Henricus de Threlkeld entered to Melmorbye in which familie of the
Threlkeld it hath ever since continued in the issue maile.[326]

[p. 33 (115)]
[D 17] Ulnesby[327] or Owsby but rightly Ulfsby, habitatio Ulfi vel
Olavi Dani, was the seat and mansion of one Olave, whom the
people commonly called Ulff, a Dane or Norwegian, that (after the
spoyle of the countey by the Danes afore the last conquest of England
by the Normans) seated himselfe there under the edge of the east
mountaines. He was one of the three sonnes of Haldan: Thorquell,
Melmor and this Ulff.[328] He and Melmor were placed in this part
of the country, but Thorquell att Thorquellbye nere Keswick.[329] The
posteritye of this Ulff were called Ulfinesbyes of this place, as the
place it self tooke name of his first building there. It seemes nere the
tyme of the conquest to have beene parted betweene two sisters, and
shortly after a moiety thereof betweene fowre sisters; for in the tyme
of Henry the third one Julian Falcard and William Armestrang held
the moietyes, and Henry le Serjeant and Patrick de Ulnesby held viii
parts, and the residue by alienacions broken in small parcells, whereof
some were given to Lannercost, some to the prior of St John Jerusalem, and others in frankmarriage and many small peeces sold.[330]
But William Armstrang's part descended iiii descents and then given
to Clement Crofton & Johan his wife by Adam Armestrang, who
gave the third part thereof to Roger Salkeld and John Beuchamp.[331]

325 Melmerby is not listed among the possessions of either Adam Parvyng (d.
1380) or his son Sir Robert (d. 1405): Cal. IPM, XV, no. 405; XVIII, no. 1176.
326 Melmerby appears to have been in the hands of the Threlkelds by 1380: see
W. Jackson, Papers and Pedigrees mainly relating to Cumberland and Westmorland, 2 vols (CWAAS Extra Series 6, 1892), II, pp. 282, 293.
327 Ousby (NY 62 34).
328 Denton's assumption that the name Ousby contains the ON personal name
Úlfr is probably correct: PNC, I, p. 228.
329 'Thorquellbye' has not been identified, unless it is an attempt to explain the
name Threlkeld.
330 On the death of Patrick de Ulvesby, 1289, it was recorded that Jeliana Falcard
had held a fourth part of one moiety of Ousby and had sold the homage of a
free tenant there to Patrick, who had also held land in Ousby from Walter de
Kempeley, Gilbert de Mora, William Armstrang, Henry Long and partners,
and Henry son of Jeliana: Cal. IPM, II, no. 699. For the grants to Lanercost,
see Lanercost, nos. 165–9.
331 Sybil wife of William Armstrong held one eighth part of the town of Ousby
in 1334, when Adam Armstrong, William's kinsman, was her heir: Cal. IPM,
VII, no. 581.

And Thomas Wershipp gave John Raughton and he to Roger Salkeld an 8th part thereof. Alice and Margarett Salkeld, heires & daughters desend to their husbands' children, John Crackenthorpp & Thomas Plumbland. And John Crofton, Clement's son, gave the two third parts to William Threlkeld and Katherine his wife.

[*p. 34 (116)*]

[D 18] Langwathby villa <u>sive</u> habitatio Waldeofi longi.[332] It is called in the records at Westminster Long-Waldeofby where it is also recorded that King Hen. the first gave it to Henry filius Sweeni together with Edenhall.[333] Howbeit this towne did not soe long continue with him nor his posteritye, for the king held it as regium dominicum. King John had it in possession. Hen. 3 gave it to Alexander, king of Scotts, in part of CC^{li} land granted to the Scotts anno domini 1237 in the 27th of his raigne by composicion for release of Cumberland and Northumberland, and other things in demand. The king of Scotts enjoyed it untill John Balioll forfeited those lands, thenceforth they did continue unto Ric. 2 tyme in the crowne but he granted those in Cumberland to Radulf Nevill, earle of Westmorland, and Johan his wife and the heires of their bodyes, whose grandchild Richard, earle of Warwick, did forfeit them to Edw. 4, who granted them to the duke of Gloucester his brother, afterwards king by the name of Ric. 3. And ever since this and the rest have continued regium dominicum.[334]

[D 19] Edenhall, aula ad Rivum Eden,[335] as aforesaid was given to Henry filius Sween, the second brother of Adam. It stands on th'other side of the river, and in the forrest of Englewood. It is now th'inheritance of the best house and familie of the Musgraves, whose auncestor Thomas Musgrave had it by marriage of William Stapleton's second daughter and coheire in Hen. 6th tyme. And before, the Stapletons held it from the first yeare of Edw. 3 five descents, by

---

332 Langwathby (NY 56 33). The suggested derivation is fanciful: the name is a topographical one, referring to its situation at a crossing point on the river Eden: ON *lang* + *vað* + *bý* ('settlement by the long ford'): *PNC*, I, p. 219.
333 Henry son of Swein's holdings in Langwathby and Edenhall are recorded in the Pipe Rolls from 1159: *VCH Cumb.*, I, p. 339.
334 Langwathby was part of the honour of Penrith, granted to the king of Scots in 1242 and deemed to have reverted to the English crown in 1307 after John Balliol's rebellion: see M. F. Moore, *The Lands of the Scottish Kings in England* (London, 1915), pp. 7–9.
335 Edenhall (NY 56 32). The second element of the name is probably OE *h(e)alh* ('corner, nook'), rather than 'hall': *PNC*, I, p. 190.

the marriage of Julian one of the ii coheires & daughters of Robert Turpe, whose father Adam Turp was but a child of seaven yeares old in Hen. 3 tyme at the death of Robert his father who then dyed seized thereof.[336]

[*In margin:*] Mariota Stapleton; 39 H. 6 Willm; 11 H. 6 Wm; 3 R. 2 Wm; 36 Ed 3 Wm [=] Julian filia et heraed Roberti; Robt Turpe;[337] Robt Turpe; Adam Turpe; Robt Turpe; Adam.

[*p. 35 (117)*]

[D20] **Ravenwik**,[338] villa in angulo curvato ad flumen Raven,[339] is now the lands of the provost and fellows of Queene's Colledge in Oxford, whose prediccessors had them of one of their founders Robert Egglesfeild, sometymes chaplane to K. Edw. 3's wife named Philippa, he endowing the colledge as cheife founder called the same Queene's Colledge.[340] The said Robert had Ravenwik in the first yeare of K. Ed. 3[341] and one Thomas Staveley and Margarett his wife in the 20 of Ed. 1st.[342] The Staveleys, auncestors to the said Thomas Staveley, held it from the conquest, for Henry the first gave it to one Adam de Staveley & his heires, tenend' per cornag' de Rege.[343] That river is called Raven of the violent fall and runing thereof. < N.B. > Adam Staveley was lord of Dent and Sedbergh.

---

336 See *Cal. IPM*, I, no. 928 (fragmentary inquest, temp. Hen. III; date lost, on death of Robert Turp) and *Cal. IPM*, VII, no. 126, which names the daughters and heirs of Beatrice and Robert Turp in 1328 as Joan, aged 16 years, and Juliana, aged 14 years. The 'Testa de Nevill' records that Robert de Brus held half a knight's fee in Edenhall, which had been granted to his ancestor, Peter de Brus by King Henry: *Book of Fees*, p. 197. For the descent of Edenhall, see F. W. Ragg, 'The earlier owners of Edenhall', *CW2*, 13 (1913), pp. 199–227. See also R. M. Blakely, *The Brus Family in England and Scotland 1100–1295* (Woodbridge, 2005), pp. 137–8.

337 H: 'Julian fil' et heres Turpe' followed by the final four names as in M.

338 Renwick (NY 59 43).

339 Raven Beck may, rather, be a back-formation from Renwick, which is from ON personal name *Hrafn* and OE *wīc* ('farm'): *PNC*, I, p. 236.

340 For Robert de Eglesfeld (*c*. 1295–1349), founder of Queen's College, Oxford, in 1341, see J. M. Kaye, 'Eglesfeld, Robert de', *ODNB*; J. R. Magrath, *The Queen's College* (Oxford, 1921), pp. 1–13. Eglesfeld's grant of Renwick to Queen's College is printed in Nicolson and Burn, *History and Antiquities of Westmorland and Cumberland*, II, pp. 434–5n.

341 1 Edw. III = 1327–8. The source has not been traced.

342 cf. FF Cumb. 26 Ed. I [1297–8] (*CW2*, 7 (1907), p. 231, no. 159).

343 See *Book of Fees*, p. 199.

[D 21] **Harskeugh**, superior silva,[344] is a village or stead neare Ravenwik, now the lands of Henry filius Christoferi filii Domini < Thomae > Dacre militis, who held it by purchase from K. Hen. viii[th] & was belonging to the priory of Lannercost. The prior's predicessor had it of the gift of Dame Ada de Engaine, filia Willelmi filia Radulfi Engaine.[345] Her son Hugho de Morvill filius Simoni < Morvill > confirmed it to the prior in K. H. 2 tyme or in the begining of K. John's raigne.[346] And before it belonged to Kirkoswold as parcell of that seignory. The channons used it for cattle < and > the mountaines for sheepe pasture, and thereupon I should think that stony hill to be called Caregg-monach' in old evidence and now corruptly Cattermanak, but that the word Carrock is Brittish or Irish and therefore some deale more auncient. By some others religious, therefore haveing right there, it hath beene soe named before the conquest.[347]

[*p. 36 (118)*]

[D 22] **Hudlesceugh**, capreolarum silva,[348] was in times past a woody place on the common pasture of Kirkoswold where the towneshipp of K. and the lord thereof wintered the heards of young goates, but now the wood is gone and the place is < become > a little village demised to tennants. In K. John's tyme one Robert de Hudleskeugh held it of the Morvills, lords of Kirkoswold, and then one Radulph Dentolff in Westmorland gave a part thereof to the house of Wetherall for Sir Hugh Morvill's soule (that kild the Thomas Beckett, archbishopp of Canterbury), his landlord sometyme of the same or the feoffor that gave it to his auncestor.[349] And the prior presently granted it to Robert de Salkeld by consent of Robert then abbott of York, and to any of Robert S. sonnes in heritage whom he would

---

344 Haresceugh (NY 610 428). The name is more probably 'hare wood' than 'higher wood', as suggested by Denton: *PNC*, I, p. 216.

345 For the charter granting *parva Haresco*, 1167x1182, see *Lanercost*, no. 33.

346 Ibid., no. 34, dated 1194x1199.

347 This name survives as Scarrowmanwick (NY 58 47), the second element of which may, indeed, refer to monks. Modern scholarship interprets the name as a compound of ON *skálir* ('huts, shielings') and either a personal name (possibly Irish *Meanach*) or Gaelic *manaich* ('of the monk'): *PNC*, I, p. 250.

348 Huddlesceugh (NY 59 42). Place-name scholars interpret the name as 'Hudd's wood': *PNC*, I, p. 216. It is not clear on what grounds Denton interpreted the first element as *capreolus* ('young goat; kid'): 'hud' is not recorded as a dialect term for goat in the standard sources.

349 *Wetheral*, no. 179. The grantor's name, Ralph de Hoff, has been garbled by Denton.

make choice off.[350] I take the same Robert Salkeld to be called Robert de Hudleskeugh, because he then dwelt there.

[*p. 37 (119)*]

[D 23] **Kirkoswold**,[351] ecclesia Sancto Oswaldo sacra, the name of the towne and parish there of very auncient tyme hath beene tearmed, and the castle there built by the Engaynes, lords of Burgh, Isall, Henriby and Kirkoswold. It was first founded by Radulfe Engayne, but farr short of that beautye and state it had afterwards by his successors. Sir Hugh Morvill in K. John's tyme enclosed the park in the second yeare of his raigne by the king's lycence;[352] and Radulphus de Levington that marryed Ada filia Johannae Morvill filiae et coheredis Hughonis Morvill, added thereunto a part of Gamelsby & Glassonbye. Thomas filius Thomae de Multon and John de Castre that marryed the widdow of Thomas Multon of Gilsland in Ed. 2 tyme. But the Lord Thomas Dacres that marryed the heires of Greystock did finish it & mote it about with great charges which notwithstanding in the third descent after him is now in a manner altogether become ruinous.[353] It was first parcell of the seignory of Adam filius Sween filii Ailrich, and granted forth with a daughter to Trivers, lord of Burgh, cheife forrester of fee of Englewood forrest, by whose daughter Ibria wife of Radulf Engayne it came to him. This lordshipp did conteine Kirkoswold, New Staffoll or Stafle, Raven-wik, Harskeugh, Hudlesceugh, Little Croglin, and Kabergh alias Langbargh,[354] and all the lands and wastes towards the east mountaines from the river Eden on the west, betwene Croglin water on the north and the little rill < Dale > Raghon-beck on the south that devides from Glassonby and Gamelsby. The heires of Adam filius Sweene were Yorkshire men therefore not regarded there and th'owners of Kirkoswold commanders, and after the makeing of Magna Charta and the rebellion Roger Montebegon mean lord, < they >[355] held it of the king in baronia mediately.[356]

350 *Wetheral*, no. 180.
351 Kirkoswald (NY 55 41).
352 2 John = 1200–1: see *Rot. Chart.*, p. 11.
353 For Kirkoswald castle, see Curwen, *Castles*, pp. 150–3. The descent of the castle's ownership is discussed in T. H. B. Graham, 'Extinct Cumberland castles, part IV', *CW2*, 12 (1912), pp. 164–78.
354 The last is represented on the modern map by Caber Farm (NY 567 464).
355 M: 'then'.
356 H: 'imediately'.

[p. 38 (120)]

[D 24] Staffle[357] lyes betweene Kirkoswold and Ainstaple, from the river Eden to the mountaines. It is a fee of Kirkoswald and gave name to a familie of gentlemen soe called. The issue maile ended about ..... tyme and then the inheritance fell to .....[358] daughters which did transferr it by their marriage to the Chambers, Mulcasters, and Blennerhassetts of Carliell.

[D 25] Croglin parva[359] stands in the same parish and towneshipp and is a fee of Kirkoswald. It was aunciently the Beuchamps, till K. H. 7 tyme, and then the Dacres lord paramount purchased it to their seignory. Aunciently towards the tyme of King Hen. the first one Uchtred held a part thereof, and Dame Ibria de Trivers and others. And afterwards one Elias de Croglin, William his son, William filius Willelmi his nephew who gave some part of the same to the house of Wedderhall, which Roger Beuchamp confirmed, that is the 5th part of the towne now (as I think) called < Cringle-dyke. >[360]

[p. 39 (121)]

[D 26] Kirke-Croglin,[361] lacus ad rupem, is the name of the river that divides Gilsland from the baronny of Gilsland[362] at the head thereof, and after it comes towards Ainstaffle it turnes to Staffle and devides them untill it be received of Eden. It's soe called of two Brittish words careg a rock and lyn a water, for it falleth fourth of stony hills.[363] Of these words is corruptly framed the present name Croglin, which gives name to the towne and church. It was aunciently[364] the frehold of one Philipp Hastings, in whose issue maile it decended untill Ed. 1 tyme and then Croglin and his other lands in Westmorland fell to

357 Staffield (NY 54 42).
358 In M the figure '3' has been inserted in the space in a different hand.
359 Little Croglin is identified by Thomas Denton with the Croglin Hall estate (centred on Croglin Low Hall, NY 555 450), a mile downstream from the village: Denton, *Perambulation*, pp. 345–6.
360 M: 'Cringledale'. For the grants of Croglin, see *Wetheral*, nos. 149–54. There were separate grants of Crindledyke (NY 55 43), including one from Roger de Beauchamp: ibid., nos. 171–3.
361 Croglin (NY 57 47). Oxford, Bodleian Library, MS Gough Scotland 4, f. 19 contains a copy of the entry for Kirk Croglin in a hand of *c.* 1700.
362 This phrase, clearly an error, occurs in M, H (where the first reference to Gilsland is, however, crossed out) and Bodleian, MS Gough Scotland 4.
363 Denton suggests a derivation from the Celtic *carreg* ('rock') + *llyn* ('lake'). Modern scholars prefer to see the name as a compound of ON *krókr* ('bend') and OE *hlynn* ('torrent'): *PNC*, I, p. 183.
364 'Hen 2' is written in the margin of M and Bodleian, MS Gough Scotland 4.

his daughters, marryed to ..... Wharton, auncestor to the now Lord
Wharton and to Warcopps;[365] but now the Lord Wharton holds it all
to himselfe. It is part of Gilsland and holden of the lords thereof. One
of those Hasteing was with King .....[366] at the seige of Jerusalem, and
received a grant of the king there of lands which the king gave him
in England. The Lord Wharton's cote is the armes of those Haste-
ings, but he hath added to them a border of ore charged with lyon's
<u>pawes</u> in saliter about the Hasteings cote, which is a manche argent
in a feild sable.[367]

[D 27] < **Comb-rew** >[368]

[p. 40 (122)]
[D 28] **Castle Carrock.**[369] *The first freeholder of Castle Carrock that
I read of was one Eustace de Vallibus, to whom Hubbert de Vallibus, lord of Gilsland, gave it in Hen. 2 tyme, & Haiton also. This
Eustace gave a carracut in Haiton and another in Castle Carrock to
the house of Lannercost.*[370] <u>It is called Castle Carrock</u> quasi castrum
de rupe[371] and was in Hen. 2 tyme the inheritance of one Robert de
Castlecarock and after him successively it descended to Robert his
son and to Richard his grandchild, whose son Robert was the last
of that name inheritor thereof. He dyed in Ed. 1 tyme and left three
daughters and heires which he begatt on the body of Christian de
Crokdake, aunt and one of the two coheires to John filius Johanni
filii Adam Crokdake, viz: Johan wife of Thomas Newbiggin, Christian wife of Michael Appulby, and Margery wife of William Egglesfeild.[372] Newbiggin's part descended to three daughters & heires,
Hellen uxor Ricardi Hale, Margarett uxor Thomae Hale, and Alice

---

365 Henry de Wharton ('Querton') was lord of Croglin in 1326: *Cal. IPM*, VI, no.
     693.
366 'Rich 2d' inserted in a different hand in M, though Richard I is presumably
     meant.
367 Bodleian MS Gough Scotland 4 adds 'This adicion was granted by Edwd the
     sixt to Thomas Lord Wharton for his service done agt the Scotts at Solom-
     moss.'
368 No account of Cumrew (NY 54 50) has been located.
369 Castle Carrock (NY 54 55).
370 See *Lanercost*, no. 30. The section marked here by asterisks occurs at the end
     of the entry for Castle Carrock in H.
371 Denton interprets Carrock as Celtic *carreg* ('rock'), whereas modern place-
     name scholars prefer Welsh *caerog* ('fortified'): *PNC*, I, p. 75.
372 For the descent of Castle Carrock in the thirteenth century, see T. H. B.
     Graham, 'The eastern fells', *CW2*, 19 (1919), pp. 101–2.

uxor Johannis Hale, all of Kirkby Thore.[373] [*In margin at this point:* Gamel de Castle-Carock test to a deed of Wm filius Odard in cout'[374] de Wedderhall.[375]] Alice part came to the Lothers of Crookdake and from them to the Musgraves of Crookdak, now owners. Margarett's part by a daughter named Alice uxor Collinson fell to two daughters, Johan uxor Gilberti Carleton and Margarett uxor Johannis Betham of Thrimby. And in the iiii[th] descent Elizabeth Bethom, then heire, uxor Roberti Salkeld had issue Roger who sold it to Lough. I find noe issue of the eldest sister Hellen Newbiggin, but one William < Kitchin >[376] who sold the ix[th] part of Castle Carock to Ranulph Dacre that married Multon's heir. The purparty of Christian Castle-carock fel by her daughter named Christian to William Ritson, and by their daughter Mariott to[377] Thomas Alanbie, and by their daughter to John de Westlevington, and by his daughter Elizabeth to Alexander Highmoore, whose heire in the 3 or 4th descent sold it to Dacre. The 3d coheire part Margery uxor Egglesfeild.

[D29] **Haiton**, villa in colle,[378] was frehold in Hubbart Vaulx tyme who gave it to Eustace Vaulx his cosne, and so continued 4 descents.[379] The lord thereof had a daughter & heir maryed to John filius Roberti < filii > Ankelm[380] de Denton.

[*p. 41 (123)*]

[D30] **Farleham**[381] hath aunciently beene a fee of Gilsland, and was granted by ...... lord of Gilsland to one Walter de Windsor in Hen. 2 tyme, brother to Alexander de Windsor being soe called because they dwelt at Windsor, but they were both brethren to one William de

---

373 'Thore' is crossed out in M. When John son of Thomas Newbiggin died in 1330, his sisters Margaret (then 11 years old), Alice (5 years) and Helen (8 years) were his heirs: *Cal. IPM*, VII, no. 314.
374 Reading unclear: 'cartulary' may be intended. H reads 'court rolls' and 'in early thetker [*sic* for 'charter'?] de Wedderhall' where this section is repeated at the foot of the account of Castle Carrock.
375 *Wetheral*, no. 36.
376 The reading of this name is unclear in M: it appears to read 'Kitaim'.
377 H: 'this daughter marry'd to ...'.
378 Hayton (NY 50 57). Denton appears to interpret the first element of the name as 'high'; hence his gloss *villa in colle* ('settlement in the high ground/hill'). Modern place-name scholars regard the first element as OE *hēg* ('hay'): *PNC*, I, p. 88.
379 H: 'some descents.'
380 M: 'John fil' Robert Anklun'.
381 Farlam (NY 55 58).

Kers-mer the ...... of Willitred filius Haldan sometyme lord of Catter-
leing, which King Hen. 2 gave to Hubbart Vaulx after he had seized
it (because Willitred tooke part with King Stephen) as forfeited. And
therefore in K. John's tyme the said William de Kersmira brought
a writt of mort d'ancestor against William Vaulx filius Huberti and
Robert son of the said William, then lords of Catterlen, but could
not recover the land. The sayd Walter de Windsor had issue another
Walter and his son called Adam de Farleham held the land in < 23
of > Ed. 1 tyme;[382] and in Ed. 3 tyme Johannes de Farleham held
it who gave it to Ranulf Dacre and Margarett Multon his wife the
lo[rds] of Gilsland, and to their heires after John de Farleham's death
and of one Andrew Latton. Thenceforth it hath continued as demesne
to the lords of Gilsland.[383] The sayd Walter Windsor gave for armes a
saltier sable in feild de argent. There are some of that surname left at
this tyme which are descended from one John de Windsor, brother to
the second Walter Windsor, to whom he gave Farleham parva. John
had issue Rayner and Solomon, and < Rayner had Barnard the father
of Richard, which Salamen and > Richard endowed the houses of
Wetherall and Lannercost with lands in Little Farlehame.[384]

[*p. 42 (124)*]

[**D 31**] **Brampton**[385] in Gilsland was for the most part demeasne
lands and the towne was a long tyme a markett towne, first granted
soe to be by K. .... to ...... lord of Gilsland, and soe continueth to this
day.[386] Att Brampton the lords doe yearely keepe the courts leets and
view of frankpledge for the whole baronny of Gilsland now, howbeit
the head and cheife seat was at Irthington in the Vaulxes' tymes and
Multons'. The towne is now all customary tennancyes or demeasnes
for the Dacres have wrung out all the freeholders of Irthington and

---

382 Adam de Farlham held £8 of land (location unspecified) from Thomas de
Multon of Gilsland by service of half a knight's fee in 1295: *Cal. IPM*, III, no.
285 (p. 185).
383 For the descent of Farlam, see T. H. B. Graham, 'Farlam and Cumwhitton',
CW2, 19 (1919), pp. 92–5.
384 A grant of land in Little Farlam to Lanercost Priory by Solomon son of David
and Bernard son of Raum (or Ratmer) was confirmed by Walter de Windsor
[1194x1220]: *Lanercost*, nos. 107, 75.
385 Brampton (NY 53 61).
386 Henry III granted a market and fair at Brampton to Thomas de Multon and
Maud his wife in 1252: *Cal. Charter R 1226–57*, p. 407.

Brampton save < Corkby >[387] and some few small tennancyes of the meaner sort of people.[388]

[D 32] Comb-catch convallis ad dorsam collis,[389] is now a farme in Brampton parish and is demeasne. It stands in a bottome on the backside of a hill, and is environned with hills and woodground. In K. Hen. 3 and Edw. 1st's tyme one Robert < Delmore >[390] held it as a fee of Brampton by knights service; and after him one John Delmoore and John his son in Edw. 3 and Rich. 2 tymes.[391]

[p. 43 (125)]

[D 33] Naworth Castle[392] is now the principall seate of the baronny of Gilsland, and hath soe beene from Edw. 2 tyme. In the 36 of Ed. 3 Margarett daughter and heire of Thomas Multon (last of that name lord thereof), dyed seized thereof;[393] and before that tyme I doe nott read of it. The auncient capitall mannor house of Gilsland was at a place in Irthington parish called the Castle-stead, where as yett is to be seene the ruines of the castle where Gill filius Bueth dwelt, and which Hubbart Vaulx had of the guift of Henr. 2.[394] And it was called the mannor of Irth-oon-towne, < contractly >[395] Irthington: villa ad

---

387 M: 'Crosbye', but Corby is meant.
388 Queen's College MS [12], p. 249, provides a fuller explanation of this statement: 'The townsmen are now for the most part customary tenants, the freeholds of the antient possessors as well here as in other parts of the barony being by the greatness and authority of the family of Dacres gott out of their hands and their heirs forced in process of time to accept of customary tenures, so that the greatest part of the barony with Irthington aforesaid is now converted into coppyhold tenements onely excepting Corby and a considerable number of small freeholds of the meaner sort of people'.
389 Cumcatch (NY 547 612). Denton is correct in interpreting the first element as Brittonic *cumbā* ('valley') but the thinking behind his translation of the second element ('on the back of a hill') is not clear. Modern scholars have been unable to identify the second element: *PNC*, I, p. 66.
390 In M the name has been altered to 'Delmoore'; as first written, it appears to be 'Delmeare'.
391 John Delamore exchanged lands with William Dacre, lord of Gilsland, in 1386, receiving land at Cumcatch in return for lands near Naworth: DUL, Howard of Naworth, C9a/2.
392 NY 559 625.
393 Inquisition, 1362: *Cal. IPM*, XI, no. 317 (p. 254).
394 For the motte at Irthington (NY 499 615) see D. R. Perriam and J. Robinson, *The Medieval Fortified Buildings of Cumbria* (CWAAS Extra Series XXIX; Kendal, 1998), p. 159.
395 M: 'contrartly'.

rivum Irthin. The river gave name to the towne, castle and mannor.[396]
The lords thereof suffered it to decay as a thing of rude edification,
and of the ruins thereof built Naworth which in success of tyme was
bettered by the owners and by like tyme through negligence more
then age begins now to decline and loose the beautye and strength
which it lately had, as all such worldly things doe which are subject
to tyme.[397]

[D 34] Denton[398] villa in profundo. The place in Gilsland where
Denton stands is a great deepe valley. The Irish call deepe in their
language Daein. Upon that Irish word the place was so named by the
Saxons Daein and the first habitacions there Daein-towne.[399] There
are two Dentons ther. Over Denton which is in Northumberland and
now the Widderingtons' lands and stands beyond the great bottome;
and Neither Denton in Cumberland, late the Dacres' lands, which
stands in the low. Both of them are parcell of the baronny of Gilsland.
The first possessor that I read of was one Weskopp, to whom Hubbert
de Vallibus, lord of Gilsland, gave Denton in or about Hen. 2 tyme.
Westcopp gave it to one Gillesbueth or Bueth-barne, otherwise that
Gillesbueth [*p. 44 (126)*] and Bueth-barne was but one person.[400] He
had issue Robert filius Bueth, who dyed without issue. His sisters
were marryed to Addock lord of Booth Castre and to < Eustace
Vaulx > the lord of Haiton in Gilsland; th'one had Over Denton and
th'other Nether Denton, which was two moietyes then by partition.
Haiton's part was given to John filius Roberti filii Ankdin or Asktill[401]
de Denton, and Robert brother to the sayd John marryed the heire to
th'other part. The said Robert filius Bueth was their mother's brother.
He gave the church to the house of Wetherall, and after his death
one David filius Terry and Robert filius Asktile, gave it to the house
of Lannercost, whereupon grew great suite till the controversie was

---

396 Denton's explanation of the place-name is correct: *PNC*, I, pp. 91–2.
397 Naworth Castle is generally agreed to be a new creation of the fourteenth
century: see Curwen, *Castles*, pp. 213–18 and sources cited in Perriam and
Robinson, *Medieval Fortified Buildings*, pp. 166–7.
398 There were two vills at Denton: Nether Denton, centred on Denton Hall (NY
578 630), and Upper Denton (NY 61 65).
399 Denton's interpretation of the name is broadly correct, though his etymology
is wrong: Denton is OE *denu* + *tūn* ('settlement in the valley'): *PNC*, I, p. 81.
400 Gille Bueth and Bueth Barn were two separate individuals. For the grant of
the vill of [Nether] Denton to Bueth Barn by Wescop son of Gille Bueth, see
above, section A43, note 328.
401 H: 'Ankelm or Asketill'.

ended by mediacion of the pope's legates who devided the profitts betweene them and gave the presentation of the vicarage to the bishopp.[402] Over Denton 7º Ed. 1[403] was given by Richard Stonland[404] and Elina his wife to John Witherington with whose issue maile it remaines at this day. Nether Denton descended from the sayd John filius Roberti filius Anctin to John and to Richard Denton knight, his son's son, whose daughter Margarett wife to Adam Copeley of Bateley in Craven, had it in marriage 17 Ed. 2.[405] John filius Adam had issue Richard Copeley whose daughter Issabell wife to Adam Denton filius Thomae del Hall had Denton from her father Richard Copeley in marriage in Henr. 4 tyme.[406] Thomas Denton Esq, now of Warnell, the son of Thomas filius Johannis holds Warnell in exchange for Denton, made in the 23 K. Hen. 7th by the said John and Thomas with the Lord Dacre,[407] which John Denton was son to Richard filius Thomae filii Adam filii Thomae del Hall as aforesaid.

[*p. 45 (127)*]

[D35] Lannercost and Walton.[408] Lannercost (ad costeram vallis),[409] was first a land or plaine in that glen or valley att the foote of a banck or riseing ground where the Pights wall standeth;[410] and Walton was soe named of the first habitacions there, built at that part of the

402 The grant [1164x1181] of David son of Terri and Robert son of Anketin was of the church of Upper Denton; the dispute was over the church of Nether Denton, which had been granted to Lanercost by Bueth Barn and confirmed by his son, Robert, who also granted it to Wetheral: *Lanercost*, nos. 45–6, 57, A2; *Wetheral*, no. 121. The history of the dispute is outlined in *Lanercost*, p. 98n.
403 7 Edw. I = 1278–9.
404 H: 'Stowland'.
405 The date is incorrect; it should read 19 Edward III (1345–6): FF Cumb. 19 Edw. III [1345–6] (*CW2*, 7 (1907), p. 238, no. 254).
406 This descent appears to differ from that given by Thomas Denton in his account of the Denton family, which states that Thomas of the Hall of Carlisle purchased Denton Hall from Sir Richard Denton in the reign of Edward II. Thomas Denton notes: 'I have seen the Deed of purchase where he is called *consanguineus dicti Richardi Denton*, by which I conceive he might be Brother, or Son, to John Grandfather to Sir Richard': Manx National Heritage Library, MS 5A, p. 5.
407 The exchange was by indenture dated 25 Oct. 1506: DUL, Howard of Naworth, C66a/1.
408 Lanercost (NY 55 63); Walton (NY 52 64).
409 Lanercost is now interpreted as a Brittonic place-name, the first element being *llanerch* ('grove'); the second element is obscure: *PNC*, I, p. 71.
410 i.e. Hadrian's Wall.

wall, at the Conquest a great forrest and wast ground. And in Hen 2 tyme they were granted by Robert filius Hubberti Vaulx, lord of Gilsland, to the prior and covent of Lannercost, which was there first by him founded in the honour of Mary Magdalene, in these tearmes: Landam de Lannercost et villam de Walton, and bounders them by certaine lymitts. He gave them also the church of Woalton, of Irthington, of Brampton, of Karlatton and Farlham, with the chapell of Treuermain and the lands of Warth-Colman, Rosswrageth, and Appletreethwait, and divers libertyes for the goods in his forrests and commons thereunto adjoyning at Lannercost.[411] Then about the yeare of grace 1116,[412] they begun to build the scite of the priory and the church, whereunto in success of tyme they moved the gentlemen to give much land and revenue, to have their bodies buried there, and for their soules' health. The Engaines and Morvills in Harskeugh, the Windsors in Corkbye and Farlham, Dentons in Denton, Vaulx in < Hayton, >[413] Giltsdale, and in Triermain, Newtons and Robert de la Sore in Grinsdall,[414] and many others in divers parts of the countrey, untill they had gotten a goodly stipend for every person in the priory, and enough to defray their extraordinary charge. The greatest cause that moved [this][415] Robert Vaulx was the death of Gill filius Buethe, auncient lord of the baronny of Gilsland, whom the said Robert had caused to be slaine under trust at a meeting sett for agreement betweene him and Hubbertt Vaulx father to Robert to whom the king had given Gill's patrimony because he tooke part with the Scotts, as the history reporteth.[416]

[*p. 46 (128)*] Howbeit the deed and charter made to the prior by the said Robert is pro anima regis Hen. 2 et Huberti patris mei et Graeciae matris < meae > &c.[417] It was disolved by King Hen. 8th

---

411 The priory's foundation charter (*Lanercost*, no. 1) can be dated to 1165x1174.
412 This incorrect date was repeated in the eighteenth-century transcript of the Lanercost cartulary: see *VCH Cumb.*, II, p. 152n. The original manuscript of the cartulary gives a traditional foundation date of 1169 which tallies with the charter evidence: see *Lanercost*, p. 4; Summerson and Harrison, *Lanercost Priory*, p. 5.
413 M: 'Halton'.
414 For these charters see *Lanercost*, nos. 33–5 (Haresceugh); 31, 72, 125 (Farlam); 51–63 (Denton); 7, 27 (Hayton); 25, 284 (Geltsdale); 1, 43–4, 70 (Triermain) and 93–104 (Grinsdale).
415 Both M and H read 'the', which has been amended in M to read 'this'.
416 The 'history' cited by Denton as the source of this tradition (which is not accepted by modern historians) has not been identified.
417 See *Lanercost*, no. 1 (p. 53).

and given to Thomas Dacres knight, and now Henry Dacre filius Christoferi filii Thomae enjoyeth the same.[418]

[D 36] Askerton and Whithill[419] was first given by ...... lord of Gilsland to Sir Roger Vaulx his ..... to whom succeeded his son William filius Roger, but after his death thenceforth it was always demeasne lands and not freehold, but the lord had certaine bondmen and villaynes which laboured in the towne to the lord's use in Ed. 3 tyme < and before. > But now there is a little stone peele where the land-serjeant of Gilsland doth reside, that commands & leads the inhabitants of the baronny in the lord's service for the queene against Scottland, and hath the demeasne lands there.[420] The residue is demised to customary tennants. In the Lord Dacre's tyme there was a baliff.

[D 37] Burdoswold[421] was in King John's tyme and some deale before the freehold of Walter Bavin, William Bavin & Radulf Bavin. They did successively hold it and gave part thereof to the house of Wetherall, and land in Comquinton to the house of Lannercost.[422] After in Ed. 1 tyme one John Gillett held land there;[423] but now and of long tyme before the lords of Gilsland have redeemed the frehold and demised it to tennants.

[D 38] Fenton.[424] William de Windsor x^{li} terrae ibidem 23 Ed. 1 de Thoma Multon per 4 partem feodi.[425] Roberti Tilioll et Margaret uxor ex < dono >[426] Rogeri filii Willelmi carracut ibm per xv^{tum} partem feodi militis.

---

418 For the Dacres of Lanercost, see Summerson and Harrison, *Lanercost Priory*, pp. 44–50. Henry Dacre (d. 1624) succeeded his father, Sir Christopher, in 1593.

419 Askerton Castle (NY 550 692); White Hill (NY 537 658).

420 For Askerton Castle, see Curwen, *Castles*, pp. 344–6; E. L. Warre, 'Askerton Castle', *CW2*, 24 (1924), pp. 149–55.

421 Birdoswald (NY 615 663).

422 'Comquinton' is an error for *Cumquenecath* (in Kingwater) where Walter Beivin granted land to Lanercost *c.* 1180 x *c.* 1210: *Lanercost*, nos. 144, 147.

423 See inquisition after death of Thomas de Multon, 1295: *Cal. IPM*, III, no. 285 (p. 186).

424 Fenton (NY 503 560) in Hayton parish.

425 Inquisition, 1295: *Cal. IPM*, III, no. 285 (p. 186).

426 M: 'Dom'.

Willm' de Windsor tenet Fenton de Margaret Dacre per < x >⁴²⁷
partem feodi < 36 >⁴²⁸ Ed. 3.⁴²⁹ Finis levat inter Johannem Warwick
<u>quer'</u> et Johannem Tillioll & Margarett uxor de d[*imidium*]⁴³⁰ de
Fenton manerii et terra in Haiton 33 Ed. 1.⁴³¹

[*p. 47 (129)*]

[D 39] Tryermaine⁴³² was at the conquest a fee of Gilsland. One
Gillandeus was lord thereof. He stood against the Conqueror, and his
son and heire Gilmor gott his owne peace with Randall Meschienes,
lord of Cumberland, and his brother William Mescheins, and quietly
enjoyed it in King Henry the first dayes, and built the first chappell theire (of wood) by the lycence of the first bishopp of Carliell,
Athelwold, and by consent of < Enoc >⁴³³ then parson of Walton kirk,
in whose parish it was. He made his cosne Gilamor the first chaplein
thereof, after which chaplaine succeeded one Daniell, and after him
Augustine that lived in the tyme of Thomas parson of Walton, which
Thomas became a channon in Lannercost <u>when [*it was founded*], and
then the rectory was appropriate to Lannercost</u>.⁴³⁴ After the death or
banishment of Gillamor, lord of Tryermaine and Torcrossok, Hubert
Vaulx gave Tryermaine and Torcrossok to his second son Ranulf
Vaulx, which Ranulf afterwards became heir to his elder brother
Robert the founder of Lannercost, who dyed without issue. Ranulf
being lord of all Gilsland gave Gilamor's lands to his owne younger
son named Roland, and lett the baronny descend to his eldest sonne
Robert filius Ranulf.⁴³⁵ Roland had issue Alexander and he Ranulf,
after whom succeeded Robert and they were named Rolands successively that were lords thereof untill the raigne of Edw. the 4th. That
house gave for armes: in a feild vert a bend dexter chekey d'or et
gules.

---

427 The figure is rendered as an ampersand in M.
428 Figure rendered '3ˢ' in M.
429 Inquisition, 1362: *Cal. IPM*, XI, no. 317 (p. 256).
430 M: 'Dg'; H: 'devi'; 'dimidium' is meant.
431 FF Cumb. 34 Edw. I [1305–6] (*CW2*, 7 (1907), p. 231, no. 175).
432 Triermain (NY 595 668).
433 M: 'Enor'.
434 The phrase 'it was founded' (supplied by Gilpin MS (*Accompt*, p. 143) and
  Fleming 1 MS [4], p. 50) is to be preferred to the reading 'he was commanded'
  in M. For the history of the chapel of Triermain, as recorded *c.* 1237, see *Laner-*
  cost, no. 346.
435 Roland de Vaux (d. before 1256), lord of Triermain, was probably an illegitimate brother of Robert (II) de Vaux of Gilsland: *Lanercost*, no. 43n.

[D 40] < **Highstedash** >

[D 41] < **Spadadam** >[436]

[*p. 48 (130)*]

[D 42] Kirkcambok[437] Eccl[e]sia ad convallem paludis. The place where Cambogh stands was named Camb-bogh-glan by the first inhabitants, whereupon the Romanes framed this name Camboglana and now Cambok and Cammo'k corruptly.[438] The nature of the soile and forme of the place caused the first < name, >[439] for there is a great bog or fenny-mire in a bottom or law round hole in that glan or dale nere unto the towne. The first possessor that I read of was one Alfred de Cammok in K. Henr. 2 tyme. Afterwards in Henr. 3 tyme and Edw. 1st the Tirryes: one Richard Tirry held it of Thomas Multon then lord of Gilsland, by the 8th part of a knight's fee[440] and after him Thomas de Leversdale, and Thomas his sonne. In 36 Edw. 3 William Stapleton and Robert de Leversdale;[441] in 22 R[s] 2[442] and Stapleton's part descended to the Musgraves with other the Stapleton's lands and a daughter.

[*p. 49 (131)*]

[D 43] Stapleton[443] was first demeasne of Gilsland and granted very auncientlye forth as a fee to the lords of Kirklevington. Richard de Levington dyed seized of a moiety thereof in the 34 of Hen. 3.[444] From him it descended to Radulf Levington who by Ada Gernon his wife (daughter to < Sir > Richard Gernon th'elder, and to Johan Morvill the second coheire and daughter to Sir Hugh Morvill) had

---

436 No accounts of Highstead Ash (NY 599 692) or Spadeadam (NY 585 706), both in Kingwater, have been located.

437 Kirkcambeck (NY 534 689).

438 Denton's attempt to link Camboglanna, the Roman name for Birdoswald, to Kirkcambeck is almost certainly incorrect. Modern place-name scholars interpret Camboglanna as Celtic *cam* ('crooked') + *glann* ('bank'); and Kirk-cambeck as 'the place on Cam Beck marked by a church': *PNC*, I, p. 56; III, p. 512.

439 M: 'named'.

440 Inquisition, 1295: *Cal. IPM*, III, no. 285 (p. 185).

441 See inquisition after the death of Margaret de Dacre, 1362: *Cal. IPM*, XI, no. 317 (p. 255).

442 In 1399 (23 Ric. II) William Stapleton and the heir of Robert de Leversdale held land in Kirkcambeck: *Cal. IPM*, XVII, no. 1324 (p. 516).

443 Stapleton (NY 50 71).

444 Inquisition, 1250: *Cal. IPM*, I, no. 199. For the subsequent descent of the lands of the lords of Kirklinton, see above: A39 (Kirklinton), C14 (Skelton).

issue Hawisse the wife of Sir Eustace Balioll. Hawise dyed without issue, therefore Stapleton and other the Levingtons' lands fell to her father's six sisters; soe became Matild de Carik her heir of Stapleton. Roland Carrick her son gave it to Pieres Tillioll in Edw. 3 tyme. And at that tyme the Stapletons held th'other moiety which descended to the Musgraves, and th'other moiety to the Morresbyes and Covills, Tilliolls' heires.

[D44] < Harper Hill >[445]

[D45] **Leversdale**[446] was first given to one Bernard le Fleming by Robert filius Hubert, lord of Gilsland in K. Hen. 2 tyme. He had two sonnes Robert and Walter which did successively inherit. After them William de Leversdale in the latter end of Hen. 3 tyme. He dyed 24 Ed. 1.[447] Then Thomas his sonne entered who had issue Thomas. In Edw. 2 tyme Henry de Malton in the right of Margarett his wife[448] and after him Thomas Malton 36 Edw. 3.[449] Then Thomas St ...

[D46] < Newby >[450]

[p. 50 (132)]

[D47] **Karlatton**[451] stands in Gilsland but < no >[452] part thereof. In Henrey the second's tyme one Gospatrick filius Makbenok held it of the king and payd fiftye markes.[453] Mak-ben-og was an Irish man and took part with King Stephen, therefore his son Gospatrick < filius junioris uxoris >[454] compounded with King Hen. for his father's liveing. After him King John gave it to Robert Ross of < Wark >[455] in Tindall, and Sowerbye and Hubbertby, untill the sayd Robert Ross recovered his lands in Normandy, which he lost in the king's service.

---

445 No account of Harper Hill (NY 501 716), in Stapleton parish, has been located.
446 Laversdale (NY 477 625).
447 Inquisition, 1296: *Cal. IPM*, III, no. 317.
448 Inquisition, 1326: *Cal. IPM*, VI, no. 678.
449 See inquisition after death of Margaret de Dacre, 1362: *Cal. IPM*, XI, no. 317 (p. 255).
450 No account of Newby (NY 47 58) has been located.
451 Carlatton (NY 52 52). A seventeenth-century account of Carlatton, incorporating much of Denton's narrative, is preserved in DUL, Howard of Naworth, C44a/3.
452 M: 'in'.
453 See Pipe Rolls 1158–9: *VCH Cumb.*, I, p. 339 (where he is named Gospatric son of Mapbennoc).
454 In Ferguson's edition (*Accompt*, p. 145) 'filius junioris uxoris' is given as the interpretation of the name 'Mac-ben-og'.
455 M: 'Marck'.

Henry the third took them from him and gave them to Alexander, king of Scotts, and his successors who held the same untill the king seized them for the revolt of John Ballioll, king of Scotts, since which tyme it was regium dominicum untill Rich. the 2's tyme who granted the same to Radulph Nevill, earle of Westmorland, and Johan his wife. After him it descended to Richard his son, earl of Salisbury, and from him to Richard, earle of Warwick his son, slaine att Barnett, after whose death King Edw. the 4th gave it to his brother Richard duke of Gloucester, being after king; and syeth that tyme it continued the possession of the crowne.[456] I read of one Ughtred de Carlatton and after him Robert de Karlatton in Henry the third and Edw. the first's tyme but whether they held any freehold there it appeares not.

[p. 51 (133)]

[D 48] **Ughtredby**,[457] habitatio Ughtredi, is the name of a little village in Brampton[458] parish in the baronny of Burgh. The place was soe named afore the Conquest of one Ughtred that first builded there, but what familye he was of it appeares not.[459] It was the inheritance of one Hildred of Carliell in Henry the second's tyme and descended as < his > other lands in Comquinton to his two grandchildren Richard and Robert, the sonnes of Odard filius Hildred, lord of Bampton. Robert had issue Adam and he Eudo, whom in the eleaventh of King Henry the third gave to Walter de Bampton, David Marshall, Robert de Wampole and Margarett his wife (sister and heire to Richard filius Ricardi filii Troit) the heires and successors of Richard Carliell fower carrucatts: Ughtredby and Little Bampton, two in Comquinton and one in Combersdale, in particion of Hildred lands, or satisfaccion for their parts of the same.[460]

[p. 52 (134)]

[D 49] **Raughton and Gaitskale.**[461] Raghe is the name of a river which takeing his .... runneth headlong by Thistlethwaite, Stockhillwath and Gateskaile, where it is received into Cawdey. The Ragh is which

---

456 The descent of Carlatton followed that of the other estates granted to Alex-ander king of Scots in 1242 and subsequently known as the honour of Penrith, namely: Penrith, Castle Sowerby, Great Salkeld, Langwathby (above, D18), and Scotby.

457 Oughterby (NY 29 55), a hamlet in Kirkbampton parish.

458 *Sic.* [Kirk]Bampton is meant.

459 Denton's interpretation is sound, the first element being the OE personal name *Ūhtrēd*: *PNC*, I, p. 143.

460 FF Cumb. 11 Hen. III [1226–7] (*CW2*, 7 (1907), p. 220, no. 29).

461 Raughton (NY 390 476); Gaitsgill (388 467).

signifyes running. The village Raughton < now standing >[462] on the hilside there (whose feilds adjoyneing make the east banks of Raugh at the foote of the river) doeth take name thereof.[463] And the hamlett Gateskale was first but a whinny place where the inhabitants of Raughton made skales and sheeles for their goates, which pastured on the blossomes of the whins there, though now it is inhabited and converted to tillage meadow and pasture.[464] About the Conquest it was all forrest and waste ground untill a great purpresture was there inclosed by < one > Ughtred filius ...... and rented to the king,[465] to be holden in fee farme and by serjeanty for keeping the eyryes of hawkes (which bred in the forrest of Englewood) for the king.[466] And therefore the Raughtons give the sparhawk in their cognisance.[467] The armes in the margent were borne by John Raghton and William Raghton his brother in King Edw. the third's tyme.[468] Their first auncestor Ughtred aforesaid had issue Roger, Richard and William, whose issue successively were called to their surnames Raughton of the place where they dwelt. Roger gave part of his land there to his brethren, and every < one > of them encreased their possessions within the forrest of Englewood by <u>renting purprestures</u>[469] to [*p. 53 (135)*] the king at Sebergham, Raughton, Gaitskale, Breckin-thwaite, and else where. One of their posteritye gave Little Raughton feild to the bishopp of Carliell. The last of Roger's name gave the mannor of Raughton to Margarett Stapleton his wife and her heires, for want of issue betweene them, whereupon William Stapleton her brother of Edenhall became her heire of Raughton, and by the Stapletons' heir generall, it fell to the Musgraves who enjoyed the same, till Humphrey Musgrave sold it to the tennants in fee.[470]

---

462 M: 'notwithstanding'.

463 In margin of M: 'villa ad rivum Raghe'. Denton is correct in interpreting Raughton as 'settlement on Roe Beck', but the name of the beck means 'boundary stream' (ON *rá* + *á*) rather than deriving from a word referring to speed: *PNC*, I, pp. 25, 134.

464 Denton's interpretation of the name Gaitsgill is correct: *PNC*, I, p. 133.

465 H: 'entred to the king', with 'Wm Rufus' in margin.

466 In 1212 Raughton was held by Henry, Thomas and Reginald by serjeanty and keeping the king's eyrie of hawks in the forest of Carlisle. It had been granted to their ancestor, Edwin, by Henry I: *Book of Fees*, I, pp. 197–8.

467 H: 'the family of the Raughtons give the spar'ehawke in that coat ensign'.

468 In the margin a sketch of arms: a bend cotised.

469 H has a blank here.

470 In margin: 'Raughton once the Musgraves'. For the Raughton family, see T. H. B. Graham, 'Vills of the Forest, Part II', *CW2*, 25 (1925), pp. 303–10.

[*p. 54 (136)*]

[D 50] **Wythope** salicium convallis.[471] Withope was a waste parcell of Allerdall above Derwend, adjoyneing to the same where it becomes a great lake and part[472] lyes betweene Emelthwaite[473] and Thornethwaite. Dame Alice Lucye, the second daughter and coheire of Richard Lucy and wife to Allane a Multon, second sonne to Thomas Multon, that marryed the widdow of Richard Lucy, gave Wythoppe and halfe of Whinfell nere Lorton, the eight part of Broughton and certaine corne out of Aspatrick milne, and three messuages and twentye acres of land in Caldbeck, unto John Lucy her sonne by the sayd Alane Multon, whom she named Lucye and not Multon, because that Lucy was the greater familye, and for that her elder sister Amabill, which marryed Lambert Multon did continue the name and armes of Thomas Multon their father in the familye of Egremont, she caused her children to be named Lucy and gave Lucyes' cote to her posterytye. She reserved of Wythop a penny rent service or a paire of gloves and after it was inhabited it was worth x^{li} per annum.[474] < The residue was worth viii^{li} ii^s ii^d per annum > and thereof she reserved a rent service of iii^d per annum. The said John Lucy lived in the tyme of Henry the third and Edw. the first and dyed about the 8th yeare of Edw. the 2.[475] Hugh Lowther the son of Hugh Lowther after the death of the said John Lucy enjoyed Wythopp, for in the 8th yeare of Edw. 2, Christian the widdow of the said John Lucy sued him for her dower in Wethopp.[476] It descended in the Lowthers' issue maile [*p. 55 (137)*] unto Sir Richard Lowther, now knight, according to the pedegree in the margent.[477] And the sayd Richard Lowther, sold the same in the fowerth yeare of King James the first of that name king of England, anno domini 1606, unto Richard Fletcher of Cockermouth, petty-chapman,[478] the son of

---

471 Wythop (NY 19 28). Denton's interpretation is correct: Wythop is from OE
      wiðig + *hop* ('withy valley'): *PNC*, II, p. 457.
472 H: 'that'.
473 H: 'Embletwhait'. Embleton is meant.
474 See inquisition *ad quod damnum*, 1307: PRO, C143/64/10. The grant of
      Wythop to John de Lucy *c.* 1260 survives in CRO, D/Van/Wythop deeds/1.
      For the early history of Wythop, see A. J. L. Winchester, *Landscape and Society
      in Medieval Cumbria* (Edinburgh, 1987), pp. 39–40, 95–6.
475 8 Edw. II = 1314–15.
476 Hugh Lowther (d. 1338) married Margaret, daughter of John de Lucy: H.
      Owen, *The Lowther Family* (Chichester, 1990), p. 20.
477 Neither M nor H has a pedigree in the margin here.
478 H: 'merchant'.

Thomas, the son of Henry Fletcher, who now enjoyeth the same to him and his heires for ever and holdeth the same by the said services of Henry now earle of Northumberland, as heir to Henry Peircy first of that name earle of Northumberland, to whom Maud Lucy his wife and last heire of the Lucye lands of that name in the xxth yeare of Richard the second gave the seignory of Allerdale.[479]

[D 51] **Embleton**, villa Amabiliae.[480] Embleton lyes above Derwent next unto Wythopp in a dale betweene Withopp and Seatmurthow on the < N. W. >[481] side of Wythopp. In the tyme of King Richard the first it was part of the demeasne of Allerdale, and then Robert Courtney and Dame Alice Romley his wife, one of the three daughters and coheires of William fitz Duncane (lord of all Allerdale ward from Dodden to Shark and Wampole), gave Embleton to Orme de Irebye, a younger son of Gospatrick filius Ormi fillii Kettelli < lord > of Seaton and Workington, and free common of pasture in Dockwray and Wythopp.[482] This Orme de Irebye was seated at High Ireby [*p. 56 (138)*] which his father Gospatrick gave him. Of that place his issue and posteritye took their surname and were called Irebyes. The hamlett of < Embleton >[483] continued in their name and possession untill the tyme of King Edward the third, according to the pedigree in the margent.

And in the 39th yeare of that king < Sir > John de Kirkby, knight, held it in fee.[484] And in the 22th yeare of King Richard the seconds [*sic*] one Jeoffrey Tillioll, in the right of Alice his then wife.[485] In the 19th of Hen. the 6th[486] an assisse of novell disseisin by Eleoner filia Roberti Ross militis and others versus James Kellome et Katherine

---

479 The Lucys' Cumberland estates passed by Maud (d. 1398), sister and heiress of Anthony de Lucy (d. 1368), to her second husband, Henry Percy, 1st earl of Northumberland: *Complete Peerage*, VIII, p. 254; IX, p. 712.

480 Embleton (NY 17 30). Denton is probably correct in regarding the first element as a personal name, but OE *Eanbald* is more likely than the medieval Amabilla, which he suggests: *PNC*, II, pp. 383–4; *Dict. LDPN*, p. 109.

481 M: 'northeast', but Embleton lies north-west of Wythop.

482 FF Cumb. 7 Ric. I [1195–6] (*CW2*, 7 (1907), p. 218, no. 2), printed in full in *Cal. Docs. Scotland*, I, no. 233.

483 M: 'Ireby'.

484 See inquisition after death of Thomas de Lucy, 1365: *Cal. IPM*, XII, no. 17 (p. 18).

485 See inquisition after death of Maud wife of Henry, earl of Northumberland, 1398: *Cal. IPM*, XVII, no. 1247 (p. 469).

486 19 Hen. VI = 1440–1. H gives date as 18 Hen. VI (1439–40).

uxor, for Embleton. And in 32 of Hen. 6th the said James Kellome and Katherine his wife recovered halfe the land against the said Elioner Ross.[487] In the 12th of King Ed. 4th John Pawlett held the same of the earle of Northumberland.[488] It is now the inheritance of Thomas Brathwaite, a lawyer.

[*In margin of p. 137:*] Ric.' 3 [*sic, for '1'*] Orm de Ireby; Thomas; H. 3 Wm; H. 3 John; E.1 Thom' qui vendidit; E.2 Willm.
[*In margin of p. 138:*] Jo. Kirkby kt bought of Jo. Ireby. Jeffrey Tillioll & Alice his wife [*followed, after a space of a few lines, by:*] Sir John Skelton's daughter & heire mater Marquiess' Winchester natus 1 Ric. 3 on nativit domini.[489]

[*p. 57 (139)*]
[D 52] Newton Regny[490] is a mannor < & >[491] village in the forrest of Englewood. It is called Regny of one William de Regni sometyme owner of the same. In the xxxiiith of King Henry the second William de Regny was impleaded in a writt of right by one William de Lasscells for a knight's fee of land in Newton Regny,[492] but did not prevaile for John Reigny succeeded after William his father, 4 Regis Johannis,[493] and William his son & dyed 4 Ed. 1.[494] Then th'inheritance fell to fower sisters and their heires: Elizabeth or Issabell uxor ...... Horseley a 4th part; Nicholas de Walton a fowerth part; Robert Kirkby and < Johan his wife >[495] a 4th part; and Hugh Littlecombe & Johan his wife and Robert Bruce and Alice his wife a 4th part.[496] But all their

---

487 FF Cumb. 33 Hen. VI [1454–5] (*CW2*, 7 (1907), p. 248, no. 359).
488 12 Edw. IV = 1472–3.
489 Gilpin, p. 104 (referring to the last sentence): 'in the MS. in marg[in] there is this note here'. The statement is puzzling: no connection between the Skeltons and William Paulet (1474/5?–1572), created marquis of Winchester in 1551, is known. His mother was Alice, daughter of Sir William Paulet of Hinton St George, Somerset: L. L. Ford, 'Paulet, William', *ODNB*; *Complete Peerage*, XII, p. 757.
490 Newton Reigny (NY 47 31).
491 M: 'a'.
492 cf. Pipe Roll, 33 Hen. II [1187]: *VCH Cumb.*, I, p. 361.
493 4 John = 1202–3.
494 Inquisitions, 1275: *Cal. IPM*, II, nos. 151, 239.
495 M: 'John'.
496 In the two inquisitions taken after the death of William de Reigny in 1275 his heirs were named as Joan wife of Robert Grubbe/Cribbe; Joan wife of John de Locun/Hugh Litilcombe; Alice wife of William le Pruz; Nicholas de Walton; and Elizabeth de Horsy/Isabel de Horshey: *Cal. IPM*, II, nos. 151, 239.

estates were in Robert Burnell, bishopp of Bathe, for in the 18th of
Edw. 1 he gave the manner by fyne unto Hugh de Lowther[497] who
dyed 10 Edw. 2[498] and left Hugh Lowther his son and heir his successor.[499] In the 44 Ed. 3 yeare Hugh Lowther the son of Sir Hugh and
Margarett his wife was found heir.[500] After <u>him</u> succeeded Robert
Lowther who dyed 8[to] Henry the sixt, and < after > Robert Lowther
entered Hugh Lowther that dyed the 15th of Edw. the 4th.[501]

[*In margin:*] 33 H. 2 Wm Reigny; 4 Jo. Jo. Reigny; 4 Ed 1 Wm Reigny;
4 coheires and < 18 E. 1 >[502] Robt Burnell episcopus Bathen' < qui >
vendid. 10 E. < 2 >[503] Hu. Lowther; 1 E. 3 Hugh < Lowther >, miles;
Ed. 3 Hugh; H. 6 Robt; Ed. 4 Hugh; Sir John Lowther, H. 8; Sir
Richard, Eliz; Sir Christ., Jac.[504]

[*p. 58 (140)*]
[D 53] **Dalemaine**, dominicum in valle,[505] is now the mansion house
of ...... Laton, Esq., and the name of the village adjoyneing to his
< tenents' farmes >[506] there. It is holden of the baronny of Greystock
per cornage and other services as a fee of the same. The first that I
read of which possessed the same was John de Morvill and Nigill
his sonne, and Walter the son of Nigill. In the 38th of Henr. 3[507] Sir
Richard de Layton, knight, was lord thereof and of Aldbye, in whose
issue maile it hath continued till this tyme according to the pedigree

---

497 FF Cumb. 18 Edw. I [1289–90] (*CW2*, 7 (1907), p. 229, no. 145).
498 Inquisition, 1317: *Cal. IPM*, VI, no. 14.
499 For the Lowther family in the fourteenth and fifteenth centuries, see Owen,
     Lowther Family, pp. 6–49.
500 Sir Hugh Lowther (IV) (*c.* 1326–1385) inherited after the death of his father,
     Sir Hugh (III), who died *c.* 1366, and his mother Margaret de Whale, who
     died Nov. 1369: Owen, *Lowther Family*, pp. 25–6.
501 Inquisitions: Robert Lowther, 1430; Hugh Lowther, 1475: see *Cal. IPM*, XXI,
     no. 345; Owen, *Lowther Family*, p. 45.
502 In M the date is written between 'episcopus' and 'Bathensis'.
503 M gives date as 10 Edw. I.
504 In H this marginal pedigree is repeated at the foot of the account of Newton
     Reigny.
505 Dalemain (NY 477 269). Since the name is recorded in the twelfth century,
     the second element is unlikely to represent the modern 'main(s)' in the sense
     of 'demesne land'. Place-name scholars have suggested that it means 'Mani's
     valley': *PNC*, I, p. 187.
506 M: '... his farmers there.'
507 H gives date as 18 Hen. III. The reference is probably to the inquisition after
     the death of Robert son of Thomas de Greystoke in 38 Hen. III (1253–4),
     which is now very badly stained and largely illegible: PRO, C132/16/9. The
     calendar (*Cal. IPM*, I, no. 314) gives few details.

in the margent, and though his land be holden in knight's service I doe not find any heire to have beene ward of his house. They give for armes ....[508]

[*In margin:*] John Morvill, H. 2; Nigill, 10 Jo. Regis; Walter, 44 H. 3 *and* Roger Laton, 10 E. 3;[509] Wm Laton, 33 E. 3; Tho. Laton, Ed. 3; Hen. 49 Ed. 3;[510] Wm Laton, 14 H. 6.

[*p. 59 (141)*]

[D 54] **Abbey of Holme Cultram.**[511] The Holme Cultram was demeasne of Allerdall, a waste forrest ground replenished with red deere, att the Conquest, for Ranulf de Meschiens gave the barony of Allerdale to Waldeiff the son of Gospatrick, earle of Dunbar, and bounded the same by the rivers of Derwent and Wampole, betweene < which >[512] two rivers the Holme Cultram lyes. Howbeit it seemes by the charters of the abbey that it was the soile and inheritance of Henry earle of Carlile, son to David king of Scotts, that dyed before his father, for Malcolumbe the Maiden succeeded his grandfather David in the kingdom of Scottland, as eldest son to the sayd Henry and next heire to the king. In the tyme of King Stephen, when he usurped the state of England, this Earle Henry gave two parts of Holme Cultram to the abbotts and monks there and granted the third part thereof to Alane the son of Waldeof aforesaid for his hunting there, which Alane then lord of Allerdale gave instantly the sayd third part of the same to the abbey as that which the said Henry fitz David had given him at the foundacion of the abbey. And Waldeof the son of the said Alane consented to the grant with his father which the said Henry confirmed as David & Malcombe aforesaid did his graunt to the monks.[513]

---

508 *Sic.* Neither M nor H provide details but Hutton John MS [6], p. 63, reads: 'they give for arms, Sa[ble] on a bend Arg[en]t 3 Escalops Gulets'.

509 H gives the date as 10 Edward II.

510 The pedigree in H omits Henry and assigns the date 49 Edward III to Thomas Laton.

511 The Cistercian abbey of Holme Cultram stood at Abbey Town (NY 17 50), the focal point of the extensive parish and lordship of Holme Cultram, which covered the coastal lowlands between Allonby and Kirkbride.

512 M: 'the'.

513 The charter of Earl Henry, dated in the Chronicle of Melrose to 1150, is calendared in *Holm Cultram*, pp. 91–2, no. 260; the confirmations by David and Malcolm are ibid., nos. 261–2. For the history of Holm Cultram abbey see *VCH Cumb.*, II, pp. 162–73.

At the death of King Stephen[514] Henry fitz Empress, the second of that name king of England, entered to Cumberland, which Stephen had before given to David king of Scotts, and therefore the monks acknowledged him their founder and he granted them by his charter totam insolam [*sic*] de Holme Cultram and Raby by their right boundes, timber and [*p. 60 (142)*] pasture in the forrest of Englewood, which his guift King Richard and John his sonnes and successors in the kingdome < allso > confirmed, with many libertyes expressed in the letters pattents without mention of any acts done by the < king of > Scotts.[515] It was then bounded by a little syke of water that falls into Wampole at Kirkbride ascending[516] that rill unto Corkley as the moss and hard ground mett. Thence through the midle of the moss betweene Wathholme and Lawrenceholme and soe cross the moss and wood to Anterpotts. Thence downe Waver till it receive Crombok; thence upp Crombok till it receive Witheskeld, so upp that side[517] unto the head thereof, then turneing west unto a syke that compasseth Mealdrig on the north and west side till it fall into Pow Newton, soe as Pow Newton falls into the sea, thence alongest the coast unto the foote of Wampole, and so upp Wampole unto Kirkbride aforesaid.[518] All this was the first foundacion of the kings, wherein they had forrest, but the monks presently erected five grainges for husbandry, at Raby, at Mawbergh, at Skinburne, at < Calfhow >[519] & turned all into tillage, meadow & pasture. Shortly after this Gospatricius the son of Orme gave them a part of his mannor of Seaton, vizt. Flemingby and the chappell there and the towne of Kelton, and his son Thomas a fishing in Derwent. He exchanged also with them Waitcroft for the said Kelton, which his

514 In margin of M: '1154'.

515 The charters of Henry II, Richard I and John are calendared in *Holm Cultram*, pp. 73–4, nos. 208–10.

516 This bounder is defective in H, which notes in the margin: 'Here the manuscript out of which this was transcribed is torn.'

517 Gilpin MS (*Accompt*, p. 60) reads 'syke'.

518 These are the bounds detailed in the confirmation charter of Richard I in 1189: *Holm Cultram*, p. 73, no. 209.

519 M: 'Culshaw', but Calvo is meant. In the margin a list of the granges: 'Old Grainge; graing de Tearmes; Maybergh; Skinburne; Raby'. The granges are represented on the modern map by Raby (NY 18 51), Mawbray (NY 08 46), Skinburness (NY 12 55), Calvo (NY 14 53) and Tarns (NY 11 47). The 'old grange' probably lay close to the abbey: *Holm Cultram*, p. 116.

father gave them.[520] Sir Hugh Morvill gave them his rectory of Burgh which they did soone approprite to their house; and his daughter Johan and his successors a salmon fishing in Eden and so much land in Burgh as they had there; also a grainge and to every carracutt of land there a net for fishing in Eden.[521] Sir Hugh Morvill gave also the pasture in Lazonby for 500 sheepe, ten kyne &10 oxen, and certain land and < for the young cattle & > sheepe their < ofspring >[522] of a yeare old.[523]

[p. 61 (143)]

Reginald Carliell gave them Newbye on the moore, which his cosne Richard filius Ricardi filii Troit gave him.[524]

Robert Torp gave them land and pasture for 700 wedders in Edenhall.[525]

Richard de Elneburgh and William fitz Symon Skelflings, lords of Alneburgh and Deerham, gave them a fishing at the mouth of the river Alne.[526]

Henry fitz Arthur filius Godard, lord of Milham, gave them Bakeley[527] in Millam which is belonging to Seaton nunery there.[528]

Sir Gilbert fitz Gilbertt de Dundraugh gave land and pasture for 600 sheepe in Distington; and Adam de Harraes att Branstibeck and Hugh Morresby in Distington.[529]

Robert de Bruce his fishing in Torduff in Annandale.[530]

Odard de Wigton gave them pasture in Wigton for a bow of kyne.[531] Waldevus filius Gamelli < filii Whilp > gave them a grainge in Kirkby-thore.[532]

---

520 In margin of M (but not H): 'Milleburna uxor domino Gilberti.' For the charters of Flimby, Kelton and Waitcroft: see *Holm Cultram*, pp. 18–20, nos. 49a–e.

521 *Holm Cultram*, pp. 1–9, esp. nos. 2, 12.

522 M: 'osperidge'.

523 *Holm Cultram*, pp. 9–10, no. 26.

524 *Holm Cultram*, p. 11, no. 31.

525 *Holm Cultram*, pp. 16–17, no. 44.

526 *Holm Cultram*, pp. 26, 30, nos. 65, 79.

527 *Sic*, for 'Leakley', which was the alternative name for Seaton nunnery: see *VCH Cumb.*, II, p. 192.

528 *Holm Cultram*, p. 31, no. 83.

529 *Holm Cultram*, pp. 32–4, nos. 87, 89, 91.

530 In margin of M and H: '1257' but the date of the grant is before 1191: *Holm Cultram*, p. 34, no. 93.

531 *Holm Cultram*, p. 44, no. 115, where the pasture right is stated to be for 10 cows and their calves, 2 horses and 10 swine and their young.

532 For the charters concerning the monks' property in Kirkby Thore, see *Holm Cultram*, pp. 61–8, esp. nos. 157, 160.

Adam filius Ketell de Newton gave them common of pasture in Newton.[533]

Thomas de Bromfeild and Adam his son land and pasture in Bromfeild.[534]

Margarett filia Johannis de Wigton the rectory of Wigton which they appropriated.[535]

King John and his brother Rich. the first gave Hylekirk and libertyes in the forrest of Englewood; and Henry the third Fryer Hall in Caldbeck.[536]

Lambert de Waverton and other freeholds there gave much land in Great Waverton and many others in diverse parts of this countye.[537]

Richard, earle Strongbow, and John de Crucy land and libertyes in Ireland.[538]

[*p. 62 (144)*]

Ughtred fitz Fergus, lord of Galloway, gave them the towne of Kirkgunyon there; and diverse others in Scottland, as William fitz Michaell de Kirkonell, lands in Kirkonell; Patrick fitz Thom' de Workington, Lochertor or Lochertores;[539] the bishopp of Glasco the chappell of Kirkginian;[540] < Duran >[541] fitz Christina Mayby in Kirkonell.[542]

Thus in short tyme they encreased their possessions to a great revenue yearly which maintained a lord abbott and ..... monks. They built there a church and the whole scite of the abbey of free stone which continued till these our tymes. King Henry the 8th tooke downe the habitacions and made the church to serve the inhabitants

533 *Holm Cultram*, p. 68, no. 191.
534 In margin of M: 'Ed. 3', though the charters concerning Bromfield are all from the thirteenth century: *Holm Cultram*, pp. 79–82, nos. 234–247a.
535 H: 'with the appropriacion'. For this grant, see: *Holm Cultram*, p. 45, no. 115c; T. H. B. Graham, 'Margaret de Wigton', *CW2*, 29 (1929), p. 87.
536 *Holm Cultram*, p. 76, no. 217; also pp. 73–4, no. 209. Friar Hall in Warnell, Caldbeck, originated in the grant to the monks of half the 'close of Warnel' by the parson of Caldbeck, confirmed by Henry III in 1232: ibid., p. 77, nos. 220–1.
537 *Holm Cultram*, p. 40, no. 103.
538 *Holm Cultram*, pp. 95–7, nos. 267a; 268.
539 H: 'Lochenter or Lachertor'. Loch Kindar (NX 97 64) or Loch Arthur (NX 90 68) may be meant.
540 For these grants of property in Galloway, see *Holm Cultram*, pp. 47–56, esp. nos. 120 (Kirkgunzeon); 116 (Kirkconnel); 127 ('Lochentur'); and 136 (chapel of 'Kyrkewinnin').
541 M: 'Durard'.
542 In margin of M: '1244'. For the charter in question see *Holm Cultram*, pp. 56–7, nos. 142–3, where the date is given as before 1234.

as a parochiall church, but now the same also is utterly defaced for the steeple lately fell downe through age, and < they > casually burnt the church with fire.[543] The rectory Queene Mary gave to the university of Oxford,[544] and the seignory of Holme Cultrum remaines yett in the king's hands, but all the other lands and commodityes in England are sold to strangers by the king's predicessors.

[p. 63 (145)]

[D55] **Waverton parva nunc Lasson-Hall.**[545] Little Waverton, now called Lassonhall, is within the baronny of Wigton, and holden of the same by .... It is the inheritance of Sir John Dalston of Dalston, knight, the son of John Dalston, son of Thomas, who bought the same of ...... Pennington of Mulcaster. The Penningtons enjoyed it .... decents from ...... who had it by .... in the tyme of King .... from the ....

In the 8th yeare of Edw. 2 John de Malton held it of the lady Margarett, the < sole > daughter & heire of Sir John de Wigton, being then valued at x^{li} per annum.[546] And in the < 32 > yeare of Ed. 1,[547] Sir Henry Malton, knight, bought by fyne levyed of John de Canton and Alice his wife,[548] the daughter and heire of ...... and then Hellen late wife of one Elias de Braiton[549] held it in dower for life, the inheritance being in Alice the wife of the said John Canton. In the 31 of Ed. 1 it was in the king's hand by the death of John de Mulcaster alias John de Easton, and by the forfeiture of Alice filia Benedict de Mulcaster next heire to the sayd John de Mulcastre de sanguine.[550] In the 6 yeare of Ed. 1[551] Alannus de Lasscells and Issabell his wife by deed indented and was impleaded then for the same by William Spar-

---

543 The steeple collapsed on 1 Jan. 1600–1 and the fire, started when a live coal and a candle were taken into the roof to search for a chisel, occurred in 1604: *Holm Cultram*, pp. 178–9.
544 The rectories of Holm Cultram and Newton Arlosh were among several granted to the university in 1554 to boost its revenues: J. McConica, *The History of the University of Oxford, Volume III: the Collegiate University* (Oxford, 1986), p. 141.
545 Lessonhall (NY 22 50).
546 Inquisition, 1315: *Cal. IPM*, V, no. 531(p. 299), though no reference is made there to the value of the estate.
547 M gives date, incorrectly, as 22 Edw. I.
548 FF Cumb. 32 Edw. I [1303–4] (*CW2*, 7 (1907), p. 231, no. 173).
549 H: 'Bramton'.
550 Inquisition, 1303: *Cal. IPM*, IV, no. 138.
551 6 Edw. I = 1277–8. H gives date as 8 Edw. I (1279–80).

ling and Alice his wife and her two sisters. Of that Lasscells it was called Lasscellhall, and since corruptly Lassonhall.[552] Before them the Wavertons held it according to the pedegree in the mergent from Adam de Parva Waverton who lived in the tymes of King Richard the first and King John as a fee of Wigton. Adam was testis to a deed of gift anno domini 1203.

[*In margin:*] Sir <u>Jo' Dalston m'</u>; <u>Jo' Dalston, ar</u>; <u>Tho. Dalston, ar</u>; <u>Pennington</u> [*4 lines space*] Jo' de Waverton; Hen Malton; Jo' de Malton; Sir Hen' de Malton; Alice uxor Jo' Canton; Jo' Mulcastre [*2 lines space*] Alane Lasscells & Issabell uxor eius [*3 lines space*] <u>Robt'</u>; <u>Radus'</u>; <u>Serley</u>; [*1 line space*] <u>Adam de parva Waverton.</u>[553]

[*p. 64 (146)*]
[D 56] <u>Waverton Magna.</u>[554] <u>Great Waverton, id villa ad Waver,</u>[555] <u>is a hamlett and fee of Wigton. It was aunciently a forrest ground and asserted by the posterity of the first baron of Wigton, which of the place took the surname and were called de Waverton, as namely Gamell de Waverton, Lambert, Serlo, Ketell, Gerrard and others, whereof some of them gave parts then to the abbey Holme Cultram to have their bodies buried there.</u>[556] <u>Alsoe the Thursebyes being forresters of fee in Allerdale rented diverse parts thereof to the king which from them descended to the Boyvells.</u>

*< 8 > Ed. 2 Lambert de Waverton 4 partem valenc' per annum xx[s] et ix[s] libt' redd'.[557] <u>Anno Ed. 4[to] 12[o] heredes John Waverton 8s 1d pl Adam Laithes qui vendidit.</u>[558]
Robert Dikes 8 partem valenc' xxx[s].[559]

---

552 Modern place-name scholars agree that the first element of Lessonhall is probably a surname, so Denton's interpretation may be correct: *PNC*, I, p. 159.

553 Gilpin MS, pp. 185–6 (printed in *Accompt*, p. 66) contains a version of this descent in reverse order.

554 Waverton (NY 22 47).

555 Denton's interpretation of the place-name is correct: *PNC*, I, p. 159.

556 Lambert son of Gillestephen of Waverton; Lambert son of Lambert and Adam son of Gamell are recorded in *Holm Cultram*, pp. 39–40, nos. 101, 103.

557 Inquisition, 1316, after death of John de Wigton (d. 1315): *Cal. IPM*, V, no. 531 (p. 299). In H the section marked here by asterisks occurs immediately after the account of Little Waverton. Gilpin (p. 186) notes beside this paragraph: 'MS. in a later hand'.

558 12 Edw. IV = 1472–3. The source of this statement has not been located.

559 This entry is from the inquisition of 1316: *Cal. IPM*, V, no. 531 (p. 299).

William Dikes 5 part'
Heredes Clement Skelton vi^t part'[560]
John Hormesby viii partem valenc xxx^s
William Osmodersley xii partem valenc' 40s
Symon de Whinhow xii partem < val' > 40s
John de Bothell xii partem < val' > 40s.*[561]

560 In H, this and the preceding line (which are not from the inquisition of 1316) are placed at the end of the section.
561 The final four entries are from the inquisition taken in 1316, after the death of John de Wigton (d. 1315): *Cal. IPM*, V, no. 531 (p. 299).

[*p. 527*]

[**E1**] Within this great barony of Copland, now called Egremond, are diverse knights' fees, which are mannors of them selves, holden of Egremond Castle, or of the lordes thereof as heires to the foresaid William de Mescheins or their assignes, as the tenors of their charters do report, or prescription hath gained by consent of lord and tenant. Amongst which mannors the lordship of Millum is the first, and of greatest libertyes; conteining < allso > in itselfe diverse manors which are holden of Millum (as Millum is of Egremont) immediately, with som difference of service.

This mannor reacheth from the river of Dudden unto Eske, tenn long miles in length, and from the sea, unto the further side of the mountaines about six miles in breadth, in forme (after a sort) thre-square and most inhabited alongst the rivers of Dudden & Eske, and towardes the sea-coste. The rest is forrest grounde, hills & great mountaines, best fitting for sheep & pasture.

< **Millum** >[2] Millum Castle, the ancient seat & capital mansion of this mannor, is plac'd at the foote of the river Dudden, which through length of time threatneth ruine. Howbeit the lords thereof make it yet their dwelling place and aboade, holding themselves content that the old manner of strong building there (with the goodly demeisnes and commodityes which both sea & land afford them, and the stately parke full of huge oakes and timber, woods and fallow deere) doe better witness their ancient and present greatness & worth, than the painted vanityes of our times doe grace our new-upstartes.

This great manor (in the time of King Henry 1) was given by William Meschiens, lord of Egremont, to .... de Boyvill, father to Godard de Boyvill, named in ancient evidences Godardus Dapifer, who being

---

1   This is the title at the head of the transcript in H. The transcript printed below is that in M. It is separate and in a different hand from the body of Denton's text and is prefaced by: 'Note. There are som loose sheets writt in a fair hand with fair margin, put in the Ancient copy (penes Dr Denton) which are not Part of the copy, but of a fair transcript collected out of it & (as I thinke) prepared for the Press, being writt more compendiousely & in a similar stile. Qu. If the rest can be found.' and 'It belongs as I thinke to § 3 of page the 6 [*i.e. paragraph 3 of p. 6 of the first part of the main text: section A3 above*] and Reacheth to .... Beginning and continuing thus'.

2   Millom Castle (SD 171 813) was the caput of Millom seigniory.

lord of Millum did give unto the abot & moncks of Furness a carucate of land there with the appurtenances call'd [*p. 528*] yet to this
day Monk-Force, which Arthurus filius Godardi confirmed unto the
abby, and after him in like sort his son & heire Henry fitz Arthure,
reserveing only the harts & hindes, wilde-boares and their kinds,
with all ayeryes of hawks.[3]

But whatsoever the lord of Egremont William Meschiens reserved in
the first grant to the Boyvills, whether demeisne or forrest libertyes,
Dame Ceciley Romeley, one of the coheires of William fitz Doncane,
& his eldest daughter, countiss of Albemarle (to whose purpartye
this Millum was allotted by partition) gave and fully confirmed the
same to the said Arthure fitz Godard, and to Henry his son & their
heires by her charter yet extant, under seale, bounding the same
thus: Dedi & concessi Henrico filio Arthuri et heredibus jus heredi-
tarium scilicet totam terram et totum feodum inter Esk & Doddon
cum < pertin' >[4] &c.; Dame Hawise, countess Albemerle, her sole
daughter & maryed to William de Mandevill, advised her said
husband allso to confirme it.[5]

And for recognition of the grant made to the Boyvills, Arthure &
Henry his son by Dame Ceciley the countess, they paid to King
Henry the second for a post-fine an hundreth poundes and five
couple of houndes, which the records doe terme decem fugatores.[6]

< Millum > The lords of this segnory of Millum have very anciently
held the same with great libertyes, and had jura regalia there; John
Hudleston did prescribe thereof in the twentyeth year of King Edw.
the first and was allow'd before Hugh de Cressingham in the pleas
of Quo Warranto holden for the king.[7]

The Boyvills held the same in their issue maile from the time of King
Henry the first untill the reign of King Henry the third above an

---

3   For the charters of Godard and his grandson Henry, see *The Coucher Book of
    Furness Abbey*, Vol. II, part ii, ed. J. Brownbill (Chetham Society new series 76,
    1916), pp. 522–3. See also *PNC*, II, p. 449.

4   M: 'pertys'.

5   The location of these grants of Millom, if they survive, is not now known.
    These and other references to charters in sections E1 to E6 suggest that Denton
    had access to early material from Millom seigniory which may no longer
    survive.

6   Pipe Rolls from 28 Hen. II (1182): *VCH Cumb.*, I, p. 353 *et seq.*

7   For the liberties claimed by John Hudleston in 1291–2 see *Placita de Quo
    Warranto*, ed. W. Illingworth (London, 1818), p. 123.

hundred years, viz : .... Boyvill, first lord; Godardus Dapifer, his
son; Arthure fitz Godard; Henry fitz Arthure; William fitz Henry;
Adam fitz Henry, brother and [*p. 529*] heire to William, and after,
Adam's sole daughter & heire Johan Boyvill, wife to the said John
Hudleston, knight, transfer'd the inheritance to the Hudlestons
whose heires mailes enjoy it at this day.

The first Boyvill gave to his second son William Boyvill, the manor
of Kirsanton with the appurtenances, whose posterity enjoyed the
same till the reigne of Ed. the second.

The second lord of Millum, Godardus, gave Munk-force aforesaid
to the abbay of Furnace, and the churches of Butle & Whittingham
and all the parishes betwene the River Eske & the parish of Millum
to the abby of St. Marye's of Yorke, to which abby his wife Matilda
also gave Andersett, now called Agnes Seat.[8]

Arthurus filius Godardi third lord of Millum, confirm'd his father's
grant of Munk-force, and of the premisses to the abbayes of Yorke &
Furnass, and granted to Furnass the service of Kirsanton in Millum,
which Robert Boyvill his cosan germain then held of him, and presently after did morgage the same to the abbot of Furness untill he
return'd from the Holy-land.[9]

Henricus filius Arthuri filii Godardi, fourth lord of Millum, confirm'd
his ancestors grants, & enfeofed Radulfe Corbett & his heires of
the manor of Brettaby, with the appurtenances in Millum. He gave
Risthwaite[10] in Dunnersdale, to one Orm filius Dolphini, and Leakley
to Henry filius Willelmi in frankmariage with his daughter Gonilde
Boyvill, with sheales for her cattle & common of pasture in Crochbeeghe and the forrest, which Gonild afterwards gave to the abbay
Holm-Cultrum, but it is now parcell of the possession of the late
nunnes of Seaton.[11]

All the residue of the fees in Millum were thus granted by the Boyvills
(lords of Millum), to their younger children & friends [*p. 530*] and by

---

8   *Coucher Book of Furness*, Vol. II, part ii, pp. 522–3; *St Bees*, nos. 76 (Godard's gift
    of churches of Bootle and Whicham); 39–41 (confirmations of Matilda's grant
    of Annaside).
9   For Arthur's grant of Kirksanton, see *Coucher Book of Furness*, Vol. II, part ii, p.
    514.
10 H: 'Kaisthwaite'. This place-name has not been identified.
11 For the grants of 'Leakley' (now Seaton SD 107 900), see *Holm Cultram*, p. 31,
    nos. 83, 85; *VCH Cumb.*, II, p. 192.

the Hudlestons & theire heires accordingly, som as mannors, som as
lesser frehold, as, namely, Ulfhay,[12] granted to one Ulff filius Evardi,
whose posterity enjoy'd it untill the time of K. Hen. 3. Ulff had issue
.........,[13] Aylsward, and Ketell. Ailsward paid to K. Hen. the second
in the 27th year of his reigne xx markes for a fine assessed on him
for an attaint.[14] Ketell had diverse sonnes, Benet, William & Michael.
Benett liv'd in King John's time. He had a son named Alan. But now
the land is reduced into demeisne again, and the lord of Millum Mr.
Huddleston and diverse of his ancestors have made there a parke
inclosd for deere, which yet to this day is called Uffhay-Parke.[15]

[E2] **Thwaites (M)**.[16] Thence along downe the river of Dudden
stands the mannor of Thwaites < between the river and the mountains, now the ancient seat of Joseph Thwaits of Ulnerigg, Esqr., and
of this place he and his ancestors have their surnames Thwaits. >
And the place being a stony mountanous countrey is not alltogether
every way fit for tillage meadow & pasture, but in severall parts and
peeces (as they are marked by nature) differing in forme or quality of
soyle, or otherwise inclos'd by the inhabitants from the barren wast
of the fells. Such pieces of land are now & of old called thwaites
in most places of the shire, somtime with addition of their quality,
as Brekanthwaite of fearns, Sivithwate of rushes, Stanythwaite of
stones, Brenthwaite of burning with the sunn, Reedthwait from
colour of the soyle, Overthwaite of higher lying, Moorthwaite of the
heath, Sowerthwaite of the wet soyle, Langthwaite of the forme in
length and diverse other.[17]

This mannor was an ancient fee, holden of the lord of Millum, for a
dowry was by Ellen the wife of John Boyvill, q' et Michael de Corney,

---

12 Ulpha (SD 19 93) in Dunnerdale.

13 The space marks are interlined.

14 Pipe Roll, 27 Hen. II (1181): Efward son of Ulf renders account of 20 marks *pro
   falso dicto*: *VCH Cumb.*, I, p. 351.

15 Ulpha Park (SD 18 91) covered the rocky ground between Logan Beck and
   Blea Beck.

16 The name Hallthwaites (SD 180 855) records the location of the manor house
   of Thwaites. The township stretched north to Thwaites Fell (SD 17 90).

17 Denton's gloss on the understanding of ON þveit ('a clearing') in the sixteenth
   century is full of interest. In M this paragraph includes several insertions in
   square brackets, which are probably Thomas Machell's work and are not
   found in H. One, referring to Denton's explanation of the name 'Brenthwaite'
   reads: 'Tho som believe in these northern parts that the Sunn never shines'.

passed by fine levied 35 Hen. the 3, of lands in Thwaites.[18] And John Hudleston impleaded William the sonne of John Thwaites, for 200 acres of pasture there anno Edw. 1 xvi°.[19]

The gentlemen of this family doe bear for armes a cross argent fretty gules in a field .... which seemes to me to be derived from the Huddleston's coate of whom they hold the mannor.[20]

[In Holkham MS, sections E7–E9 (Muncaster, Ravenglass, Drigg and Carleton) are placed here.]

[*p. 531*]

[E3] Whitcham.[21] **(M)** At the west end of Donerdale, near the fells foranenst Millum, stands Whitcham or Wicheham alias Whittingeham which all (or the most part thereof) was another fee holden of Millum, and (as I take it) the place tooke that name of one Wyche, the first feoffee of the same.[22] He liv'd about the time of K. H. 1. Two of his sonnes, William filius Wyche and Godfrey, were witnesses to a morgage of Kirsanton, in the time of King Hen. 2. But their issue generall brought the land into other familyes about the time of King H. 3, for then one Radulf de Bethom had the land, & the 6° of Ed. 1 he granted estovers to John, parson of Whitcham, in his woods there.[23] And one Rob. filius Radulphi de Bethom, warranted lands in Sellcroft and Saterton, in Millum, ix° Ed. 1.[24] But the mannors of Selcroft[25] & Whitcham, were in another family nono Edwardi secundi, as appeareth by a fine thereof levyed betwene William Corbet & Alicia his wife q[uerentes], and John de Corney deft.[26]

[E4] Whitbeck Lordship.[27] Some deal westward under the mountains standes the church or chapel of Whit-beck, which William Morthing, lord of Whitbeck, gave by fine levyed to the prior and

18 FF Cumb. 35 Hen. III [1250–1] (*CW2*, 7 (1907), p. 224, no. 86).
19 16 Edw. I = 1287–8.
20 H reads '… to whom they sold the mannor of Thwaits'.
21 Whicham (SD 13 82).
22 Whicham ('Whit(t)ingham' in early sources) is an early OE name, meaning 'village or homestead associated with *Hwita*': *Dict. LDPN*, p. 366; cf. *PNC*, II, pp. 443–4.
23 FF Cumb. 6 Edw. I [1277–8] (*CW2*, 7 (1907), p. 228, no. 120).
24 9 Edw. I = 1280–1. The locations of these lands are Silecroft (SD 13 81) and 'Satherton' (the north-east end of Whicham parish around SD 16 85).
25 In margin: 'Selcroft (M)'.
26 FF Cumb. 9 Edw. II [1315–16] (*CW2*, 7 (1907), p. 233, no. 188).
27 Whitbeck (SD 11 84).

covent of Conyngsseat in the xlvth year of King Hen. the 3.[28] These
Morthings and Corbets were anciently seated in Millum. I have seen
of their names in evidences and writeing made in the time of King H.
(or Ed.) the second, and to have bin men of good worth and quality
then, as namely one Will' de Morthing, & John de Morthing, Will'
Corbet, and Radulf Corbett. Diverse of the Corbetts seated themselves in Scotland, in those famous warrs of King Ed. 1, where their
posterity remain to this day.

[*p. 532*]

[E5] **Butle.**[29] Next unto Whitbeck, in the common high-street, more
towards the west is Butle, where of old stood a mansion of the family
of the Cowplands. They beare for armes, or, a bend sable, on a canton
& 2 barrs gules. I have seen a register of their descent, namely: Sir
Richard Cowpland, knight; Alane his son father to Richard, who
dyed seised hereof in the 26th year of King Ed. 1,[30] and left his estate
to John his son, father to another Richard Cowpland. They continued
in the issue maile till the time of Richard the second and King Henry
the iiiith & now their lands are transferr'd into other familyes.

[E6] **Corno (M).**[31] The mannor of Corney lyes next Butle in Millum,
more towards the north-east under the mountaines upon the top of
< the > lesser hills. Corney is called allso Cornhow, and Corno. Of
this place, the posterity of Michael le Falconer (& himselfe) tooke
the sirname of Corney, for they had feofment there anciently in the
times of King John and of Hen. the 3. And nearer the sea westward is
seated the nonery of Seaton,[32] of the endowment of the ancient lords
of Millum confirmed by the barons of the seigniory of Egremont to
the nunns there, which did continue untill by the late suppression of
abbayes the king had it given, who granted that scite & lands there in
Millum unto his servant Sir Hew Askewgh and his heires. But now it
is the Penningtons' lands. This knight descended from one Thurston
de Bosco, who lived in the dayes of King John, and had feofment
from the lords of Kirsanton at a place then call'd the Akeskewgh (or

---

28 For the grant of the advowson to Conishead Priory, the Augustinian house
   near Ulverston, see FF Cumb. 45 Hen. III [1260–1] (*CW2*, 7 (1907), p. 226, no.
   108).

29 Bootle (SD 10 88).

30 Inquisition, 1297–8: *Cal. IPM*, III, no. 449.

31 Corney (SD 11 91).

32 In margin: 'Seaton nunnery'. For this monastic house, see *VCH Cumb.*, II, pp.
   192–4.

Oakewood),[33] and from a poore estate was raised to that honor & preferment by his service to King Hen. the viii in his house ordinary, and in the feild at the seige of Bullen & warrs in France.[34]

[*p. 533*]

[E7] < **Mulcastre** >[35] The next fee unto Millum, holden imedately of the barony of Egremont, is Mulcaster, now the mansion of Mr Joseph Penington Esqr.[36] It is vulgarly named Monkastre but of old in evidences written Mule-castre & Meol-castre. The ancient house are those old ruines there called the Old Walls;[37] for their present dwelling place is a later erection, made by the Peningtons, much better & more conveniently sett for state and avoydance of the ayre's < sharp >[38] distemper from the sea. The mannour is bounded-in betwene that river Eske & a little rill or beck called Mite. It is in forme a long ridge or riseing-ground of hills from the foote of Eske, extended long betwene those rivers unto the great and vast moun- taines belonging to Egremont in Eskedale, Wastdale & Myterdale. There are not many under fees belonging to the mannour.

[E8] Ravenglass,[39] now a village, anciently a green of fearnes, whence it hath its name of < the two words > Reinigh, fearnes & Glass, green, deriv'd from the Irish,[40] stands there at the water side, where, by a grant made by King John to Richard Lucy, lord of Egremont (anno eius regni x°) is yerely kept a fair & a market in right of the haven there of lord paramount.[41] But the said Richard Lucy, in the same

---

33 FF Cumb. 4 John [1202–3] (*CW2*, 7 (1907), p. 219, no. 9); *St Bees*, p. 439n. Neither calendar gives the location of the land (half a carucate) granted in Kirksanton.

34 For Sir Hugh Askew (d. 1562), see C. R. Hudleston, 'Millom families: part ii', *CW2*, 93 (1993), pp. 90–2. In H the transcript ends here, the material below having been placed between sections E2 and E3, and is followed by 'NB. Here ended the fouer leaves that were stiched in.'

35 Muncaster (SD 10 96).

36 Joseph Pennington (1564–1641) was the son and heir of William Pennington (d. 1573): J. Foster, *Penningtoniana: Pedigree of Sir Josslyn Pennington, fifth Baron Muncaster of Muncaster* (London: privately printed, 1878), table before p. 1.

37 Walls Castle was the bathhouse of the Roman fort at Ravenglass: see W. G. Collingwood, 'Roman Ravenglass', *CW2*, 28 (1928), pp. 353–66; M. L. Brann, 'A survey of Walls Castle, Ravenglass', *CW2*, 85 (1985), pp. 81–5.

38 M: 'shap'.

39 Ravenglass (SD 08 96).

40 Modern place-name scholarship accepts an Irish derivation but interprets the name as a compound of *rann* ('part, lot or share') and the Irish personal name *Glas*: 'Glas's part or share': *PNC*, II, p. 425.

41 For the market charter of 1208 see *Rot. Chart.*, p. 26.

year, confirm'd by fine levyed to the mesne lord and tenants all the land & fee of Ravenglass, namely to Alan Penington, William fitz Hugh & Roger filius Edwardi, to hold the same of the said William and his heires.[42] And gave them moreover estovers to make them [p. 534] fishgarthes in the river Eske, to this day continued.[43]

The Peningtons have long enjoy'd the mannor and other landes there nigh adjoyning. But their ancestors tooke the sirname of Penington in Lancashire. They were for the most part knights successively, & men of great valour in the king's services, on the Bordures and Marches, and in other expeditions where it pleased the king to command them.

That old ruin'd castle of Mulecastre was so named because it stoode near unto a barren < wast >[44] ground at the foote of Eske called Eske-meil or mule. The Mulecastres have their sirnames of it, written aunciently de Mulcastre. That name Mule and Meil is common to diverse places there, as this meil-of-Eske, Kirksanton Meil, Cart-meill & the mule of Galloway & allso Millum it selfe.[45] These stand near the sea and are commonly low depressed ground & champaine under mountains & promontoryes into or at the sea & merse-groundes, and named mule as the mouth or enterance from sea into a river or such like place in the sea shore.[46]

[p. 535]
[E9] < **Carleton & Dregg** >[47] Between Myte and the river Irt and the sea is Carleton & Dregg, another fee of Egremont, now the Peningtons' land.

---

42 FF Cumb. 10 John [1208–9] (*CW2*, 7 (1907), p. 219, no. 19).

43 Fishgarths were fish weirs in which baskets were set to catch migratory species: see A. J. L. Winchester, *Landscape and Society in Medieval Cumbria* (Edinburgh, 1987), pp. 108–10.

44 M: 'vast'.

45 In M, numbers are written above these words, thus: allso (4) Millum (1) it (2) selfe (3), pointing to the word order in H, which reads 'Millum it selfe allso'.

46 The term Denton is discussing is the ON *melr* ('a sandbank'), found in Eskmeals and Cartmel, for example, but he is confusing it with ON *muli* ('a headland or promontory'), found in Mull of Galloway and, possibly, Muncaster. Millom is derived from neither: it means 'at the mills': *PNC*, II, p. 414.

47 Carleton was that part of Drigg parish between the rivers Irt and Mite, focused on Hall Carleton (SD 071 978); the village of Drigg (SD 07 99) lies north of the Irt.

Carleton was first villa rusticarum, a towne of husbandryes & then called Carleton, but after it was made a demeisne.[48]

Dregg had great store of oakes in the elder times, & thereof the Scotts & inhabitants at and before the Conquest called the manor Dreg of Derig or Dergh, which is oaks in that Scottish & Irish language. Mutch old blown wood beaten downe with the windes from sea and yet digged up out of mosses & wet ground there. And diverse other places in the country & Scotland allso have so got their names from Derig or Derghe; as Glenderghe in Scotland, Dundragh in Cumberland; and in our English, Aickton, Aikhed, Aikskeugh.[49]

48 Denton's interpretation is broadly correct: the first element of Carleton is OE *ceorl* or ON *karl*, both of which mean 'peasant': *PNC*, II, p. 377; III, p. 481; *Dict. LDPN*, p. 67. For a discussion of Carleton names in Cumberland, see C. Phythian-Adams, *Land of the Cumbrians* (Aldershot, 1996), pp. 26–7.

49 The terms Denton is discussing are Gaelic *darach* and ON *eik*/ OE *āc* ('oak tree'). However, both Drigg and Dundraw probably derive from ON *drag* ('a steep slope'), which also has the sense of 'portage', referring, in the case of Drigg, to a place where boats were dragged ashore: *PNC*, I, pp. 139–40; II, p. 377; *Dict. LDPN*, p. 101.

APPENDIX I: MANUSCRIPT COPIES OF
JOHN DENTON'S HISTORY

The following list aims to provide a summary of the known manuscripts of Denton's history. It builds on the list drawn up by David Mawson in 'John Denton re-visited: a fresh appraisal of the manuscript transcripts of his "Accompt"', *CW3*, 4 (2004), pp. 163–74. The manuscripts have been numbered anew below, but cross-references to Mawson's numbering are included.

Series A

[1] *Machell MS* [Mawson no. 2]. CRO, Carlisle Dean & Chapter muniments, Machell MSS, Vol. 6, pp. 1–146 and 527–35. Copies prepared for Thomas Machell (1647–1698), the antiquary and rector of Kirkby Thore. On Machell's death, his antiquarian papers, including these transcripts, came to William Nicolson, later bishop of Carlisle, who had them bound into six volumes and placed in the library of the Dean & Chapter of Carlisle. Parts 1 and 2 of Denton's history (sections A, B, C and D) are on pp. 1–146; the 'four leaves' (section E) on pp. 527–35. The title page, carries *inter alia* the heading 'MS Collectiones Antiquit' Cumbriae' and the date 1670. A note reads: 'Transcribing cost me 5s.' Part 1 (pp. 1–64) is headed by a note in William Nicolson's hand: 'The following description is Mr John Denton's first part'. Part 2, separately paginated, covers pp. 83–146 of the volume. Between the two parts, on p. 81 are pedigrees showing the descent of the manors of Cardew and Dalston, written in Nicolson's hand with the note: 'Before the 2d part of Mr Denton's MS in a copy lent to me (W. Carliol) by Mr Bird of Brougham, Jun. 3 1708, there are these pedigrees.' The transcript of the 'four leaves' (section E) on pp. 527–35 is in a different (and probably later) hand and is headed 'Note. There are som loose sheets writt in a fair hand with fair margin, put in the Ancient copy (penes Dr Denton) which are not Part of the copy, but of a fair transcript collected out of it & (as I thinke) prepared for the Press, being writt more compendiously & in a smarter stile.' It is preceded (p. 527) by a note, again 'penes Dr

Denton', of '3 Collections in order to the Antiq' of Cumb', consisting of escheats, fines and pleas, which are probably John Denton's extracts from records at Westminster. See also nos [23], [24] below.

The manuscript is heavily annotated in Machell's hand, with further marginal comments by William Nicolson. There is some evidence to suggest that Machell attempted to collate this transcript with the text of a Series B manuscript: for example, in the Gosforth entry [A6] 'the wife of Robert Leyburne' has been amended to read 'the widow ...'; in Seascale [A8] 'Senhouse' has been replaced by 'Seanos'; and in Bolton [A11] the same surname has been replaced by 'Seavenhowes'. In each case the replacement approximates to the Series B version.

[2]   *Holme MS* [Mawson no. 16]. Oxford, Bodleian Library, MS Top. Cumb. c.1.

Contains Parts 1 and 2 (sections A, B, C and D, ending with Holm Cultram [D54]) but not the 'four leaves'(Section E). It is in the same (or an almost identical) hand as Machell's transcript, retaining the same pagination and page layout as MS [1], and incorporating Machell's marginalia in Part 1 (but not in Part 2). The top left-hand corner of first page of text carries the title: 'A Description of the Countye of Cumberland Booke the first' and below this 'First part.' The transcripts of Denton are followed by two later documents, 'The rights and privileges of the King Tennants within the Forest of Englewood' (carrying the signature of Thomas Denton) and 'The Boundry of the Forest of Englewood' and other, later, material in an eighteenth-century hand. The volume bears the signature 'John Holme his 1712' and, at the end of the transcript, the address 'To Mr John Holme Attorney att Law in Carlile, These'. The owner is probably to be identified as John Holme (d. 1755) of Holme Hill, Hawksdale, Dalston (see *CFH*, p. 163). The front age also bears the note: 'Bought from U. Maggs Aug 14 1888 for £1 16 0.'

[3]   *Jackson A1114.* Carlisle Library, Jackson Collection, A1114. An incomplete manuscript, covering most of Part 1 only (sections A1 to B12). It is in a hand slightly later than MS [1] and MS [2] but retains the same pagination and layout as these. The early provenance of this copy is unknown: it formed part of a bequest given to Tullie House Library, Carlisle, in 1945, in memory of Christopher Scott-Nicholson (1906–1945) by his widow.

[4]   *Fleming 1 MS*. CRO, D/Lons/L12/2/2 and 3. A late-seventeenth-century copy in two volumes, numbered 'MS. B' and 'MS. C', largely in the hand of Sir Daniel Fleming (1633-1701)

of Rydal. The two volumes are identified in Fleming's memoirs as 'a Copy of a Manuscript in Folio, writ by Mr. Jo. Denton of Cardew in Cumberland, a sticht Book, wherein is a good Account of divers Persons & Places in the County of Cumberland' (CRO, D/Lons/ L12/2/15, f. 230). 'MS. B' contains Part 1 (sections A and B) and is followed (pp. 85-9) by a transcript of section E in another hand, at the top of which Fleming has added: 'A copy of some loose sheets of Mr Jo. Denton's lent me by Mr James Bird of Brougham Anno Domini 1683'. 'MS. C' carries the title 'Pars secunda' on the cover and contains Part 2 of Denton's history (sections C and D), followed by other material, including pedigrees showing the descent of Cardew and Dalston (also found in Machell MS [1], p. 81) on p. 67; a pedigree of the Briscos of Crofton taken from 'a copy of MS. B & MS. C (lent me by Mr Rich. Jackson July 24 1690)', for which see [26] below, on p. 68; and summaries (in a different hand) of charters concerning the Lowther family estates, on pp. 69-84. The text contains most of the Series A variants, though it includes the account of Wiggonby [C10], which is omitted in most Series A manuscripts. A *terminus ante quem* is provided by the date of 1683 for the addition of the section E material at the end of Fleming's transcript of Part 1. I am grateful to Scott Sowerby and Noah McCormack for allowing me sight of their transcript of Fleming's memoirs in advance of publication, without which this copy of Denton's history would not have been identified.

[5] *Fleming 2 MS*. CRO, D/Lons/L12/2/4.
A seventeenth-century copy in a hand and layout similar to the Machell [1] and Holme [2] manuscripts, containing Parts 1 and 2 (sections A, B, C and D), though the first folio is missing and the transcript begins midway through section A2. It is identified in a modern hand as a 'fair copy' of Fleming 1 MS [4] but it does not conform in all textual variants to [4], though it does include the account of Wiggonby [C10]. It is presumably a copy which belonged to Sir Daniel Fleming, since it survives among his antiquarian papers, but it cannot be identified in the list of Fleming's manuscripts included in his memoirs (CRO, D/Lons/L12/2/15, f. 230). It is conceivable that it is the copy Fleming used in his own description of Cumberland (1671), which is printed in E. Hughes (ed.), *Fleming-Senhouse Papers* (Cumberland Record Series II, Carlisle, 1961), pp. 34-61.

[6] *Hutton John MS* [Mawson no. 9]. CRO, D/Lons/L.12/4/5/1.
Contains Parts 1 and 2 (sections A, B, C and D, ending with Holm Cultram [D54]). The manuscript is entitled 'Ancient State and History of the County of Cumberland from the Conquest to the

Reign of King James 1st' and is said (in a later hand on the flyleaf) to have been 'found amongst the ancient title deeds evidences and records of the manor of Hutton John'. It was lent by Andrew Hudleston of Hutton John to Sir James Lowther in 1771 and not returned. In 1892 it was rediscovered in Lord Lonsdale's London house, along with the manuscript of Thomas Denton's *Perambulation of Cumberland* (see R. S. Ferguson, 'The Denton manuscripts', *CW1*, 13 (1895), pp. 218–23). The transcript appears to date from the late seventeenth century: loose pages in a more modern hand are dated 1698; internal evidence suggests a *terminus post quem* of 1674 (D. J. W. Mawson, 'Another important copy of John Denton's manuscript', *CW2*, 78 (1978), p. 98).

Series B

[7] *Holkham Hall MS* [Mawson no. 10]. Holkham Hall Muniments, MS 760.
In a hand from around 1700, containing (in order) sections A, D, C, B and E. There are hints that the transcriber did not know Cumberland well: some place-names have been garbled ('Withowe' for Wythburn; 'Olenkewn' for Glencoyne ('Glenkewne' in [1])). The manuscript was discovered in the earl of Leicester's library at Holkham Hall, Norfolk, in 1922 by the earl's librarian, C. W. James, who suggested that it had come to Holkham through Lady Margaret Tufton, daughter to Thomas, 6th earl of Tufton (d. 1729), heiress to the barony of Clifford and a descendant of the earls of Cumberland, who became countess of Leicester (C. W. James, 'A copy of John Denton's MS. in the possession of the earl of Leicester', *CW2*, 23 (1923), pp. 103–8). An alternative connection, suggested by Mary Wane, is through the Denton family of Hillesden, Herts., whose members included Dr William Denton (1605–1691), who seems to have possessed a copy of John Denton's history (see below, no. [24]). He was guardian to the heirs of his brother, Sir Alexander Denton (1596–1645), whose descendant Elizabeth Denton (d. 1810) married Wenman Roberts, heir to the Holkham estate (Mary Wane (personal communication); *Complete Peerage*, VII, pp. 562–5).

[8] *Mawson MS* [Mawson no. 11]. CRO, DX 1915/2.
Apparently a sister copy to MS [7], with the distinctive rendering of the phrase 'four leaves' (section E) as 'Tower leaves'. It is described in D. J. W. Mawson, 'Another important copy of John Denton's manuscript', *CW2*, 78 (1978), pp. 97–103. A note to the reader in the

hand of the antiquary Dr Hugh Todd (*c.* 1657–1728) identifies the text as an 'imperfect account of the County of Cumberland … made by one Mr Denton of Cardew, near Carlisle, in the latter end of Queen Eliz.'s Reigne.' The transcript is undated but, on the basis of the note it contains updating the pedigree of the Brisco family of Crofton, David Mawson suggested (*CW2*, 78 (1978), p. 99) that it was made between 1690 and 1694. The provenance of this copy is unknown before 1976, when it was purchased by David Mawson of Banks, Brampton, from Michael Moon, antiquarian bookseller of Beckermet (*Catalogue 28*, item no. 51). After David Mawson's death in 2006, it was offered for sale by R. F. G. Hollett & Son, antiquarian booksellers, Sedbergh, in their winter 2007–08 catalogue (*List 150*, item no. 83) and purchased by Cumbria Archive Service. It is possible that this was the copy included in Edward Bernard's catalogue of manuscripts in Carlisle cathedral library (see below, no. [25]).

[9] *St Edmund's Hall MS* [Mawson no. 14]. Oxford, Bodleian Library, St Edmund's Hall MSS, 8/1.
A copy omitting the accounts of Cardew [D9] and Crofton [C1]. It is contained in pp. 305–435 of one of five volumes sold at Sotheby's on 20 December 1932 (lot 38). Three of the volumes contained Hugh Todd's account of the diocese and bishopric of Carlisle; this contained transcripts of various documents relating to the history of Cumberland and the diocese. The lot was sold on behalf of Lord Brougham and Vaux of Brougham Castle, Penrith, and was bought by Thorpe, who may have been a bookdealer. All five volumes were later acquired by Alfred Emden, principal of St Edmund Hall, Oxford, who presented them to the college library in 1950.

[10] *Craighall MS* [Mawson no. 15]. CRO, DX 1329/1. A manuscript prepared by Hugh Todd in 1688 for Richard Graham of Netherby, Viscount Preston (1648–1695) but probably never delivered, as a result of Preston's attainder for supporting James II. It apparently remained among Todd's personal papers, which passed by his daughter Catherine, wife of Archibald Hope, son of Sir Thomas Hope of Craighall, into the Hope of Craighall muniments (National Archives of Scotland, GD 377/162). Todd's papers were deposited in CRO by the Scottish Record Office in 1993. Inside the front board of the volume is written 'Dr Todd MSS No 1. 1889 JDH'.

Re-ordered copies

[11] *Gilpin MS* [Mawson no. 4]. CRO, DX 1915/1.
The manuscript used by R. S. Ferguson as the basis for his edition
(*An Accompt of the most considerable Estates and Families in the County
of Cumberland*, CWAAS Tract Series 2 (Kendal, 1887)). The flyleaf
bears the signature of William Gilpin (1657–1724) of Scaleby and
the date 20 August 1687 (the year has been altered, possibly from
'1678'). Gilpin's preface assigns authorship to Denton: 'The originall
MS is supposed to be writ by an ancestor of Mr Denton's of Cardew
during the time of his imprisonment (as its said) in the Tower, upon
a contest that hapned to be betwixt him & Dr Robinson then Bp. of
Carliell.' Gilpin claimed that the transcript was 'word for word with
the originall, there being no alteracions but onely in the method, the
places being here reduced under their respective baronies ...' His
source cannot be identified with either Series A or Series B manuscripts, since the text includes variants occurring in both series. Gilpin
re-ordered the entries, arranging them under each barony and struc-
turing them geographically, beginning with Millom and ending with
Liddell, Kirklintion and Linstock. He added some material of his
own, including introductions to Inglewood forest (pp. 247–8) and the
barony of the sons of Swein (p. 317), placing his additions in square
brackets and marking them with double quotation marks in the
margin. His additions were, however, printed by Ferguson without
any indication that they were not part of the original text. Gilpin also
added marginal notes identifying sections which appeared to him to
be in a later hand in the manuscript from which he was copying. He
copied Denton's text into the upper sections of each page, leaving a
generous space below, in which he added coats of arms and notes
on the subsequent descent of manors to 1687. Gilpin's manuscript
was still at Scaleby Castle in 1887. In the early 1970s, it was bought
by Michael Moon, the antiquarian bookseller of Beckermet, from Ben
Weinreb, a London bookdealer, and was purchased from Michael
Moon by Dr Andrew Thornton of Holmrook, who sold it to David
Mawson of Banks, Brampton in 2003. After David Mawson's death
in 2006, it was offered for sale by R. F. G. Hollett & Son, antiquarian
booksellers, Sedbergh, in their winter 2007–08 catalogue (*List 150*,
item no. 84) and purchased by Cumbria Archive Service.

[12] *Queen's College MS* [Mawson no. 3]. Queen's College, Oxford,
MS 282.
The manuscript appears to be an attempt to sketch out a history
of Cumberland manor by manor, using John Denton's work as a

starting point: parts of Denton's text are substantially re-written. It is headed: 'An Imperfect Account of the County of Cumberland'. Additional place-name headings have been entered to fill in the gaps in Denton's accounts for Allerdale above Derwent ward and several manorial descents have been updated to 1687, presumably indicating the manuscript's approximate date. A second hand has added a few marginal notes making corrections from 'Denton's MS'. It bears an inscription recording its donation to the library of Queen's College, Oxford, by Dr Hugh Todd, probably towards the end of the seventeenth century.

[13] *Thomas Denton MSS*
[13a] Manx National Heritage Library, Douglas, Isle of Man, MS 5A.

A small volume used by Thomas Denton (1637–1698) of Warnell as a commonplace book in the mid 1680s. It contains material found in his 'Perambulation of Cumberland' (below [13b]), including his accounts of the Isle of Man and Dublin, as well as re-ordered transcripts of part of John Denton's history, under the title: 'The Coppy of an Old Manuscript of the Etimoligies of divers Parishes, Townes, & houses in Cumberland, and also ye geneoligies, and and [*sic*] Pedigrees of many ancient Families, who were & are owners'. The extracts from John Denton are all from sections C and D, suggesting that Thomas Denton only had access to Part 2 of Denton's history at that time. The manuscript was acquired by the Manx Museum in 1923, when it purchased the library of the Manx bibliophile, George William Wood, of Streatham, London, to form the basis of what is now the Manx National Heritage Library. According to Wood, writing in 1898–9 (*Yn Lioar Manninagh*, 3 (1895–1902), p. 435) he had purchased the manuscript 'a few years ago' from the library of Thomas Noble, senior warden of the Ironmonger's Company, London, and the manuscript had formerly been in the collection of 'Dr. Percy' (probably Thomas Percy (1729–1811), for whom see R. Palmer 'Percy, Thomas', *ODNB*).

[13b] CRO, D/Lons/L12/4/2/2.
Thomas Denton's 'Perambulation', compiled for Sir John Lowther in 1687–8 (published as *Thomas Denton: A Perambulation of Cumberland 1687–8*, ed. A. J. L. Winchester with M. Wane, Surtees Society Volume 207/CWAAS Record Series XVI, 2003), reproduced the relevant sections of John Denton's history as its starting point for its parish histories. Nowhere is the source acknowledged, other than to credit the description of the boundaries of Cumberland as being

the work of 'a good antiquary' (p. 33 of the printed edition). Across his 'perambulation' of Cumberland, Thomas Denton reproduced John Denton's work almost in its entirety (with the exception of his account of Carlisle), incorporating material from sections A, B, C, D and E, suggesting that he subsequently had access to both Part 1 and Part 2 and the 'four leaves'. A comparison of key variants suggests that, like Gilpin, his source cannot be identified as either a Series A or a Series B manuscript.

Later copies

[14] *Society of Antiquaries MS* [Mawson no. 5]. Library of the Society of Antiquaries of London, SAL/MS/91.
A folio copy from a Series A manuscript, considered by Ferguson to have been made between 1734 and 1747. Its title states that it had been 'collated with a copy formerly belonging to William Nicolson, Ld Bp of Carlisle', presumably the Machell MS [1]. Appears to have been given to the Society of Antiquaries by Charles Lyttelton, bishop of Carlisle, in 1762.

[15] *Milbourne MS* [Mawson no. 7]. Carlisle Library, Jackson Collection, A151.
A copy of the Gilpin MS [11] with annotations brought down to 1749 by William Milbourne of Armathwaite Castle. Used by R. S. Ferguson in conjunction with [11] in preparing his edition of John Denton's *Accompt*, published in 1887.

[16] *Jackson A177* [Mawson no. 9]. Carlisle Library, Jackson Collection, A177.
A copy of Machell MS [1] in an eighteenth-century hand.

[17] *Rowley MS* [Mawson no. 13]. An eighteenth-century copy of a Series B manuscript, probably the Mawson MS [8], with the addition of a pedigree of the Orfeur family, brought down to 1732. Purchased in the 1950s by Mrs Myrtle Rowley of Glassonby from a Darlington bookseller. It was in the possession of Mrs Hilda Walmesley of Rickmansworth in 2003 (information from David Mawson).

[18] *Fetherstonhaugh MS*. An eighteenth-century copy of a Series B manuscript in the library at The College, Kirkoswald, identified by Richard Brockington in 2009. It appears to be a copy of – or a sister copy to – the Rowley MS [17], as it includes the pedigree of the Orfeur family to 1732, with additions in a later hand to 1790. The phrase 'four leaves' (section E) is unequivocally transcribed as

'Tower leaves', again suggesting that the source was the Mawson MS [8]. The provenance of the Fetherstonhaugh MS is unclear: Mr Timothy Fetherstonhaugh has suggested to me that it may have been acquired by his grandfather, Col Timothy Fetherstonhaugh (1869–1945), who was a keen antiquarian.

[19] *Aglionby MS* CRO, D/Ay/5/17.
An early- to mid-eighteenth-century transcript of a Series A manuscript, sections A, B, C and D. The entries for the Wavertons [D55 and D56] are in a different hand from the rest of the transcript. The source was probably the Machell MS [1], since the transcript includes Machell's marginal notes.

[20] *Jackson A171.* Carlisle Library, Jackson Collection A171.
Nineteenth-century transcript of a Series B manuscript, annotated in red by R. S. Ferguson and collated with Machell MS [1]. A note at the beginning, probably in Ferguson's hand, reads: 'The Copy of John Denton of Cardew's MS from which this was taken was most probably made between the years 1707 and [*blank*] when William Nicolson was Bishop of Carlisle, as his name is placed after Robinson's in the list of bishops, omitting the intermediate names.'

Other recorded copies

This section lists copies referred to in various sources but which can no longer be identified. In the absence of evidence for the early provenance of most of the manuscripts listed above, it is possible that some of the copies below may, in fact, be the same as others listed above.

[21] *Mawson no. 1.* Ferguson (*Accompt*, p. iii) recorded a 'very early copy' in the possession of 'the late Major Fairtlough of Roodlands, Keswick', which was then (1887) in Canada. Ferguson stated that he had copied this manuscript 'many years ago' but neither the original, nor Ferguson's copy have been traced.

[22] *Mawson no. 6.* Ferguson also recorded (*Accompt*, pp. v–vi) a vellum-bound book, measuring 7 inches by 5½ inches, then (1887) in the possession of Mr Browne of Tallentire Hall, containing a copy of John Denton's History, a copy of Hugh Todd's history of Carlisle, and documents referring to Highhead Castle and Inglewood forest. It had previously belonged to Josiah Relph of Sebergham (d. 1743) and bore his signature and a list of his linen.

[23] *Bird MS*. In his annotations to the Machell MS [1] (p. 81) William Nicolson records being lent a copy of John Denton's manuscript by Mr Bird of Brougham in June 1708. That this was a Series A copy is implied by the reference to 'the 2^d part' of Denton's manuscript in the copy lent by Bird. Sir Daniel Fleming had also borrowed material identified as 'Mr Denton's' from James Bird of Brougham: in 1682 he borrowed three books, containing transcripts of pleas and fines (CRO, D/Lons/L12/2/11), and the following year 'some loose sheets', containing section E of Denton's history (see above [4]).   Bird's Denton manuscripts have not been traced. James Bird (d. *c.* 1714) was steward of the Appleby estates of Lord Tufton.

[24] *'Dr Denton' MS*. The transcript of Section E (the 'four leaves') in Machell MS [1] (p. 527) is prefaced by the statement that these were 'put in the Ancient copy (penes Dr Denton)' but were 'not Part of the copy'. This implies that Dr Denton possessed an early copy of John Denton's history. Like James Bird (above, [23]), he also possessed copies of John Denton's collections of notes from Crown records, described as '3 Collections in Order to the Antiq. of Cumb' (CRO, Machell MSS Vol. VI, p. 525). For the identity of 'Dr Denton', see above, Introduction, p. 8.

[25] *Carlisle Cathedral MS*. In his list of manuscripts belonging to Carlisle Cathedral, Edward Bernard included as no. 610.8 'Descriptio Cumbriae Anglice: facta per D. [*sic*] Denton, armigerum de Cardew, prope Carlielum temp. Eliz. R.' (E. Bernard, *Catalogi Librorum Manuscriptorum Angliae et Hiberniae* (Oxford, 1697), p. 13). As Bernard's catalogue was published before Thomas Machell's death in 1698, it is probable that this entry refers to a copy other than no. [1] above. It may refer to one of Hugh Todd's Series B copies of the Denton manuscript. Todd had supplied Bernard with a list of manuscripts at Carlisle, including several of his own that he intended to place in the cathedral library (see D. J. W. Mawson, 'Dr Hugh Todd's account of the diocese of Carlisle', *CW2*, 88 (1988), pp. 207–24). The similarity in the wording of the phrase assigning authorship in the entry in Bernard and the preface of the Mawson MS [8] is striking: it may be that the Mawson MS was the one Todd intended to deposit in the cathedral and which, in consequence, was included in Bernard's catalogue, even though Todd did not ultimately deposit it there.

[26] *St Bees School MS*. In July 1690 Richard Jackson, headmaster of St Bees school, sent Sir Daniel Fleming of Rydal a transcript of 'the Description of Cumberland', taken from a copy he had apparently borrowed ('The Copy this was taken by is now gon from me'). Fleming entered a pedigree of the Brisco family of Crofton from this manuscript into the volume containing his own transcript of Denton's history (above, [4]) and returned the transcript, via the usher of St Bees, in June 1691 (J. R. Magrath (ed.), *The Flemings in Oxford*, Volume II (Oxford, 1913), pp. 294–5). I am grateful to Richard Sharpe for drawing my attention to this reference.

Fragments

[27]   *CRO, D/Lec, box 219.* Caldbeck entry [B14] only. A late seventeenth-century copy of the Caldbeck entry, combining elements from both Series A and Series B, headed 'A discription of the parish and Mannors of Caldbecke Underfell and Upton when they came first to be inhabited and tilld.' It is signed 'George Denton' and carries the verification 'vera Copia Originall' Exa[mina]tur per me Jacobum Nicholson.' I am grateful to Professor Ron Davie of Caldbeck for drawing my attention to this document.

[28]   *Oxford, Bodleian Library, MS Gough Scotland 4, ff. 19r, 19v.* Croglin ('Kirkcroglin') [D26] and Caldbeck [B14] entries only. A late seventeenth-century copy of the entry for Croglin, followed immediately by that for Caldbeck; the latter follows the Series A rather than the Series B text. The entry for Croglin carries an addition, found in neither Series A nor Series B, recording an addition to the arms of Thomas, Lord Wharton, granted for service at Solway Moss.

[29]   *Carlisle Library, Jackson Collection A167 and A180.* Partial, nineteenth-century copies in the same, or very similar, hands: A167 covers sections A1to A43 (Cumberland bounds to Gilsland barony); A180 covers sections C1 to C8 (Crofton to Bowness on Solway) only.

APPENDIX II: SERIES A AND SERIES B MANUSCRIPTS: KEY VARIANTS

The following tables identify the major textual differences between Series A and Series B manuscripts. They are based on an analysis of manuscripts [1], [2], [3], [6], [7], [8] and [10].

Omissions etc.

Section	Variant text	Series A	Series B
A33	manors held of Papcastle	omitted	included
A39/A40	final section of descent of Rockcliffe	correctly placed in A40	misplaced in middle of A39
B2	paragraph beginning 'After the death of Richard, earl of Chester …'	omitted	included
B4	final sentence	omitted	included
B6	text from 'and that dorpe or village' to end	included	omitted
B11	marginal note re copy being 'rent'	included	omitted
B11	final sentence (at foot of p. 59)	omitted	included
B12	damaged material at foot of p. 60	omitted	included
B14	damaged material at foot of p. 62	omitted	included
B14	damaged section at foot of p. 63	omitted	included (incomplete)
C10	Wiggonby entry	omitted	included
C13	para. 4: descendants of Thomas Multon and Ada Morvill	included	omitted
D4	pedigrees at end of entry	omitted	included
D13	descendants of Adam son of Swein	included	omitted
D14	para. 2 insertion re Terriby of Terriby and nuns of Armathwaite	omitted	included
D28	first sentence	placed at beginning of entry	placed at end of entry
D39	section re appropriation of rectory	included	omitted

Section	Variant text	Series A	Series B
D47	phrase 'filius junioris uxoris'	omitted	included
D54	bounds of Holm Cultram	complete	note in margin that source manuscript torn; bounds defective.

Textual variants

A35	list of bishops of Carlisle	ends with Snowden	ends with Robinson
A36	Dalston genealogy	ends with William (and date 1670 in [2] and [3])	ends with George
B2	King Arthur's worthiness in the time of …	'British kings'	'Scottish kings'
B2	description of Castle Street	'C. street'	'Castlegait from the castle at the end thereof'
D50	description of Richard Fletcher	'petty chapman'	'merchant'

INDEX

Entries in **bold** refer to the principal accounts of places and families: individual personal names in the family genealogies have been indexed only where they occur elsewhere in the text. Marginal entries listing lords of a manor and repeating material in the body of the text are noted but have not been indexed by name. Abbreviations: dau: daughter; marr: married; s: son; w: wife

Carleton (near Carlisle), 84–5, 89; Little, 89

Carleton (in Drigg), 37, 41, **190–1**

Carleton, Joan w. of Gilbert, 160

Carlisle, 10, 18, 79, **88–93**, 111, 115, 142;
bishopric, 85; bishops (listed), 70–1, 79, 84, 143; grant to, 171
cathedral, library of Dean and Chapter, 193, 202
charter of liberties, 92
churches: St Cuthbert's, 90, 91; St Mary's, 75
dean and chapter, 138, 151
hospital of St Nicholas, 111, 126–7
nunnery, 89
priory, 84, 140; foundation, 89; grants to, 56, 59, 61, 67, 72, 74, 76, 93, 108, 112, 145, 151; priors (listed), 90–1; relics, 91
streets, 79, 92–3

Carlisle (*Carliell*) family, **138–9**; Adam, 126, 170; Christian dau. of Odard, 147; Eudo de, 127, 170; Ewan, 148; Hildred of (*Hyld*), 85, 126, 138, 140, 147, 170; Hildred, Odard s. of, 126; John, parson of Kirkland, 115; Reginald de, 86, 140, 178; Richard, 126, 170; Robert s. of Odard s. of, 126, 170; Robert s. of Robert, 115; Sapience w. of William de, 148

Carlyle family of Kinmont, 138

Cartmel (*Cart-meill*), 41, 190

Carwinley (*Carwendlow*) (in Arthuret), 72

Castle Carrock, **159–60**

Castlecarrock family, **159**; Christian, 160; Gamell de, 160

Castlerigg, 60, 66

castles: Askerton, 166; Egremont, 34; Kirkoswald, 157; Millom, 183; Naworth, 162–3

Castle Sowerby, 71, 169

Castlestead (in Irthington), 162

Castre, John de, 69, 157

Catterlen (*Catterling*), 82, 130, 161

Chambers family, 158

Charters, Alan de, 147

Chester, earldom, 81; Hugh Lupus earl of, 82; Richard earl of, 81–2, 91

Cholmeley (*Cromely*), Richard, 105

Chorry, Robert, bishop of Carlisle, 71, 86

Christian captive and Muslim maiden, story of, 18, 38–9

Christian, Duran fitz, 179

'Chronicon Cumbrie', 2, 19–20, 33n, 60n

church buildings: Holme Cultram, 179–80, St Cuthbert (Carlisle), 90, 91; St Mary (Carlisle), 75

Clapell, Cicely w. of Jordan, 128

Clebburn family, 106

Clerk, Henry, 54

Clifford, Robert, 35, 133; George, earl of Cumberland, 133

Cliftley, Henry s. of Katherine de, 114

Clifton, Great and Little, 34, 60, 66

Cocker and Derwent, lands between, 34, 36, 37, 60

Cockermouth, 60; honour, 20, 36, 64, 66

Colby (Westmorland), 135

Coldall, –, merchant in Carlisle, 125; Eleanor dau. of Richard, 125

Collanland (near Cockermouth), 66

Collinson, Alice w. of –, 160

Colvend (*Culwen*) (near Rockcliffe, Kirkcudbright), 59

Colvill (*Colvyll, Covill*) family, 97, 169; Edward, 114; John, 81; Margaret, 114; Robert, 114; Roger s. of Walter, 114

Conishead priory (Lancashire), 90, 188

Copeland (*Cawpland, Kopeland*), barony, 20, 34, 183

Copeland (*Cowpland*) family, **44**, **188**

Copeley, Adam, 164; John s. of Adam, 164; Richard, 164; Isabel, 164

Corbet family, 188; Alice, 187; Ralph, 185, 188; William 187, 188

Corby (*Kirkby; Korkby*), 82, 129, 130, 135, 140, 161, 165; Great (*Chorkby*), **137–8**; list of lords, 138

Corby (*Chorkbye*), Adam de, 137

Cormaunce, Henry de, 80

Corney, **188–9**

Corney, John de, 187; Michael de, 186

Corry (*Cary*), Eva w. of Walter, 133; Walter, 133; Walter s. of Walter, 76

Courtney, Robert de, 35, 64, 173, 145; Alice his w. *see* Rumelli

Crackenthorpe family 117; Henry, 150; John, 152, 154; Thomas, 80; William, 152

Craik-, Crake-, Crayksothen *see* Greysouthen

Crenquer, Alexander, 149, 150

Cressingham, Hugh de, 184

Crindledike (*Cringledike*) (in Cargo), 148

Cringledike (in Croglin), 158

Crochbeeghe (in Whitbeck), 185

Crofton, 56, **111–13**, 128

Crofton family, 128; Ada w. of Stephen de, 56, 128; Adam de, 118, 140; Clement, 111, 153; Helena, 140;

Millom seigniory, 37, **37–40**; **183–6**, 188, 190; castle, 17, 183; market, 40

Millom, Adam de, 38; Godith w. of Henry s. of Arthur de, 38; Gunild dau. of Henry de, 37, 38, 39; Henry s. of Arthur de, 38; Joan dau. of Adam de, 40; William de, 37, 38 *see also* Boyvill

Miterdale, 62, 189

Monceux (*Munciux*), Amand, 134

Monkbretton priory (Yorkshire), 149

Monk-force (in Whitbeck), 184, 185

Monseil, John, 150

Montacute, William, earl of Sarum, 127; Elizabeth, countess of Sarum, 127

Montbegon, Adam de, 149, 150; Clementia dau. of Roger, 150; Maud w. of Roger, 150; Roger de, 86, 149, 157

Montford, Simon, earl of Leicester, 67, 69

Moon, Michael, bookseller, 197, 198

Moorhouse, [Christopher], 51

Moresby, **55**

Moresby family, 54, 97, 169; Adam de, 49; Christopher, 80–1; Sir Christopher, 150; Hugh, 178; Margaret, 128; Thomas de, 56, 128; Ucknan, 55

Morland (Westmorland), 57; church, 135

Morpait, Mariot relict of Thomas, 127

Morthing (*Meething*) family, 188; John, 188; Richard, 43; William, 187, 188

Morvill(e) family, 165; tradition concerning mother of Sir Hugh, 102; Ada dau. of Sir Hugh, 68, 115, 131; Ada dau. of Joan, 113, 157; Helewise dau. of Joan, 113; Sir Hugh (d. 1202), 18, 67, 102, 103, 113, 156, 157, 168, 178; 'Sir Hugh' (*recte* Simon), 67; Joan dau. of Sir Hugh, 68, 113, 115, 168, 178; John de, 175; Nigel s. of John, 175; Walter s. of Nigel, 175

Mosedale, 107

Moulton (*Multon*) family, 20, 161; genealogy, **36**, **68–9**, **131**; Alan, 54, 172; Edward, 103; Elizabeth, 52; Hubert, 103; John, 50, 56, 66; John s. of Agnes Estholme, 43; Lambert, 66, 172; Margaret (w. of Ranulph Dacre), 161, 162; Margaret (w. of Sir William Leigh), 103; Margaret (w. of Thomas Lucy), 42, 66; Maud, 128; Thomas (d. 1240), 115; Thomas (d. 1270), 75, 103, 124, 157; Thomas (d. 1294), 56, 66, 128; Thomas of Gilsland, 37, 43, 44, 67, 114, 157, 166, 168; Thomas

(identity uncertain), 45; Thomas (d. 1304) *see* Lucy

Mowbray, Alexander, 98; Geoffrey, 99; Robert, 98; Roger, 98

Mulcaster family 158; Adam de, 41; Alice dau. of Benedict de, 180; David de, 41; John de, 41, 95; John de (alias John de Easton), 180; Robert de, 80, 95, 96, 115; Thomas, 95; Walter, 95, 150; William, 95; William de (alias William de Redness), 95

Multon *see* Moulton

Muncaster (*Mulcaster*), 37, **40–2**, **189**

Mungo, St, 108

Mungrisdale (*Grisedale*), 107

Murry, John, 87

Murton, 53, **53–4**

Murton, Adam de, 54; Gerard, 54; Roger, 54

Musgrave family, 146, 154, 160, 168, 169, 171; –, 142; Edward, 103; [Elizabeth] dau. of Cuthbert, 141; Humphrey, 171; Thomas, 154

Naworth Castle, 17, 20, **162–3**

Nevell, Alan de, 70

Neville family, Lords Latimer, 98; Alexander (de), 86, 149; Elizabeth w. of John, 148; Gilbert or Gilfrid and Mabel his w., 150; Joan w. of Ralph, 154, 170; John of Raby, 98; Ralph, 98; Ralph, earl of Westmorland, 148, 154, 170; Richard, 87; Richard, earl of Salisbury, 170; Richard, earl of Warwick, 170; William de, 86, 149, 150–1

Newbiggin (in Croglin), 80

Newbiggin, Helen, 160; Joan w. of Thomas, 159

Newby East (in Irthington), 130, 169

Newby West (*Newby on the Moor*) (in Cummersdale), 85, 86, 117, 127, **140**, 178; list of lords, 140

Newton in Allerdale *see* Westnewton

Newton family, **104**, 165; Adam s. of Ketel de, 179; Thomas de, 124

Newton Reigny, **174–5**; list of lords, 175

Nichol Forest, 72, 73

Nicholson, James, 203

Nicolson, William, bishop of Carlisle, 8, 11, 193–4, 200, 201, 202

Noble, Thomas, 199

Norden, John, 14, 18

Northeaston (in Arthuret?), 72

Northumberland, earls of, 36, 42, 54, 105, 109–10 *see also* Percy